Communication Across Cultures

Mutual understanding in a global world

Communication Across Cultures examines the ways in which spoken and written language may be interpreted depending on the context and expectations of the participants. Key concepts are drawn from linguistic pragmatics and discourse analysis, and studies of politeness and cross-cultural communication. The book has many examples from a variety of languages and cultures – from Japan to Germany, from the Americas to Africa, and to Australia.

This book is intended for students of linguistics and related disciplines, and interdisciplinary researchers who have no specialised knowledge of linguistics. Relevant literature and recent research are featured and explained throughout for the benefit of students who are learning how research in this field is conducted, and also for interdisciplinary researchers wishing to incorporate some of these perspectives into their own work.

Dr Heather Bowe is Senior Lecturer in Linguistics at Monash University and Director of the Language and Society Centre.

Kylie Martin is completing a PhD at Monash University on the socio-cultural situation of the Ainu language in Japan. She has lived and worked in Indonesia as well as in Japan.

Communication Across Cultures

Mutual understanding in a global world

Heather Bowe and Kylie Martin

Monash University
School of Languages, Cultures and Linguistics

CAMBRIDGE
UNIVERSITY PRESS

CAMBRIDGE UNIVERSITY PRESS
Cambridge, New York, Melbourne, Madrid, Cape Town, Singapore, São Paulo

Cambridge University Press
477 Williamstown Road, Port Melbourne, VIC 3207, Australia

Published in the United States of America by Cambridge University Press, New York

www.cambridge.org
Information on this title: www.cambridge.org/9780521695572

© Heather Bowe, Kylie Martin 2007

First published 2007

Printed in Australia by Ligare

A catalogue record for this publication is available from the British Library

National Library of Australia Cataloguing in Publication data
Bowe, Heather J. (Heather Joan), 1947– .
Communication Across Cultures: Mutual Understanding in a Global World.
Bibliography.
Includes index.
ISBN-13   978-0-521-69557-2 paperback
ISBN-10   0-521-69557-0 paperback
1. Intercultural communication.   2. Politeness (Linguistics).   3. Speech acts (Linguistics).
4. Discourse analysis.   5. Translating and interpreting.   I. Martin, Kylie.   II. Title. 302.2

ISBN-13   978-0-521-69557-2
ISBN-10   0-521-69557-0

Contents

List of figures

List of tables

Transcription conventions

Spoken discourse examples use the following conventions (following Neil 1996):

.	not a punctuation mark; final pitch contour
,	continuing pitch contour
!	exclamatory or animated intonation
? *or* ↑	rising intonation
xxxxx	inaudible or incomprehensible talk
<X word X>	uncertain hearing; the most likely text
+ *or* (·)	slight pause
+n+ *or* (n)	pause of n (number) seconds length
=, *or* : (e.g. a=ah, a:ah)	an extension of the syllable or sound indicated
[ ] *or* * *	speech overlap
(0) (0)	latching, indicates no interval between contiguous utterances such that the second latches immediately onto the first without overlapping with it
~~	speaker breaks off before completion of word

Preface and acknowledgments

T HE LINK BETWEEN linguistic form and the interpretation of meaning is multifaceted. Like light passing through a prism, the components of vocabulary, grammar, metaphor, style, politeness and inference are shaped by sociocultural practices to produce language as it is used. All of these components are brought into sharp focus in the study of intercultural communication.

Heather Bowe's interest in the multifaceted nature of language was kindled, when a student at the University of Southern California, from the interaction of the work of Bernard Comrie, Edward Finegan, Elaine Anderson, Elinor Ochs, Robert Kaplan, Osvaldo Jaeggli, Jack Hawkins and fellow students Nikko Besnier, Doug Biber, Bill Eggington, Gary Gilligan, Heather Holmback, Tsukao Kawahigashi, Keiji Matsumoto, Joyce Neu, Charles Randriamasimanana, Ian Roberts and Bonnie Schwarz.

The interest of students in the 1980s in the business applications of linguistics encouraged Heather to envisage a subject which examined the link between language form and the interpretation of similar forms in different cultural contexts. She has taught units in intercultural communication at Monash University at both undergraduate and graduate level to students from the Faculties of Arts and Business for over ten years. Heather's interest in this area has been informed greatly by the work of Michael Clyne and other colleagues in the areas of languages and linguistics at Monash, particularly by Keith Allan, Kate Burridge, Marissa Cordella, Georgina Heydon, Heinz Kreutz, Helen Marriott, Anne Pauwels, John Platt, Joanne Winter, and Farzad Sharifian, as well as past and present students from a rich variety of cultures including Margaret à Beckett, Zosia Golebiowski, Angelina Kioko, Kei Miyazawa Reid, Deborah Neil and Mingjian Zhang.

More recently, the material in this book has been a resource for subjects taught at the Monash campuses in Malaysia and South Africa, in addition to classes at the Monash campuses in the Melbourne area, and so the presentation has aimed to be more international in orientation.

Kylie Martin's interest in intercultural communication began at the University of Adelaide where she was a student of Peter Mühlhäusler, and where she completed an Honours thesis on the contemporary influences of the Javanese and Indonesian languages and cultures on each other in the context of the vernacular diversity in the Indonesian Archipelago. Kylie subsequently completed her MA, Convergence and Divergence of Bahasa Malaysia and Bahasa Indonesia – seventeen case studies of Malaysian and Indonesian international students in Australia, at Monash, under the supervision of Michael Clyne. Kylie has since taught English as a second language in Japan and contributed to the teaching of the intercultural communication units on the Monash Melbourne campuses. Kylie is currently working on research for her PhD, examining the role of the Ainu language in modern Japan.

This work has also benefited from the comments of anonymous reviewers, and from the assistance of Natalie Stroud with editing and Patti Sharp with graphics.

Heather would like to say a special thank you to her husband Robin, who made space in their mobile home so that the draft manuscript could be completed on their trip around Australia during Heather's long service leave, and has continued to support her to see this project to completion.

Heather Bowe and Kylie Martin
School of Languages, Cultures and Linguistics
Monash University, Clayton, Victoria
November 2006

1

Culture, communication and interaction

1.1   INTRODUCTION

THIS BOOK IS INTENDED as an academic reference for undergraduate and graduate students and interdisciplinary researchers who do not have specialised knowledge of linguistics. Key concepts relevant to an understanding of language issues in intercultural communication are drawn from the research areas of pragmatics, discourse analysis, politeness and intercultural communication. Relevant academic literature and recent research conducted by the authors is exemplified and explained throughout the book so that students can become familiar with the way research in this field is reported and can follow up on the ideas presented.

An understanding of intercultural communication is crucially related to an understanding of the ways in which the spoken and written word may be interpreted differentially, depending on the context. The message received is not always the one intended by the speaker or the writer. This book systematically examines sociocultural and pragmatic aspects of the language context, and discusses a wide range of factors that contribute to the interpretation of language in context. The authors argue that an understanding of how these principles interact in a given language, and in intercultural communication, is crucial to the development of mutual understanding in the global world.

Although speakers engaged in intercultural communication typically choose a single language in which to communicate, individuals typically bring their own sociocultural expectations of language to the encounter. Speakers' expectations shape the interpretation of meaning in a variety of ways. To manage intercultural interaction effectively, speakers need to be aware of the inherent norms of their own speech practices, the ways in which norms vary depending on situational factors and the ways in which speakers from other language backgrounds may have different expectations of language usage and behaviour.

Representative research methodologies are exemplified throughout the book, although there is no single chapter devoted to methodology.

1.2 CULTURE, COMMUNICATION AND INTERCULTURAL INTERACTION

Some of the key ideas relating to the study of culture, communication and intercultural communication are presented here and developed in more detail in each chapter.

CULTURE

The term culture, as we will be using it, refers to the customs and expectations of a particular group of people, particularly as it affects their language use.

 The term **culture** has a wide range of meanings today, because it has actually changed in meaning over time. Goddard (2005:53 ff.) provides an excellent account of some of these changes. In its earliest English uses, *culture* was a noun of process, referring to the tending of crops or animals. This meaning (roughly 'cultivating') is found in words such as *agriculture, horticulture* and *viviculture*. In the sixteenth century *culture* began to be used about 'cultivating' the human body through training, and later about 'cultivating' the non-physical aspects of a person. In the nineteenth century the meaning was broadened to include the general state of human intellectual, spiritual and aesthetic development (roughly comparable to 'civilisation'), giving rise to the 'artistic works and practices' meaning that which is associated with music, literature, painting, theatre and film. Goddard reports that the 'anthropological' usage of culture was introduced into English by Tylor in the late nineteenth century in his book *Primitive Culture*. Tylor defined **culture** as 'that complex whole which includes knowledge, belief, art, morals, law, custom and other capabilities and habits acquired by man as a member of a society' (Tylor 1871:1).

Goddard (2005:58) makes the point that the 'anthropological' use typically related to people living in 'other places'; however, in contemporary expressions such as *youth culture, gay culture, kid culture* the principle of differentiation has shifted entirely to the notion of different 'kinds of people'. Even so, Tylor's definition of culture seems to us to still be very relevant.

Research on intercultural communication often relates to cultural groups at the level of nations and national languages; however, we need to be aware that many of the major languages of the world such as German, English, Spanish and Arabic are spoken by people of different nationalities, often in geographically distant areas and that each national variety of these pluricentric languages will have at least some of its own codified norms (Clyne 1992; Clyne, Fernandez & Muhr 2003).

Research on **cross-cultural communication** typically compares communication practices of one language/cultural group with another, while studies on **intercultural communication** focus on features of the shared communication between speakers from different language/cultural backgrounds.

Most modern research on cross-cultural and intercultural communication takes into account that communication is affected by different aspects of the context, including cultural expectations, social relations and the purpose of the communication.

DIRECTNESS AND INDIRECTNESS

At the level of sentence grammar, mappings between one language and another can be relatively straightforward; however, even with simple sentences, the communication context can influence the interpretation of an utterance.

Grice (1975) and Searle (1969, 1975) were among the first researchers to grapple with the difference between direct and indirect messages. They identified the importance of context to the interpretation of meaning, and examined the way in which inferences can be drawn. Such analysis is even more important for intercultural communication because different sociocultural expectations may be involved. Grice's work has been criticised, more recently, for its anglocentric approach (e.g. Clyne 1987, 1994; Wierzbicka 1991, 1994a). Social interaction, cultural norms and numerous environmental factors need to be taken into account when interpreting conversational implicature (Levinson 1983:127).

Key ideas relating to the study of conversational implicature, of how people determine the literal and/or non-literal meaning of an utterance in a particular context, and the theory of speech acts, are examined in Chapter 2, along with modifications necessary to make this type of analysis relevant to intercultural communication.

POLITENESS

The relationship between directness and indirectness and politeness is examined first in a general way, and subsequently using examples from cross-cultural research on speech acts and politeness.

Different languages have different ways of marking politeness. People from some cultures tend to favour directness, while people from other cultures favour less directness. Even so, directness may also vary in relation to social context. The relationship between directness and politeness as examined by Blum-Kulka (1987:133 ff.) illustrates that while these notions may be related, they are not one and the same. This field of research suggests that politeness may be better defined as doing what is appropriate in a given cultural context. Directness and politeness are examined in Chapter 3, drawing particularly on the research paradigms of Brown and Levinson (1987), Goffman (1955, 1967), Ehlich (1992), Fraser (1990) for politeness and face, Blum-Kulka, House and Kasper (1989) and Wierzbicka (2003) for cross-cultural research on speech acts, and the research of Ide (1989, 1990), Matsumoto (1988, 1989), Meier (1995a,b) and Watts, Ide and Ehlich (1992) who challenge the universality of aspects of these paradigms. The research of Wierzbicka (1991, 2003) and Sharifian (2004) provides further insight into the ways courtesy and respect can be conveyed in different languages.

SPEECH ACTS AND POLITENESS ACROSS CULTURES

Speech acts, such as requests, may differ according to cultural preferences for directness or indirectness. For example, in the case where a person wants a favour from another person, the preferred strategy may be to hint and talk about the topic (Richards & Sukwiwat 1983). In another cultural context, it may be more appropriate to ask directly. In some cultures it is acceptable for the person asked not to respond verbally but to simply carry out the requested action. The growing body of research on the inter-relatedness between direct and indirect speech acts and politeness in different cultural contexts is examined in Chapter 4, beginning with the seminal work of the CCSARP project (Cross-Cultural Speech Act Realization Patterns, Blum-Kulka, House & Kasper 1989), which is based on discourse completion tests conducted with native speakers of eight languages. Cross-cultural variation of requests, complaints, apologies, acceptances of apologies and compliments are exemplified, drawing on the work of House and Kasper

(1981), Cohen and Olshtain (1981), Blum-Kulka (1987), Suszczyńska (1999), Clyne (1994), Cordella (1990), Smith (1992), Sugimoto (1998), Hobbs (2003) and Wierzbicka (2003).

CONVERSATIONS

People from different cultural backgrounds may have different expectations of conversation. Clyne and Platt (1990) point out that intercultural communication conflict can develop where one party considers the other to be either offensively forward or arrogantly uncooperative. Routines for greeting and leave-taking can vary considerably from culture to culture, as can the use of laughter and expectations concerning the organisation of speaker turns. Preferences for different communication channels (e.g. face-to-face communication versus the use of the telephone or email) also differ between different cultures and sub-cultures, as do the appropriate length of a speaker's turn in conversation and attitudes to interruptions and silence. These features of conversation are examined in Chapter 5, drawing particularly on the research paradigms of Schegloff (1968, 1982), Schegloff and Sacks (1973), Sacks, Schegloff and Jefferson (1974), Albert and Kessler (1976, 1978) for turn-taking, adjacency pairs, back-channelling and repetition, and exemplified by the research of Goddard (1977), Clark and French (1981) and Sifianou (1989) on telephone use in different cultures, and Gavioli (1995) on the function of laughter in different cultural contexts. Intercultural conversation is exemplified from research in the Australian workplace from Clyne (1994) and Béal (1992) and from Kjaerbeck (1998) from intercultural business negotiation in Mexican and Danish.

POWER AND STEREOTYPING

Stereotyping is the process by which all members of a group are asserted to have the characteristics attributed to the whole group (Scollon & Scollon 2001:168). We need to remember that no individual member of a group is the embodiment of his or her group's characteristics. Furthermore, people belong to a multitude of different sub-groups and thus cannot be defined by their membership to any one particular group. Cultural differences in the concept of self and others, and related perceptions of power are also important in understanding the social expectations and conventions which underlie language use. They are also used to interpret linguistic meaning in a given interaction. However, any categorisation of a group results in some level of stereotyping (El-Dash & Busnardo 2001). Thus, while linking certain characteristics to different cultures serves as a useful guide, such categorisations may lead to some level of overgeneralisation.

These topics are examined in Chapter 6, drawing particularly on the work of Fairclough (1989, 2000), Fairclough and Wodak (1997), Giddens (1982, 1993), Gottlieb (2006), Hofstede (1980, 1983, 1991), Pennycook (2001) and van Dijk (1987, 1996).

NAMING AND ADDRESSING

Modes of address and naming systems vary greatly from culture to culture. For example, among Sikh Indians, men and women may have similar 'given' names and sex is marked by the use of 'Singh' for males and 'Kaur' for females. However, in Australia, 'Singh' has been adopted as a surname by Sikh Indians (males), and has in some cases been passed on as the family surname for females as well as males in the subsequent generation. There are so many naming systems that Clyne and Platt (1990) suggest that people need to be alert, to enquire and not to be surprised about differences when they encounter people from different cultural groups.

The variety of naming practices available to identify individuals in a society are examined in Chapter 7, drawing on the research paradigms of Braun (1988), Brown and Gilman (1960), Geertz (1976) and Goffman (1968), which show how different forms of address can contribute to a person's sense of identity and the relationship between the individual and their social context.

Brown and Gilman's (1960) paper is used to illustrate the ways in which second- and third-person pronoun forms can be used to signal familiarity and formality/deference in some Indo-European languages. The ways in which nouns and pronouns of address, kinship terms, and honorifics are used as part of complex systems of familiarity, respect and deference in different languages are exemplified through the research of Suzuki (1976) and Koyama (1992) for Japanese, Geertz (1976) and Koentjaraningrat (1989) for Javanese, as well as Hvoslef (2001) for the language of the Kyrgyz Republic, one of the fifteen new states after the dissolution of the Soviet Union.

ORGANISATION OF WRITTEN DISCOURSE

Variation in the organisation of writing across cultures has been studied from a cross-linguistic perspective, particularly over the last two decades. Differences of expectation with regard to the appropriateness of topics and the sequence of topics may differ across cultures. In different cultures people may place more weight on verbal or written undertakings. Texts and arguments can be organised in different ways. There may be a preference for more or less formally oriented texts. Some cultures, such as the English culture, favour presenting ideas in a linear progression, while in other cultures the presentation of ideas may be more 'digressive' or tend towards different rhythms, such as symmetry or parallelism. The issues of cultural differences in the organisation of ideas and written discourse as observed by Kaplan (1972, 1988) and exemplified by Hinds (1980) for Japanese, Eggington (1987) for Korean, Kirkpatrick (1991) for Mandarin letters of request, Ostler (1987) for Arabic prose, and Clyne (1980, 1987) and Clyne and Kreutz (1987) for English and German are further examined in Chapter 8.

INTERCULTURAL COMMUNICATION IN PROFESSIONAL AND WORKPLACE CONTEXTS

One important intercultural communication issue in professional and workplace contexts is the practice of translating and interpreting, which needs to be sensitive to most of the issues discussed thus far in this book. Translators face a particular challenge to balance pragmatic equivalence and impartiality. Pragmatic equivalence is sensitive to the cultural and linguistic norms of the respective languages. Some central issues relating to the practice of translating and interpreting (e.g. Widdowson 1978; Larson 1984) are examined in Chapter 9, along with some examples of translation challenges in advertising.

The medical and legal professions, which rely heavily on question and answer sequences, are also particularly problematic for intercultural communication, whether or not interpreters are involved. Different cultural norms may pertain to the way questions and answers are posed, and there are also other issues that are specific to each of these professions. These are discussed with reference to the research of Davidson (2000), a case study of medical interpreting in the United States, and Pauwels, D'Argaville and Eades (1992) relating to the provision of evidence by Australian Aboriginal clients in the courtroom.

Different cultural expectations may also shape the behaviour and interpretation of different parties engaged in intercultural business negotiation. This is also exemplified in Chapter 9 with reference studies reported by Marriott (1990) for a Japanese–Australian business encounter, and by Spencer-Oatey and Xing (2003) for a Chinese–British business encounter.

TOWARDS SUCCESSFUL INTERCULTURAL COMMUNICATION

Research on spoken discourse in the Australian multicultural workplace by Monash researchers (e.g. Clyne 1994; Bowe 1995; Neil 1996) involving participants from different cultures who are engaged in natural communication in a language that is not a first language to any of the speakers, has shown that individuals can develop ways to construct a 'common ground' and avoid many of the problems inherent to intercultural communication. The research findings of Bowe's study of automotive manufacturing workers, and of Neil's (1996) study of hospital ancillary staff, reported in Chapter 10, illustrate that speakers involved in intercultural communication on a daily basis find ways to use language creatively and collaboratively to ensure that the intended message is received and that potential miscommunication is circumvented.

Giles' (1977:322) notion of accommodation, and Sharifian's notion of conceptual renegotiation (Sharifian forthcoming), are also examined to illustrate dimensions of the way in which individuals can adapt to the challenges of intercultural communication.

The book concludes with some cautious optimism. Although, in the early stages, individuals may approach intercultural communication through the ethnocentric prism of their own immediate culture and misread the intentions of their intercultural communication partners, as they become more aware of the ways in which sociocultural conventions shape language use, individuals may be more able to understand intercultural communication and communicate more effectively.

SUGGESTED FURTHER READING

Goddard, C. 2005 'The lexical semantics of culture'. *Language Sciences* no. 27, pp. 51–73.

Neil, D. 1996 *Collaboration in Intercultural Discourse: Examples from a Multicultural Australian Workplace*. Frankfurt am Main: Peter Lang, Chapter 2, pp. 27–68.

Scollon, R. & Scollon, S. Wong 2001 *Intercultural Communication: A Discourse Approach* 2nd edn. Oxford: Blackwell, Chapter 7, pp. 122–37.

2

Direct and indirect messages: The role of social context identified by Grice and Searle

AT THE LEVEL OF SENTENCE GRAMMAR, MAPPINGS between one language and another can be relatively straightforward; however even with simple sentences, the communication context can influence the interpretation of an utterance. It is at the level that might be called 'reading between the lines' that cultural differences may arise and these may contribute to misunderstandings in intercultural communication. In this chapter we will examine some of the ways in which we can identify and understand aspects of this complexity.

During the 1950s and 1960s the philosopher John L. Austin, his pupil H. Paul Grice and other like-minded scholars including John Searle, tried to explain how people draw inferences in everyday communication. These researchers came to be known as 'ordinary language philosophers' (Thomas 1995:29).

Austin (1962, 1970) attempted to determine the distinction between what a speaker says, what the speaker actually means, and what the hearer thinks the speaker means. Austin's initial work on the communicative intent, form and effects of utterances was outlined in his paper *How to do Things with Words* (1962). This work has formed the basis for much research into this aspect of language, an understanding of which is also crucial to the study of intercultural communication.

The following example illustrates one of the ways in which an English speaker may 'read between the lines' in a conversation.

On arriving home from school, a teenage child says to his mother:

'I've come straight home from school today.'

The child's mother is a bit taken aback! She is puzzled by what the child means, why he said it – if it was really true, what else he might have been doing.

9

What is it about such a statement that raises so many questions and leads the hearer to draw the implicature that the comment has something other than its literal truth value? It is questions like these that Grice set out to explore.

2.1 GRICE'S MAXIMS

Grice (1975) identified four expectations that adult English speakers seem to use in interpreting literal and implied meaning in a conversation. He called these expectations **conversational maxims,** which work together with a general principle he called the **Cooperative Principle**.

Grice's maxims (1975:45–7) can be summarised as follows:

Quantity: Make your contribution as informative as is required (for the current purpose of the exchange).

Do not make your contribution more informative than is required.

Quality: Do not say what you believe to be false.

Do not say that for which you lack adequate evidence.

Relevance: Be relevant.

Manner: Avoid obscurity of expression.

Avoid ambiguity.

Be brief.

Be orderly.

Cooperative Principle:

Make your conversational contribution such as is required, at the stage at which it occurs, by the accepted purpose or direction of the talk exchange in which you are engaged.

These maxims represent **norms** that hearers can expect speakers to have followed, if they are engaged in **cooperative conversation**. (Grice stated the maxims as imperatives, but we need to understand that he was intending them as normative rules of interaction.) Allan (1991) makes the good point that the maxims should be regarded as 'reference points for language interchange' and not as 'laws to be obeyed'. In effect, we use these norms as a base, against which conversational exchanges can be compared. When we encounter communication that does not meet these norms, we then search for **non-literal interpretations (conversational implicatures)**.

The above example about the mother's suspicion when her son said that he had come straight home from school can be accounted for with reference to Grice's maxim of **Quantity**: *Make your contribution as informative as is*

required. Do not make your contribution more informative than is required.
If it was usual that the mother expected her son to come straight home
from school, then any comment stating that to be the case would be over-
informative and superfluous. Thus, when the son's comment appears to
state the obvious, an alternative interpretation is invited, or, implied.

The following example further illustrates how the maxims assist in determining the difference between the level of literal meaning and the level of
implied meaning.

Trevor climbs a ladder to fix a broken tile on the roof. When he reaches
the roof, he accidentally kicks the ladder and it falls to the ground, leaving
him stranded.

> Jason: Do you want me to put the ladder back so you can climb
>   down?
> Trevor: (on the roof)   No! I just want to hang around up here all
>   day!

In terms of Grice's maxims, there ought to have been no need for Jason's
question. It was obvious from the context that Trevor would need Jason to
replace the ladder. So in terms of Grice's maxim of **Quality**, Jason's question
was asking the obvious. It was superfluous in the context and therefore it
flouted the maxims of **Quantity** and **Relevance**. In return, Trevor replies
using sarcasm. His reply was literally untruthful, hence, also flouting the
Quality maxim.

Jason would be able to interpret Trevor's reply as sarcasm using the
maxims and the cooperative principle. When Trevor's reply was not a direct
answer to Jason's question, the **Cooperative Principle** would require Trevor
to find a suitable interpretation other than the literal meaning, and he could
thus conclude that the reply was an instance of sarcasm.

Levinson (1985:102) provides the following additional example:

> A: Where's Bill?
> B: There's a yellow VW outside Sue's house.

Levinson suggests that B's contribution, taken literally, fails to answer
A's question, and thus seems to violate at least the maxims of **Quantity** and
Relevance. B's utterance could then be interpreted as a non-cooperative
response, ignoring A's concerns by changing the topic. Yet, Levinson suggests, it is clear that despite the *apparent* failure of cooperation, we try to
interpret B's utterance as nevertheless cooperative at some deeper (non-
superficial) level. We do this by assuming that it is in fact cooperative, and
then by asking ourselves what possible connection there could be between

the location of Bill and the yellow VW, and hence arrive at the suggestion (which B effectively conveys) that, if Bill has a yellow VW, he may be in Sue's house.

This inference can arise because of the underlying assumption of cooperation, which allows us to reinterpret an apparently contradictory or irrelevant comment in terms of something that would make sense in the context. It is this kind of inference that Grice calls a **conversational implicature.**

Grice (1975:49) also recognised that language-users sometimes fail to observe the four maxims. A maxim might not be observed if, for example, a person deliberately tells a lie or cannot speak clearly for whatever reason (i.e. speaking while eating, a person with stage fright, etc.). Grice listed three methods by which a speaker could fail to observe a maxim:

- flouting a maxim
- violating a maxim
- opting out of a maxim.

Of these categories, 'flouting a maxim' is the one which has received the most interest. Grice was mainly interested in those situations in which a speaker blatantly fails to observe a maxim with the deliberate intention of causing an implicature. In such contexts, the speaker, however, does not intentionally mean to deceive or mislead the hearer, only to induce the hearer to search for an additional meaning to that of the expressed meaning. Grice termed this process by which the implicature is produced **flouting a maxim.**

Grice (1975) was principally concerned with **conversational implicature** as distinct from **conventional implicatures**, which are signalled by words such as *but, even, therefore* and *yet* which remain the same regardless of situational factors. The implied meanings of **conversational implicatures** vary according to the context of what is spoken. Social interaction, cultural norms and numerous environmental factors need to be taken into account when interpreting conversational implicature (Levinson 1983:127).

However, Grice's work has been criticised for its anglocentric approach (e.g. Clyne 1987, 1994; Wierzbicka 1991, 1994a). Sperber and Wilson (1986) have attempted to overcome this English bias by identifying **relevance** as the key factor in determining how people draw inferences in a given context. Sperber and Wilson's **relevance theory** is sometimes employed as an alternative to the Gricean anglocentric approach (see Jary 1998).

Alternatively, we might assume that each language/culture may have different settings for Quantity, Quality, and Manner.

Clyne in his discussion of the **intercultural application** of Grice's Cooperative Principle and four Maxims has proposed the **revisions** as summarised below (Clyne 1994:194–5):

Quantity: *A single maxim* – 'Make your contribution as informative as is required for the purpose of the discourse, **within the bounds of the discourse parameters of the given culture.**

Quality: *Supermaxim* – 'Try to make your contribution one for which you can take responsibility **within your own cultural norms**'.
Maxims
(1) 'Do not say what you believe to be in opposition to your **cultural norms of truth, harmony, charity and/or respect.**'
(2) 'Do not say that for which you lack adequate evidence' (probably DUBIOUS even in informal Anglo contexts).

Manner: *Supermaxim* – 'Be perspicacious' (retained in its original form).
Maxims
(1) 'Do not make it any more difficult to understand than may be dictated by questions of face and authority' (see Chapter 3).
(2) 'Make clear your communicative intent **unless this is against the interests of politeness or of maintaining a dignity-driven cultural core value, such as harmony, charity or respect.**'
(3) 'Make your contribution the appropriate length required by the nature and purpose of the exchange and the **discourse parameters of your culture.**'
(4) 'Structure your discourse according to the **requirements of your culture.**'
(5) 'In your contribution, take into account anything you know or can predict about the interlocutor's communication expectations.'

Clyne's formulations are designed to accommodate the differences between **form-based** cultures (in which highly structured, hierarchical, linear means of written and spoken forms of communication are preferred) and cultures where **content and knowledge** are core values (e.g. Eastern European, German), and in which a greater amount of information is often preferred.

In Chinese and Vietnamese, the notion of cooperation entails saying only a small amount in order to avoid conflict, whereas in some cultures such as Jewish, Israeli and African–American cultures, contrariness (and therefore saying a lot) and immodesty are considered to be cooperative (Clyne 1994:12).

Grice's third maxim of Manner is regarded as being the most 'culturally limiting' of all the maxims (Clyne 1994:193). The concept of **orderliness** is highly valued in form-oriented cultures such as the Anglo-based cultures of England, the United States and Australia and is closely connected with the concept of linearity in writing. In cultures such as Vietnamese, Japanese and Javanese, where implicitness or non-assertiveness is a core value, the maxim of 'Avoid obscurity of expression' can be regarded as being meaningless. Cam Nguyên (1991:43) has identified what she terms the Vietnamese 'tolerance for ambiguity'. This **tolerance for ambiguity** is accompanied by a preference for a **circular** discourse structure, which involves merely suggesting examples of an implicit perception and continually returning to this perception to expand upon it. Ide (1989) also postulates that the 'tolerance for ambiguity' relates to the tendency of **indirectness** at the pragmatic level of some East (and South-east) Asian languages. The additional fifth maxim of Manner was added by Clyne (1994:195) to address the problem of whether it is/should be the speaker's culture or the hearer's culture which determines the communication patterns.

Furthermore, Clyne (1994) proposed the 'revised' maxim of Quality in order to overcome the European bias in the meaning of 'truth'. Clyne (1994:193) suggests that the European notion of 'truth' as an absolute value is not regarded as being of vital importance in such cultures as Vietnamese and South-east Asian Chinese, and argues that in such cultures 'in any competition with harmony, charity or respect, "truth" not only need not, but should not, be a criterion'. In South-east Asian communities, the core value of harmony directly contrasts with the Western European/Middle Eastern perception of 'truth'.

Notwithstanding the above criticisms and revisions, Grice's approach has served as a basis for an enormous amount of research in the area of pragmatics and, in its various adapted forms, has been the basic theoretical framework for much of the studies into intercultural communication. Grice's framework provides a necessary bridge in overcoming the gap between what is expressed, what is actually meant by the speaker (the intended meaning) and how the hearer perceives that meaning. Without a framework like Grice's it is difficult to map the difference between the expressed (**literal**) meaning of an utterance and its **implied** meaning in a given context.

In order to account for the fact that the interpretation of non-literal meanings by the hearer may not necessarily coincide with the intentions of the speaker, Austin (1962) and Searle (1969) characterise utterances in the following way (explanations in brackets provided by the present authors):

Locution: **the actual form of the utterance**
(what is actually said)

Illocution: **the communicative force of the utterance**
(what was intended by the speaker in making the utterance)

Perlocution: **the communicative effect of the utterance**
(what the hearer interprets as the meaning intended by the utterance)

This characterisation of the tripartite nature of communication helps us to see how miscommunication might occur. Even when the Speaker and the Hearer come from the same culture, there is the possibility that the **message received** may not equate with the **message intended**. The likelihood of miscommunication increases greatly when the Speaker and the Hearer come from different cultures and may have different expected **norms**.

2.2   SPEECH ACTS

In the context of his work on the communicative intent, form and inter-pretation of utterances, Austin (1962) established a distinction between **statements** (called constatives by Austin), which are utterances that may be assigned a truth value, and **performatives**, which he claims have no truth values but perform actions whose successful completion rests on felicity conditions (see Allan 1986, 1994). Searle (1979) further subdivides performatives into five subcategories:

Types of Speech Acts

Assertives: Stating: an act which commits the speaker (S) to the truth of the proposition (P).

Directives: Commanding and requesting; attempts by the speaker (S) to get the hearer (H) to do something.

Commissives: Promising and offering: acts which commit the speaker (S) to a future act (A).

Expressives: Thanking, forgiving, blaming, complaining, apologising: acts in which the speaker (S) makes known his/her attitude about a proposition to the hearer (H).

Declarations: Baptizing, naming, appointing, sacking: acts which bring about correspondence between the propositional content and the reality.

(Searle 1979:12–29)[1]

In his 1969 monograph entitled *Speech Acts*, Searle characterises a number of Speech Acts in terms of what he refers to as their **Propositional Content**; and identifies certain **Preparatory**, **Sincerity** and **Essential Conditions** under which each speech act can be reasonably used or in his terms '**felicitously performed**'. These are provided in Table 2.1.

To understand Searle's 'Table of Speech Acts', we can examine the characterisation of **Requests**, which Searle classifies as a type of **Directive**. Recall that with all Directives, the onus is on the Hearer to do something.

REQUESTS

Searle characterises **Requests** as having a **Propositional Content** in which the uttering of a request aims to bring about a **Future act (A) of the Hearer (H)**. This can be contrasted with a promise, for example, which relates to a future act (A) of the Speaker.

Searle lists the following **Preparatory Conditions** and necessary prerequisites for a request to be felicitous: that the Hearer (H) **is able to do the act (A); and it is not obvious** to both the Speaker (S) and the Hearer (H) that the Hearer (H) will **do the act (A) in the normal course of events of his own accord**. Searle uses the term **felicitous** to mean 'well motivated', or 'well formed'.

Searle specifies the **Sincerity Condition** that the Speaker (S) **wants** the Hearer (H) **to do the act (A);** and the **Essential Condition** that a Request counts as **an attempt** to **get** the Hearer (H) to **do the act (A)**.

Searle notes in the comments section that the other directives **Order** and **Command** have the additional **Preparatory Condition** that the Speaker (S) must be in a **position of authority** over the Hearer (H), and that the authority relationship affects the **Essential Condition** because such directives count as an **attempt** to get H to do A by virtue of the authority of S over H.

Most of these conditions seem to be intuitively sensible. However, they can also explain, for instance, why a person might feel affronted when

Table 2.1. Speech acts

Types of rule	Request	Assert (state that)	Question	Thank (for)	Advise	Warn	Greet	Congratulate
Propositional content	Future act A of H	Any proposition P	Any proposition or propositional function	Past act A done by H	Future act A of H	Future event or state, etc., E	None	Some event, act, etc., E related to H
Preparatory	1. H is able to do A. S believes H is able to do A. 2. It is not obvious to both S and H that H will do A in the normal course of events of his own accord.	1. S has evidence (reasons, etc.) for the truth of P. 2. It is not obvious to both S and H that H knows (does not need to be reminded of, etc.) P.	1. S does not know 'the answer', i.e. does not know if the proposition is true, or, in the case of the propositional function, does not know the information needed to complete the proposition truly (but see comment below). 2. It is not obvious to both S and H that H will provide the information at that time without being asked.	A benefits S and S believes A benefits S.	1. S has some reason to believe A will benefit H. 2. It is not obvious to both S and H that H will do A in the normal course of events.	1. S has reason to believe E will occur and is not in H's interest. 2. It is not obvious to both S and H that E will occur.	S has just encountered (or been introduced to, etc.) H.	E is in H's interest and S believes E is in H's interest.
Sincerity	S wants H to do A.	S believes P.	S wants this information.	S feels grateful or appreciative for A.	S believes A will benefit H.	S believes E is not in H's best interest.	None.	S is pleased at E.
Essential	Counts as an attempt to get H to do A.	Counts as an undertaking to the effect that P represents an actual state of affairs.	Counts as an attempt to elicit this information from H.	Counts as an expression of gratitude or appreciation.	Counts as an undertaking to the effect that A is in H's best interest.	Counts as an undertaking to the effect that E is not in H's best interest.	Counts as courteous recognition of H by S.	Counts as an expression of pleasure at E.

Table 2.1. (*cont.*)

Types of rule	Request	Assert (state that)	Question	Thank (for)	Advise	Warn	Greet	Congratulate
Comment	*Order* and *command* have the additional preparatory rule that *S* must be in a position of authority over *H*. *Command* probably does not have the 'pragmatic' condition requiring non-obviousness. Furthermore in both, the authority relationship affects the essential condition because the utterance counts as an attempt to get *H* to do *A* in virtue of the authority of *S* over *H*.	Unlike argue, these do not seem to be essentially tied to attempting to convince. Thus 'I am simply stating that *P* and not attempting to convince you' is acceptable, but 'I am arguing that *P* and not attempting to convince you' sounds inconsistent.	There are two kinds of questions, (a) real questions, (b) exam questions. In real questions *S* wants to know (find out) the answer; in exam questions, *S* wants to know if *H* knows.	Sincerity and essential rules overlap. Thanking is just expressing gratitude in a way that, e.g., promising is not just expressing an intention.	Contrary to what one might suppose advice is not a species of requesting. It is interesting to compare 'advise' with 'urge', 'advocate' and 'recommend'. Advising you is not trying to get you to do something in the sense that requesting is. Advising is more like telling you what is best for you.	Warning is like advising, rather than requesting. It is not, I think, necessarily an attempt to get you to take evasive action. Notice that the above account is of categorical not hypothetical warnings. Most warnings are probably hypothetical: 'If you do not do X then Y will occur.'		'Congratulate' is similar to 'thank' in that it is an expression of its sincerity condition.

(Searle, J. R. 1969:66–7)

someone they know well asks them to do something they had already intended to do and which the speaker knows is routinely expected of them. For example, a request such as *Would you please remember to tidy your desk before you leave* uttered in a context in which the Hearer always leaves his/her desk tidy and the Speaker knows it, could cause a serious affront.

The importance of preparatory conditions for some requests can be seen in examples where the Speaker actually ascertains the ability of the Hearer to do an act before making a request. This is often the case before a request is made. For example: *Are you going to be attending class on Thursday? Would you mind collecting the assignment details for me?*

SPEECH ACT CONDITIONS AND THE STRUCTURE OF INDIRECT SPEECH ACTS

In his discussion of the relationship between Direct and Indirect Speech Acts, Searle (1969, Chapter 3) points out that the forms of **Indirect Speech Acts** are routinely built upon **speech act conditions** as illustrated by the following.

There are a variety of ways to ask someone at the dinner table to **pass the salt**:

1. Pass the salt (please).
2. Can you pass the salt?
3. Can you reach the salt?
4. Would you mind passing the salt?
5. I would appreciate it if you would pass the salt.
6. Would you pass the salt?

The first request is a **direct request**, which takes the form of an **imperative**, with the possible addition of *please*.

The next two requests are based on the **Preparatory Condition**. Literally these requests have the form of a question about the **Hearer's ability to do the act**.

The fourth one relates to the **Hearer's attitude to the proposed act**, and is also related to the **Preparatory Conditions**.

The fifth request is a statement and relates to the **Sincerity condition** – that the Speaker **wants** the Hearer to perform **the act**.

The sixth request seems to also relate to the **Essential condition** – and counts as an **attempt to get** the Hearer to do **the act**.

Searle (1975) observes that **indirect speech acts** have both a **primary illocutionary force** and a **secondary illocutionary force**. This is obvious to English-speaking children who may counter the indirect request *Can you pass me the salt?* with a reply such as *I can but I won't*. Searle argues that mutually shared background and the principles of cooperative conversation (proposed by Grice) provide the means by which the utterance *Can you pass me the salt?* can be regarded as having the primary illocutionary force of a request. He argues that indirect speech acts have, in addition, a secondary illocutionary force, relating to the literal form of the utterance, in this case a question about the Hearer's ability to pass the salt. Searle suggests that some sentences 'seem to be **conventionally used as indirect requests**'.

The important role of the culturally oriented assumptions of mutually shared background and cooperative conversation explains where interpretations might be misconstrued in certain contexts, including intercultural contexts.

In a survey of middle managers in businesses in the eastern area of Melbourne conducted in 1995, we found that the most frequently used request forms were variants of (2) and (6) with the addition of the word *please* as given in (7) and (8):

7. Can you pass the salt please.

8. Would you please pass the salt.

It is interesting that the addition of the word *please,* which occurs only in requests, seems to remove the secondary illocutionary force almost entirely. It would be inappropriate to interpret *Can you pass the salt please* as a simple question.

Table 2.2. The grammatical form of direct commands and requests

Directives	Example	Grammatical form
– commanding action	Close the door!	Imperative
– requesting action	Please close the door.	Please + imperative
– requesting information	What time is it?	Question (WH)
	Where are you going?	Question (WH)
	Is it time to finish?	Question (yes/no)
	Is the door closed?	Question (yes/no)
	Do you like ice-cream?	Question (yes/no)

The examples in Table 2.2 show that the **Imperative** (with or without *please*) is the basic grammatical form used for **commanding** and **requesting** action, whereas information requests contain either **interrogative pronouns** (*when* words in English) or the **inversion of the subject and the auxiliary** in Yes/No questions. The supporting auxiliary *do* is required if the sentence has no other auxiliary.

Direct directives are actually used relatively infrequently in the languages of the world. **Indirect forms** are more common. In contexts where direct forms are used, they tend to be employed among similarly aged siblings, friends, and other equals.

Bargiela-Chiappini and Harris (1996), who analysed 32 authentic texts written by and to the managing director of an international joint venture, found that the forms of requests tended to vary according to whether the request was of a 'routine' type or whether it was more complex (which they labelled 'relational').

Table 2.3 illustrates the more restricted set of request forms that they found were used in 'routine' contexts, compared with the broader, more elaborate set of request forms used by the managing director.

Table 2.3. Request form-types

Form-type ('routine' texts)	Occurrences	Form-type ('relational' texts)	Occurrences
please + imperative	3	please + neg. imperative	1
would you please	3	please + imperative	1
please could you	3	you will need to	1
could you	1	they should ensure that	1
can you please	1	I suggest you enclose	1
I would be grateful if you would	1	I suggest we discuss	1
I would be obliged if you would	1	I would like to see	3
it is intended to add	1	will you please	2
		could you please	1
		can you please	1
		can we please	1
		I would be grateful if	1
		I would be grateful if you could	4
		I would appreciate your	1
		I would v.m. appreciate your	1
		I believe it would be worthwhile	1
		I would be grateful if you would	2
		perhaps you may like to	1
		perhaps we could	1
		perhaps we can	1

(from Bargiela-Chiappini & Harris 1996:644)

2.3   SUMMARY

In this chapter we have seen how the frameworks of Grice and Searle can provide a basis to explain how speakers use context to interpret language forms. We have also seen how some aspects of Grice's framework need to be modified to be cross-culturally applicable.

Additional examples of the speech acts of request, complaint and apology in different cultures are examined in Chapter 4.

2.4   REVIEW

1. **Key Terms:** Speech acts (direct and indirect), locution, illocution, perlocution, Cooperative Principle, maxims of conversation (Quality; Quantity; Relevance; Manner), conversational implicature, inference, assertive, directive, directness, indirectness, norms.

2. **Key Ideas**
   Having read this chapter you should:
   a. understand the difference between direct and indirect speech acts;
   b. appreciate how people of different cultures may draw different inferences from the same utterance;
   c. be aware of the significance of such cultural differences for intercultural interaction.

3. **Focus Questions**
   a. **'Flouting the Maxim'**
   Consider the following extract from Section 2.1:

   > . . . in those situations in which a speaker blatantly fails to observe a maxim with the deliberate intention of causing an implicature. In such contexts, the speaker, however, does not intentionally mean to deceive or mislead the hearer, only to induce the hearer to search for an additional meaning to that of the expressed meaning. Grice termed this process by which the implicature is produced 'flouting a maxim'.

   Provide an example of 'flouting a maxim'. Indicate the social interaction, cultural norms and environmental factors which influence the interpretation of its conversational implicature.

   b. **Speech Acts**
   Using Searle's (1979) subdivision of performatives, provide an example for each of the five types of speech acts. Indicate their Propositional Content as well as the Preparatory, Sincerity and Essential Conditions for each type of Speech Act (use Table 2.1 as a guide).

c. Indirect Speech Acts

(i) Provide an example of an indirect speech act and describe its primary illocutionary and its secondary illocutionary force using Searle's (1975) definition (see section 2.2). Explain the influence of the cultural assumptions of mutually shared background on the interpretation of this indirect speech act.

(ii) How could this indirect speech act be misunderstood in an intercultural context? Give an example of the linguistic and cultural context in which it could be misconstrued.

4. Research Analysis: Grice's maxims

a. Consider the following maxims as defined by Grice (1975:45–7) and revised by Clyne (1994):

Manner: Avoid obscurity of expression
Avoid ambiguity
Be brief
Be orderly
Manner: *Supermaxim* – 'Be perspicacious'.

Maxims

1. 'Do not make it any more difficult to understand than may be dictated by questions of face and authority.'
2. 'Make clear your communicative intent unless this is against the interests of politeness or of maintaining a dignity-driven cultural core value, such as harmony, charity or respect.'
3. 'Make your contribution the appropriate length required by the nature and purpose of the exchange and the discourse parameters of your culture.'
4. 'Structure your discourse according to the requirements of your culture.'
5. 'In your contribution, take into account anything you know or can predict about the interlocutor's communication expectations.'
(Clyne 1994:194–5)

(i) Why are Clyne's (1994) revisions of the maxim of Manner regarded as being more appropriate for interpreting utterances in an intercultural context?

(ii) Why is Clyne's fifth maxim of Manner important to the interpretation of an utterance in intercultural contexts? Provide an intercultural communication example that might illustrate this.

(iii) Is the concept of 'orderliness' highly valued in your culture? Describe the appropriateness of Grice's 'be orderly' in your daily communication patterns.

(iv) Based on your answer to the previous question, do you think Clyne's revisions relating to 'be orderly' overcome the limits of Grice's maxim? Give reasons for your answer.

b. Now further consider the extract taken from the above discussion regarding the Maxim of Manner (see section 2.1):

> Cam Nguyên (1991:43) has identified what she terms the Vietnamese 'tolerance for ambiguity'. This 'tolerance for ambiguity' is accompanied by a preference for a 'circular' discourse structure, which involves merely suggesting examples of an implicit perception and continually returning to this perception to expand upon it. Ide (1989) also postulates that the 'tolerance for ambiguity' relates to the tendency of 'indirectness' at the pragmatic level of some East (and South-east) Asian languages.

(i) Would you describe your own culture as having a 'tolerance for ambiguity'? Give reasons.

(ii) How does having a 'tolerance for ambiguity' or a lack of 'tolerance of ambiguity' affect the discourse structures in your culture?

(iii) Describe some possible negative perceptions and consequences which may arise in an intercultural communication context where there are two people, one from a culture that values ambiguity, another from one which values a higher level of certainty. Provide at least two strategies of how such negative perceptions and consequences may be overcome and successful intercultural communication can occur.

5. Research Exercise

There are a variety of ways to ask someone at the dinner table to *pass the salt*.

1. Pass the salt (please).
2. Can you pass the salt?
3. Can you reach the salt?
4. Would you mind passing the salt?
5. I would appreciate it if you would pass the salt.
6. Would you pass the salt?

Using the above example as a guideline, conduct a survey of at least five people to determine their interpretation of different request forms and their literal and non-literal meanings. You can use the above request forms of English, or design your own request forms using a language that you know well.

NOTE

1 Searle (1979) uses the term *illocutionary act,* where he earlier used the term *speech.* The latter term is used here because it has subsequently received wider use.

SUGGESTED FURTHER READING

Grice, H. P. 1975 'Logic and conversation'. In Cole P. & Morgan J. (eds) *Syntax and Semantics 3: Speech Acts.* New York: Academic Press.

Levinson, S. C. 1983 *Pragmatics.* Cambridge: Cambridge University Press.

Searle, J. R. 1969 *Speech Acts.* Cambridge: Cambridge University Press.

Searle, J. R. 1975 'Indirect speech acts'. In Cole P. & Morgan J. (eds) *Syntax and Semantics 3 (Speech Acts).* New York: Academic Press.

3 | Politeness and face

ALL SOCIAL GROUPS HAVE **preferred ways of speaking** – for example, contemporary English greetings may include:

> Hi, What's up? How's it going? G'day (Australian English), How are you? Hello, How do you do?

While *How do you do?* would be highly valued at a formal occasion, it would not be a good way to greet your friend in the morning. You would need something less formal, more cool, more humorous – even perhaps a loud groan! In this chapter we will examine what makes an utterance appropriate in a given social context but not in another. This basis will contribute to an understanding of parallel complexity in intercultural communication.

Most languages have differing styles of communication according to:

- levels of familiarity (e.g. family, friends, acquaintances, strangers)
- levels of formality (e.g. extremely formal to informal)
- types of situations (e.g. professional, business, sport, private, public)
- relative age
- gender.

Getting these levels correct is often called **socially appropriate behaviour** or **politeness**.

Many people tend to think of politeness as the use of extremely formal language, but most linguists perceive politeness as a continuum of **appropriate communication**. Fraser (1990:220) cites the following example from the 1872 version of *Ladies' Book of Etiquette and Manual of Politeness* to illustrate the general folk perception of equating 'politeness' with 'good manners':[1]

> . . . avoid topics which may be supposed to have any direct reference to events or circumstances which may be painful.

> [in the event a lady unintentionally raises a troublesome subject, she is instructed that] in that case, do not stop abruptly, when you perceive that it causes pain, and above all, do not make the matter worse by apologizing; turn to another subject as soon as possible, and pay no attention to the agitation your unfortunate remark may have excited.

> Never question the veracity of any statement made in general conversation:

> . . . if you are certain a statement is false, and it is injurious to another person, who may be absent, you may quietly and courteously inform the speaker that he is mistaken, but if the falsehood is of no consequence, let it pass.

One of the key points that this etiquette advice advocates is that one should try to avoid upsetting people. This notion of avoiding conflict or confrontation is an integral element of appropriate language usage, finding its way into the language of almost all social groups – and it is this that is generally recognised as 'politeness'.

3.1 THEORIES OF POLITENESS: BROWN AND LEVINSON

One of the major approaches to politeness is Brown and Levinson's (1978) theory of politeness phenomena (revised slightly in 1987). This model consists of three basic notions – **face, face-threatening acts (FTAs)** and **politeness strategies**. Brown and Levinson's account of politeness was based on the analysis of three unrelated languages and cultures, namely English, Tamil (a Dravidian language) and Tzeltal (a language of the Mayan family of Central America) and was claimed to have universal applicability.

FACE

The central concept of **face** is derived from both the English folk perception of 'being embarrassed or humiliated, or "losing face"' (Brown & Levinson 1987:61) and from the work of Goffman (1955, 1967). In Brown and Levinson's terms, the concept of 'face' refers to the desire that all people have to maintain and defend their own self-image.

The second basic notion of Brown and Levinson's model is the concept of **face-threatening acts** *(FTAs)*.

Face is something that can be lost, maintained or enhanced, and any threat to face must be continually monitored during an interaction. It is believed to be in everyone's best interest that face be maintained.

Brown and Levinson (1987:24) suggest that some acts are intrinsically **threatening to the face** and require softening. Therefore, language-users develop politeness strategies to reduce the face loss that may result from an interaction that is face-threatening.

Brown and Levinson (1987:61) make a distinction between positive and negative face; which they define in a way that many find counter-intuitive, but which is still widely used in the literature. Brown and Levinson's definitions are as follows:

Positive face: the positive consistent self-image or 'personality' (crucially including the desire that this self-image be appreciated and approved of) claimed by interactants.

Negative face: the basic claim to territories, personal preserves, rights to non-distraction – that is, to freedom of action and freedom from imposition.

Regardless of the problems with this terminology, the key observation is that politeness has two important aspects; preserving a person's positive self-image and avoiding imposing on a person's freedom.

The above aspects of *face* can give rise to the following four types of **face-threatening acts**, identified by Brown and Levinson (1987:65–6):

- Acts threatening to the Hearer's Negative Face (freedom of action): e.g. ordering, advising, threatening, warning
- Acts threatening to the Hearer's Positive Face (self image): e.g. complaining, criticizing, disagreeing, raising taboo topics
- Acts threatening to the Speaker's Negative Face (freedom of action): e.g. accepting an offer, accepting thanks
- Acts threatening to the Speaker's Positive Face (self image): e.g. apologizing, accepting a compliment, confessing.

Brown and Levinson (1987:74) suggest that the assessment of the seriousness of a face-threatening act involves the following factors in many and perhaps all cultures:

D the *Social Distance* between the Speaker and the Hearer (i.e. the degree of familiarity and solidarity they share, or might be thought to share)

P the *Relative Power* of the Speaker with respect to the Hearer (i.e. the degree to which the Speaker can impose on the Hearer)

> **R**   the *Absolute Ranking* of the imposition in a particular culture (both in terms of (1) the expenditure of goods and/or services by the Hearer, (2) the right of the Speaker to perform the act; and (3) the degree to which the Hearer welcomes the imposition).

Brown and Levinson (1987:80) illustrate the interaction of these variables by citing the subsequent examples.

In the case of requests for 'free goods' or small services (low imposition (R)) between members of the public (P not relevant), then either of the following might be used by the Speaker on account of the relative Social Distance between the Speaker and the Hearer:

> 1. *Excuse me, would you by any chance have the time?*
> 2. *Got the time mate?*

It is Brown and Levinson's intuition (1987:80) that (1) would be used where the Speaker and the Hearer were distant (speakers from different parts, for instance), and (2) where the Speaker and the Hearer were close (either known to each other, or perceptibly 'similar' in social terms).

In regards to the P variable (relative power), D and R being more or less constant and having small values (e.g. if the Speaker and the Hearer know each other and the imposition is for free goods), then either of the following might be used depending on the relative power between the Speaker and the Hearer:

> 3. *Excuse me sir, would it be alright if I smoke?*
> 4. *Mind if I smoke?*

Brown and Levinson (1987:80) suggest that (3) might be said by an employee to his boss, while (4) might be said by the boss to the employee in the same situation.

(Now that smoking is less widely acceptable, the contexts in which such utterances would be appropriate are more restricted, yet we believe the comparison still holds.)

In regards to the R variable (degree of imposition), Brown and Levinson (1987:81) provide the following illustration; supposing P is small and D is great (e.g. the Speaker and Hearer are strangers), and P and D are held constant, then either of the following might be used depending on the degree of imposition (R):

> 5. *Look, I'm terribly sorry to bother you but would there be any chance of your lending me just enough money to get a railway ticket to get home? I must have dropped my purse and I just don't know what to do.*
> 6. *Hey, got change for a quarter?*

Brown and Levinson suggest that both might be uttered at a railway station by a frustrated traveller to a stranger, but that their intuitions are that in saying (5) the Speaker considers the FTA to be much more serious than the FTA in (6). 'Our conclusion is that in the ranking of impositions in Anglo–American culture, asking for a substantial amount of money without recompense is much more of an imposition than a request to search one's pocket for change' (Brown & Levinson 1987:81).

The third basic notion of the Brown and Levinson model relates to the choice of **Redress Strategies**, which are employed when the weight of the imposition is perceived as being face-threatening. Brown and Levinson acknowledge that the degree to which a given act rates as face-threatening as well as the social importance to distance and power, are culturally determined, and may differ according to the situation within a particular cultural environment (1987:76–9). However, they do assert that P, D and R 'seem to do a remarkably adequate job in predicting politeness assessments' (1987:17).

Brown and Levinson's schematic representation of possible politeness strategies is summarised in Figure 3.1. The top options (e.g. Do the face-threatening act) are considered appropriate if the imposition is relatively small, whereas the bottom options (e.g. Don't do the act) are appropriate if the risk to face is high.

Brown and Levinson's model thus tries to account for choices that speakers make in avoiding threats to a hearer's self-image (positive face) or freedom from imposition (negative face). The model assumes that in choosing how to phrase speech acts that may threaten the hearer's positive or negative face, a speaker takes into account the factors of: relative power between the speaker and hearer (P), relative social distance between the speaker and hearer (S), and the relative degree of the imposition involved (R). Meier (1995a:346), in a somewhat negative analysis of Brown and Levinson's model, suggests that Brown and Levinson's claim for the universality of the concept of face is only made 'to the extent that positive face wants and negative face wants are common to all people, as is a mutual knowledge of face, a social pressure to attend to it, and the presence of principles governing the realization of indirect speech acts'.

While researchers tend to agree that the notion of *face* seems to be a key principle underlying politeness in all cultures, it may not be a principle that all members of a community are consciously aware of. Within our own immediate contacts, we may all know people who are not aware of any concept relating to face and face-saving, yet use politeness strategies that reflect the concept of face. It would seem that individuals in some cultures can acquire conventionally polite ways of speaking and interacting as a result

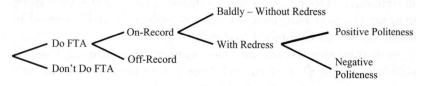

If Low Face Risk to the Participant

If High Face Risk to the Participant

Explanation of terms

On-record – when only one intention can be identified by the participants
e.g. 'I promise that I will pick you up at 4 o'clock'.

If the participants decide that 'I' (the Speaker) has unambiguously declared the intention of committing the above future act, then it is regarded as 'on-record'.

Off-record – the avoidance of direct impositions
e.g. 'I'm out of cash. I forgot to go to the bank today'.

Baldly, without redress – involves undertaking an act in the most direct, unambiguous and clear manner
e.g. 'Clean your room' ('Do X!').

People will only do an FTA in such a manner if the Speaker does not fear retribution from the Hearer.

> **Redressive action** – 'gives face' to the Hearer, meaning that the Speaker tries to overcome any possible damage from the FTA by modifying their behaviour i.e. positive or negative politeness strategies.

> **Positive politeness** – strategies addressed to the Hearer's self-image (positive face), e.g. by treating him as a member of an in-group, a friend, a person whose wants and personality traits are known and liked. (Thus involving expressions of solidarity, informality and familiarity.) e.g. exaggerate interest in H, sympathise with H and avoid disagreement.

> **Negative politeness** – is oriented towards H's negative face and involves expressions of restraint, self-effacement, and formality e.g. being conventionally indirect, giving deference, using hedges, apologizing for imposing.

Figure 3.1. Possible politeness strategies
(Summary of Brown & Levinson 1987:69–70)

of social norms of communication, without understanding the notions of face that may underpin these norms. At the same time, others in the same society may be more conscious of the notions of face and face-saving.

The concepts inherent to the Brown and Levinson model have formed the basis of much subsequent research in a range of different contexts and across cultures. Brown and Levinson make reference to some of these in the introduction to the 1987 reissue of their original (1978) work, arguing that, for the most part, their key concepts still stand and are useful in illuminating cross-cultural differences (1987:1–50).

In the following sections we review some of the subsequent work on politeness, almost all of which can be seen to have been informed in some way by the work of Brown and Levinson.

3.2 DIFFERENT PERSPECTIVES ON POLITENESS

Fraser (1990) identifies four major perspectives on the discussion of linguistic politeness:

- the social norm view
- the conversational maxim view
- the face-saving view
- the conversational-contract view.

Brown and Levinson's approach, as discussed above, is represented in Fraser's 'face-saving view'. Alternative approaches are represented under the other three headings 'the social norm view', 'the conversational maxim view' and Fraser's own characterisation of politeness 'the conversational-contract view'.

According to Fraser (1990:220) *the social norm view* relates to the folk understanding of politeness in English-speaking countries. He argues that such a view:

> ... assumes that each society has a particular set of social norms consisting of more or less explicit rules that prescribe a certain behaviour, state of affairs, or a way of thinking in a context.

Impoliteness, which is equated with rudeness, occurs 'when action is to the contrary' of the norm, whereas politeness develops 'when an action is in congruence with the norm' (Fraser 1990:220). In some respects, the social norm view is consistent with contemporary approaches which view politeness as 'socially appropriate behaviour'.

The second perspective, *the conversational maxim view* is based on Grice's concepts of the Cooperative Principle and his four conversational maxims: *Quantity, Quality, Relevance* and *Manner* (discussed in Chapter 2). Fraser identifies Lakoff (1973) as one of the first researchers to adopt Grice's constructs to elaborate upon politeness. It can be inferred from Lakoff's work that 'politeness' is the avoidance of offence (Fraser 1990:223). In a later work, Lakoff claims that politeness is 'a device used in order to reduce friction in personal interaction' (Lakoff 1979:64). Lakoff (1973) proposes the following two rules of Pragmatic Competence:

1. Be Clear (essentially Grice's maxims)
2. Be Polite.

In addition, Lakoff posits the sub-maxims:

Rule 1: Don't impose
Rule 2: Give options
Rule 3: Make Hearer feel good.

Leech (1983) has also used Grice's Cooperative Principle and maxims as the basis for his approach. He has, however, elaborated his model to include politeness maxims and a set of rules, which accompany the maxims and are used to determine the degree of interaction between the maxims in a particular situation. These maxims are:

Tact Maxim
> Minimise Hearer costs: maximise Hearer benefit
> (Do not put others in a position where they have to break the tact maxim)

Generosity Maxim
> Minimise your own benefit; maximise your Hearer's benefit

Approbation Maxim
> Minimise Hearer dispraise; maximise Hearer praise

Modesty Maxim
> Minimise self-praise; maximise self-dispraise

Agreement Maxim
> Minimise disagreement between yourself and others; maximise agreement between yourself and others

Sympathy Maxim
> Minimise antipathy between yourself and others; maximise sympathy between yourself and others.

The fourth perspective, the *conversational-contract view* described by Fraser is an elaboration of a politeness model, first outlined by Fraser in 1975 and then by Fraser and Nolen (1981). The basic premise of this approach is that in a given conversation each participant has his or her own individual set of rights and obligations, which influence the flow and content of the interaction. Such rights and obligations can be renegotiated throughout the interaction and are influenced by the participant's past experiences, institutional rhetoric, as well as other factors such as the perceived status and power of the Speaker and/or Hearer.

While Lakoff and Leech use the term *maxim* in their models we note that they are employing the term *maxim* in a very different manner to Grice. Grice's maxims focus more on expectations regarding language and how information is conveyed in everyday conversations (e.g. Quantity, Quality, Relevance and Manner), whereas Lakoff's sub-maxims and Leech's maxims are more to do with interpersonal relationships.

In the last decade, researchers such as Janney and Arndt (1992) have suggested that 'linguistic politeness' should be viewed as *socially acceptable behaviour*. They make the distinction between *interpersonal politeness,* or what is termed *tact,* and *social politeness*. Their concept of *tact* is similar to that of Brown and Levinson's and is described as 'an individual's show of consideration for *alter* by addressing *alter's* (positive or negative) face needs in order to avoid conflict' (Meier 1995a:347). Social politeness, in contrast, is 'the use of social conventions for routine behavior (e.g. greetings, interrupting, leave-taking)' (Meier 1995a:347). This distinction is also employed by Blum-Kulka (1989). Blum-Kulka differentiates *tact* and *formal politeness* as expressions of *appropriate, polite behaviour* (1989:67).

Watts, Ide and Ehlich (1992) draw a somewhat similar distinction between *first order politeness* and *second order politeness*. First order politeness is described as 'commonsense notions of politeness' and is regarded as pertaining to the individual. Second order politeness, however, is characterised as the process which maintains a balance between the participants in a given interaction. Watts (1989), and Watts, Ide and Ehlich (1992) also term this second order politeness as *politic* which contrasts with the first order *polite* behaviour (see also Watts (2003) and Meier (1995a,b) for a further discussion of politic and polite behaviours).

Meier (1995a:347) points out that the approaches of Blum-Kulka (1990, 1992), Ide (1989), Ide et al. (1992), Lakoff (1989), and Ehlich (1992) all focus on similar notions to Watts' distinction between 'polite' and 'politic' behaviour. For example, Ide (1989) views the unmarked type of politeness as 'non-polite' or 'zero-polite' which corresponds with Watts' 'politic' and which contrasts with her 'plus-valued politeness' (Ide et al. 1992) or 'polite' category (Watts' 'polite' behaviour).

3.3 CRITICISMS OF BROWN AND LEVINSON

As we have seen, the model proposed by Brown and Levinson (1978, 1987) has been the subject of much subsequent research and also much comment and some criticism.

One of the key problems that we see with Brown and Levinson's politeness model is that it is concerned principally with politeness strategies in the context of face-threatening acts. Yet interaction does not exist entirely of face-threatening acts. The building of positive relationships through mutual caring and assistance over time is surely important, and is usually accompanied by the expression of mutual appreciation and praise. Such actions contribute to the building of positive face between individuals, in an ongoing way. However, Brown and Levinson's model only treats this in passing.

The second problem we see with Brown and Levinson's model relates to their characterisation of positive politeness strategies in terms of expressions of solidarity, informality and familiarity alone. Surely there are many social contexts in the English-speaking world in which affirmation of the positive self-image of an addressee who is senior in age, experience or status, or socially distant from the speaker, is overtly expressed, sometimes with formality, and deference. In other cultures, particularly Asian cultures, the expression of deference and respect is almost mandatory with addressees who are senior in age, experience or status. (In certain restricted contexts, for example, among employees who have worked together for a significant period, private exchanges might be less formal, but in public, conventional deference to seniors would be mandatory.)

To account for the under-representation of deference in the Brown and Levinson model, researchers have drawn attention to the fact that the model is based on the individual, rather than the social group. The distinction between the individual and the group has its roots with Tönnies' 1974 comparison of *Gemeinschaft* (individual) and *Gesellschaft* (society) (see de Kadt 1998:178).

Mao (1994) suggests that Brown and Levinson's concept of 'face' as an image that intrinsically belongs to the individual, to the 'self', contrasts with Goffman's original interpretation of 'face' as 'a "public property"' which is seen as given or 'loaned' to individuals depending upon the situation. De Kadt (1998) argues that this difference in the interpretation of 'face' is of great significance when discussing this concept in terms of universality, especially for non-Western cultures. De Kadt suggests that Goffman's original concept (Goffman 1967) has the advantage of better accommodating both volitional and social indexing aspects of politeness.

For instance, Goffman (1967:44) regarded 'face' as an element present in every society and indicated that:

> societies everywhere, if they are to be societies, must mobilise their members
> as self-regulating participants in social encounters.

Goffman suggested that 'each person, subculture and society seems to have its own characteristic repertoire of face-saving practices, yet these are all drawn from a single logically coherent framework of possible practices' (1967:13). Such a perspective seems to be in opposition to Brown and Levinson's concept of face in that, according to Goffman, 'face' is used in terms of 'persons' and 'societies' not just 'individuals'.

De Kadt (1998:188) found that Zulu speakers use both verbal and non-verbal means of communication to address the issue of 'face'. Greeting rituals are viewed as being compulsory and are generally performed by the subordinate person in the interaction. These greetings are followed by enquiries into the status of the other's health and wellbeing, not by the subordinate, but this time by the person of higher status. Generally, in such interactions, terms of address are used which specify the participants' roles in the coming conversation. For example, de Kadt (1998:188) reports that:

> . . . an adult male could be referred to by his wife as *baba ka Sipho,* 'father of Sipho', by pupils at the school where he teaches as *thisha,* 'teacher', by his colleagues as *mngame wami,* 'my friend', (and) by men of the same age as *infowethu,* 'my brother'.

This example shows that for the Zulu speaker, the status of the participants determines the choice of terms and phrases. In such a society the concept of *face* is one of mutuality and is paid attention to by both participants throughout the interaction.

De Kadt argues that Goffman's broader definition of 'face', in contrast to Brown and Levinson's, is thus more appropriate in understanding the social indexing and volitional aspects of Zulu politeness. 'Such a perspective diverges from the more limiting focus on FTAs, which is present in the Brown and Levinson model' (de Kadt 1998:189).

Brown and Levinson's focus on 'individual face' has also attracted much criticism from Japanese linguists. Matsumoto (1988, 1989) argues that this notion of *face* with its focus on individual territorial rights is difficult to apply to the Japanese language context. Matsumoto (1988) and Ide (1989) argue that individual rights are not so important in the Japanese culture because cultural norms focus more on the positional relation to others than with individual territory.

The politeness strategies proposed by Brown and Levinson have also encountered much criticism. Ide (1989) argues that Brown and Levinson's concept of 'face' and their distinction between positive and negative politeness strategies does not account for the Japanese notion of *wakimae* (which Ide translates as 'discernment'). She believes that Japanese social interactions do not allow for interactional choice, because social norms are predetermined by a person's place in society. According to Ide (1989), Brown and Levinson's approach does not accommodate such predetermined forms of interaction because it is not a matter of establishing the level of imposition, rather of the superior–inferior relationship in society. In this context, Goffman's original interpretation of 'face' in terms of its volitional features and social-indexing perspectives is perhaps more appropriate for such cultures.

While Ide (1989) describes 'politeness' in relation to 'discernment', other approaches to politeness have employed the term 'deference' (e.g. Adegbija 1989; Blum-Kulka 1989). Meier (1995a:348) points out that such a term is quite often used interchangeably with politeness and that this is not surprising given that 'Brown and Levinson derived their model from Goffman (1967), whose two forms of deference are transformed by Brown and Levinson into their two types of politeness strategies'.

Another criticism of Brown and Levinson's model has been the connection between politeness and indirectness. Brown and Levinson suggest that there is a direct link between indirectness and politeness – the more obscure the intention of an utterance, the more polite it is; the more direct or clear the intention, the less polite it is. House and Kasper (1981), Tannen (1981), Wierzbicka (1985, 1991, 2003), Blum-Kulka and House (1989), and Bialystok (1993) have all examined the connection between politeness and the level of indirectness and found that the relationship between these two processes differs from culture to culture. For example, in Japanese discourse there is a closer link between politeness and indirectness than in American or Arabic cultures (Takahashi & Beebe 1993). Katriel (1986) found that in the Israeli Sabra culture there is a direct connection between politeness and directness. Wierzbicka (1985) suggests that Polish society is sometimes perceived as being generally 'impolite' or 'rude' due to the usage of performatives and imperatives for advice-giving and directives. Such types of utterances can be viewed as being 'too direct' in cultures which value indirectness as the norm.

Another problem with research that compares levels of directness and indirectness is that conclusions can only be relative to the cultures which are being contrasted. For example, if German speakers from House and Kasper's (1981) study, who are regarded as being direct, are compared with Greek speakers from Pavlidou's (1991), the Germans might be judged as being indirect in contrast to a higher level of directness of the Greek speakers. The same has been said about Australians who appear to be indirect when contrasted with Hebrew and German speakers (Blum-Kulka & House 1989).

As the above studies show, it is problematic to identify cultures solely in terms of a negative and positive orientation, especially when discussing indirectness and directness. Meier (1995b:386) believes that describing cultures in relation to such orientations is misleading and 'risks perpetuating national stereotypes and "linguacentricity"'.[2]

3.4 THE STUDY OF CROSS-CULTURAL PRAGMATICS USING NATURAL SEMANTIC METALANGUAGE

Wierzbicka (1972, 1985, 1991, 2003) has developed an approach to the study of cross-cultural semantics and cross-cultural pragmatics based on the explication of the meaning of words and illocutionary acts by the use of just over two dozen lexical primitives, which she suggests are semantic universals. Wierzbicka's methodology, which draws on the ideas of seventeenth century thinkers such as Descartes, Leibnitz and Locke, who were interested in how simple words could be used to define others, uses these semantic primitives to compare differences of definition between similar words and concepts in different languages. Wierzbicka (1994b) introduced the term 'cultural scripts' to refer to her technique for articulating cultural norms, values and practices using Natural Semantic Metalanguage.

The following example of differences in approach to 'self assertion' in Japanese and English (Wierzbicka 2003:72 ff.) contrasts the Western model [cultural script] based on the 'complex of individuality, autonomy, equality, rationality, aggression, and self-assertion' with the traditional Japanese 'complex of collectivism, interdependence, superordination-subordination, empathy, sentimentality, introspection and self-denial' as characterised by Lebra (1976:257).

Wierzbicka suggests that the main difference between the two cultural perspectives with regard to self-assertion can be represented simply as:

Japanese don't say: 'I want this', 'I don't want this'
Anglo–American do say: 'I want this', 'I don't want this'.

Wierzbicka continues; Japanese culture discourages people from expressing clearly their wishes, their preferences, and their desires (what they would or wouldn't like or want), whereas Anglo-Saxon culture encourages them to do so:

| *Japanese* | don't say: 'I would/wouldn't like (want) this' |
| *Anglo–American* | do say: 'I would/wouldn't like (want) this'. |

Furthermore, Japanese culture, in contrast to Anglo–American culture, discourages clear and unequivocal expression of personal opinions:

| *Japanese* | don't say: 'I think this/I don't think this' |
| *Anglo–American* | do say: 'I think this/I don't think this'. |

Wierzbicka reports the observations of Smith (1983:44–5): '. . . the Japanese are at pains to avoid contention and confrontation . . . much of the definition of a "good person" involves restraint in the expression of personal desires and opinions'. This restraint manifests one of the greatest Japanese cultural values, called *enryo*, a word usually translated as 'restraint' or 'reserve'. 'One way to express *enryo* is to avoid giving opinions and to sidestep choices when they are offered. As a matter of fact, choices are less often offered in Japan than in the United States' (Smith 1983:83–4).

Rather than trying to translate the Japanese term *enryo* into English cultural concepts such as reserve, restraint, modesty or self-effacement, Wierzbicka (1991:76) considers the observations of Smith (1983), quoted above, and similar observations by Doi (1973:12), Mitzutani and Mitzutani (1987) and Lebra (1976) and characterises the meaning of the Japanese word *enryo* in terms of concepts such as *want, think, say, good* or *bad,* in the following way:

enryo
X thinks:
I can't say to this person: I want this, I don't want this
                                     I think this. I don't think this
someone can feel something bad because of this
X doesn't say it because of this
X doesn't do some things because of this.

Wierzbicka (2003:76) observes that in English, on the contrary, one is expected to say clearly and unequivocally what one wants, what one would like, or what one thinks. She suggests that 'uninhibited self-assertion' is allowed and encouraged in mainstream, Anglo–American culture:

as long as it doesn't come into conflict with another cherished value of the culture, that is, personal autonomy. This means that while one is allowed to say in principle 'I want X', one is not allowed to say freely:
I want you to do X
since in this case, the speaker's right to 'self assertion' would come into conflict with the addressee's right to personal autonomy.

Wierzbicka suggests that this is why English has a number of interrogative-directive devices (sometimes called 'whimperatives') such as:

Would you do X?
Will you do X?
Could you do X?
Can you do X?
Why don't you do X?

She suggests that this collection of utterances can be characterised, with some reference to the autonomy of the addressee, for example:

I want you to do X
I don't know if you will do X
I want you to say if you will do it.

Returning to Japanese, Wierzbicka cites Matsumoto's (1988) observation that even though the use of interrogative structures is more limited in Japanese than it is in English, in Japanese 'the important thing is to show deference and acknowledge one's dependence on other people rather than to avoid the imposition'.

Wierzbicka concludes that, in many situations, it is easier (in Japanese) to say 'I want you to do X' than 'I want to do X' – as long as one acknowledges one's dependence on the addressee:

I want you to do X
I know that you don't have to do it
I say: it will be good for you if you do it
I think: you will do it because of this.

Wierzbicka (2003:78) summarises the comparison as follows:

In English, if one wants the addressee to do something, it is important to acknowledge the addressee's autonomy by inviting them to say whether or not they will comply with the request. Hence the proliferation and the frequency of 'whimperatives' in English. In Japanese, interrogative directive devices or 'whimperatives' exist, too, but their scope is much narrower than in English (cf. Matsumoto 1988, Kageyama-Tomori 1976). Instead, there is in Japanese a proliferation of devices acknowledging dependence on other people, and deference to other people. Hence, the basic way of making requests in Japanese involves not 'whimperatives' (that is quasi interrogative structures) but dependence acknowledging devices (usually combined with expressions of respect) . . .

Wierzbicka observes that, by contrast, in many other languages, for example Polish, Russian, Hebrew, Italian and Hungarian, the bare infinitive is used much more freely, and the use of interrogative structures in directives is much more limited.

Wierzbicka (1972, 1980, 1991, 2003) and other scholars such as Goddard (1989, 2005), Wierzbicka and Goddard (2004), and Harkins (1990) have examined a variety of micro and macro concepts (cultural scripts) in a great number of languages incorporating an explication in terms of Natural Semantic Metalanguage. Regardless of whether one is entirely happy with Wierzbicka's method of NSM explication, this body of research on cross-cultural pragmatics is significant in terms of the comprehensive inventory of concepts that have been compared and discussed.

3.5   COGNITIVE AND CULTURAL SCHEMA

Within recent approaches of cognitive linguistics, an individual's knowledge is represented in his/her cognitive schema and, by extension, cultural knowledge is represented using *cultural schema* of the sort exemplified here from the work of Sharifian (2004).

Sharifian (2004:123–5) illustrates the way in which a cultural schema known as *sharmandegi* (sometimes translated as 'being ashamed') is evident in the Persian language (Farsi) in a number of speech acts translated literally here:

> Expressing gratitude:
>   'You really make me ashamed.'
> Offering goods and services:
>   'Please help yourself, I'm ashamed, it's not worthy of you.'
> Requesting goods and services:
>   'I'm ashamed, can I beg some minutes of your time.'
> Apologising:
>   'I'm really ashamed that the noise from the kids didn't let you sleep.'

Sharifian (2004:125) suggests that in all cases, the *sharmandegi* schema 'seems to encourage Iranians to consider the possibility that in the company of others they may be doing or have done something wrong or something not in accordance with the other party's dignity'. He further comments that the idea of a common schema underlying the various instances of the use of the expression *sharmandegi* is also supported by the observation that all those speech acts may be responded to by the same formulaic expression, such as *doshmanetoon sharmandeh basheh* literally meaning 'your enemy be ashamed'.

Sharifian relates the *sharmandegi* schema to a higher level 'overarching' cultural schema which defines a core value of culture related to social relations that he calls *adab va ehteram*, roughly glossed as 'courtesy and respect' in English. He suggests that '(t)his higher-level schema encourages Iranians to constantly place the presence of others at the centre of their conceptualizations and monitor their own ways of thinking and talking to make them harmonious with the esteem that they hold for others'.

Sharifian argues that such 'cultural schemas' are conceptual structures that develop at the cultural level of cognition, rather than the psychological level. These schemas are knowledge templates that are represented in a distributed fashion across the minds in a cultural group. Cultural schemas are abstracted from social interactions between the members of a cultural group, who 'negotiate' and 'renegotiate' these schemas across generations. Such schemas can motivate thought and behaviour that is considered to be appropriate to a particular cultural group, and suggests that '(u)nfamiliarity with such schemas may lead to discomfort or misunderstanding during the process of intercultural communication'.

3.6   SUMMARY

As can be seen in this chapter, there has been considerable research interest on the phenomenon of 'politeness' spanning the last four decades. Brown and Levinson's model has provided an important foundation for analysing linguistic politeness and has drawn research attention to the relative importance of different aspects of politeness in different societies. In particular, the importance of conventional deference associated with an addressee's position in society has been clearly documented for many cultures. The expression of deference on account of age, relationship and status is required in all areas of communication in those cultures and has motivated a two-tier approach to politeness, one tier which relates to conventional deference that applies more generally, and a second tier that involves contextually motivated variation.

Meier suggests that the study of politeness requires that we 'persist in placing language within its broader social context' (1995a:353).

The use of Natural Semantic Metalanguage to analyse cultural scripts (e.g. Wierzbicka 2003; Wierzbicka & Goddard 2004), and the analysis provided by Sharifian (2004) and others (e.g. using 'cultural schema'), provide further insight on aspects of politeness, and provide a further perspective from which to study cross-cultural communication.

3.7 REVIEW

1. **Key Terms** Face (positive and negative), politeness (positive and negative), institutional power (P), social distance (D), relative imposition (R), speech–event; formality; sincerity; cultural script, natural semantic metalanguage, cultural schema.

2. **Key Ideas**
Having read this chapter you should:
   a. be able to differentiate between positive and negative face and positive and negative politeness
   b. appreciate why different levels of politeness may be appropriate or expected in different situations
   c. appreciate the different ways in which people express politeness
   d. appreciate the significance of cultural differences in expressions of politeness and the reasons for such (e.g. different preferences for positive and negative face; differences in the ascription of P, D, and R).

3. **Focus Questions**
   a. **Face-threatening acts**
      Based on your own experience and language background, provide an example of a face-threatening act and analyse it in terms of Brown and Levinson's (1987) factors of D, P and R which can be used to assess the seriousness of a face-threatening act (section 3.1).
   b. **Different perspectives on politeness**
      Using Fraser's (1990) discussion of four different perspectives of linguistic politeness (section 3.2), which one do you believe is the best approach in understanding and analysing politeness across cultures? Give reasons for your choice.
   c. **Brown and Levinson**
      The approach of Brown and Levinson (1978; 1987) has been widely criticised by researchers.
      (i) Provide three of the key problems concerning their approach which have been identified by their critics.
      (ii) Based on your own experience and language background, do you believe that such criticisms are well founded? Give reasons for your answer.

4. Research Analysis

Consider the following extract from Wierzbicka (1991, 2003) who refers to the observations of Smith (1983:83–4) in regard to Japanese:

> . . . the Japanese are at pains to avoid contention and confrontation . . . much of the definition of a 'good person' involves restraint in the expression of personal desires and opinions (Smith 1983:44–5).
>
> This restraint manifests one of the greatest Japanese cultural values, called *enryo*, a word usually translated as 'restraint' or 'reserve' . . . One way to express *enryo* is to avoid giving opinions and to sidestep choices when they are offered. As a matter of fact, choices are less often offered in Japan than in the United States . . .

a. Would you describe your own culture and the associated linguistic communication practices as being similar to that of the Japanese? How are your own linguistic practices similar to or different from that described in the above quote?

b. In your own culture, is the avoidance of giving opinions and showing a high level of restraint in the expression of personal desires highly valued and seen as being 'polite'? Give at least two examples to illustrate your argument.

c. How would the politeness strategies of a Japanese speaker and an American English speaker in an intercultural communication setting differ from each other? How would the concept of face and the strategies used to redress any face-threatening acts differ amongst these two interlocutors?

Wierzbicka (2003, 1991:78) further describes the politeness strategies used in English and Japanese. Consider the following extract:

> In English, if one wants the addressee to do something, it is important to acknowledge the addressee's autonomy by inviting them to say whether or not they will comply with the request. Hence the proliferation and the frequency of 'whimperatives' in English. In Japanese, interrogative directive devices or 'whimperatives' exist, too, but their scope is much narrower than in English (cf. Matsumoto 1988; Kageyama-Tomori 1976). Instead, there is in Japanese a proliferation of devices acknowledging dependence on other people, and deference to other people. Hence, the basic way of making requests in Japanese involves not 'whimperatives' (that is quasi interrogative structures) but dependence acknowledging devices (usually combined with expressions of respect).

d. Based on the above quote, are 'whimperatives' commonly used in your first language? Give two examples to illustrate your answer.

e. Using the above two extracts as a guideline for your answer, why are 'whimperatives' less likely to be used as a politeness strategy in Japanese than in English?

5. Research Exercise
Conduct a brief survey of around six people from at least two different language backgrounds and ask them to define what the terms 'polite' and 'impolite' mean to them. Are the people's definitions consistent with Brown and Levinson's description of politeness strategies (i.e. positive and negative politeness strategies). Provide examples to substantiate your findings.

NOTES

1 This example was quoted by Fraser 1990 from J. S. Locke (cited in Kasher 1986).
2 The term 'linguacentricity' refers to the limitations of perspective that may result from using a single language as a model for understanding all others.

SUGGESTED FURTHER READING

Ide, S. 1990 'How and why do women speak more politely in Japanese?' In Ide S. & McGloin N. H. (eds) *Aspects of Japanese Women's Language*. Tokyo: Kuroshio Publishers, pp. 63–79.

Lee-Wong, S. M. 1994a 'Imperatives in requests: Direct or impolite, observations from Chinese'. *Journal of Pragmatics*, vol. 4, pp. 491–515.

Mao, Lu Ming, R. 1994 'Beyond politeness theory: "Face" revisited and renewed'. *Journal of Pragmatics*, vol. 21, pp. 451–86.

Meier, A. J. 1995a 'Defining politeness: Universality in appropriateness'. *Language Sciences*, vol. 17, no. 4, pp. 345–56.

Meier, A. J. 1995b 'Passages of politeness'. *Journal of Pragmatics*, vol. 24, pp. 381–92.

Zadjman, A. 1995 'Humorous face-threatening acts: Humour as strategy'. *Journal of Pragmatics*, vol. 23, pp. 325–39.

4 | Speech acts and politeness across cultures

In this chapter we build on the ideas presented in Chapters 2 and 3 and examine some of the growing body of research on the inter-relatedness between **direct** and **indirect speech acts** and **politeness** in **different cultural contexts**.

One approach to research in this area involves the comparison of speech acts used by native speakers of one language with those used by native speakers of other languages in a range of parallel contexts. The CCSARP project, which examined Cross-Cultural Speech Act Realization Patterns in eight languages (Blum-Kulka, House & Kasper 1989)[1] is a major study of this kind and is based on discourse completion tests conducted with native speakers of each language. This approach is exemplified below from parts of the CCSARP project, and also research conducted by Suszczyńska (1999).

Other research has involved language learners acquiring a second language, and has examined the extent to which their use of the second language may contain pragmatic features of their first language, or failure to comprehend pragmatic features of the second language. This area of research, which began as a branch of second language research, now forms part of the growing body of research known as **Interlanguage Pragmatics** (e.g. Kasper & Blum-Kulka 1993; Trosborg 1994).

The terms **Intercultural Pragmatics** and **Intercultural Communication** are being increasingly used to refer to both research involving native speakers and competent second language users, and also research involving participants from different cultures engaged in natural intercultural communication in a language that is not a first language to any of the speakers. Examples of research of the first type is that of Béal (1992) conducted in a French company in Australia, discussed in Chapters 5 and 10; and two examples of intercultural business meetings by Marriott (1990) and Spencer-Oatey and Xing (2003) discussed in Chapter 10. Examples of the second type of research, involving participants from different cultures communicating in a language that is not their own, is exemplified in the research of Clyne (1994), reported below in section 4.4, and that of Neil (1996) discussed in Chapter 11, which are both based on workplace communication in English by speakers from non-English-speaking backgrounds.

4.1   REQUESTS: INDIRECTNESS AND POLITENESS

Blum-Kulka (1987) examines indirectness and politeness in requests used by participants who were asked to rank a set of varied requests in terms of **directness** and also in terms of **politeness** in Hebrew and in English. The research finds that while some types of requests were ranked similarly for **indirectness** and politeness within a given language or across languages, this was not the case for all request types.

The request types consisted of a set of nine mutually exclusive strategy types postulated to represent a cross-culturally valid set, which are described and exemplified in English in Table 4.1.

The research methodology involved students who were native speakers of Hebrew or English being asked to rank a series of randomly presented requests relating to five different situations in terms of either directness or politeness. Tables 4.2 and 4.3 show the findings for the directness ratings, and the politeness ratings respectively. The scores for the category means are included in Tables 4.2 and 4.3 as a way of seeing how distinct the separation is between different strategies.

Blum-Kulka (1987:136) finds that the most direct strategy (**Mood Derivable – Imperative**) is considered the most direct and the least polite in both Hebrew and English. Within and across languages there is some variation in the other categories.

In neither language is the strategy which is judged as the most indirect judged as the most polite. In both languages **Hints** are rated as the most indirect and **Query Preparatory**, which is achieved by means of conventional indirectness, (*Could/Would you . . . ?*) as the most polite.

There is some systematic variation between languages as to the relative politeness of **Hints** compared to other forms of hedging or suggestion, with English speakers regarding **Hints** more towards the **Politeness** end of the continuum than do the Hebrew speakers. English speakers, on the one hand, regarded **Want Statements** as more polite than **Obligation Statements**, while the reverse was true for Hebrew speakers.

Blum-Kulka (1987:135) notes that request forms drawn from natural speech samples were 'stripped' of both internal and external modifications

Table 4.1. Examples of the nine request categories

Descriptive category	Examples
1. Mood derivable (imperative)	Clean up the kitchen
	Move your car
2. Performative	I'm asking you to move your car
3. Hedged performative	I would like to ask you to move your car
4. Obligation statement	You'll have to move your car
5. Want statement	I would like you to clean the kitchen
	I want you to move your car
6. Suggestory formulas	How about cleaning up?
	Why don't you come and clean up the mess you made last night?
7. Query preparatory	Could you clean up the mess in the kitchen?
	Would you mind moving your car?
8. Strong hints (A)	You've left the kitchen in a right mess
9. Mild hints (B)	We don't want any crowding
	(as a request to move the car)

(from Blum-Kulka 1987:133)

Table 4.2. Directness scales in Hebrew and English for the nine request types

HEBREW		ENGLISH		
Strategy type	**Mean**	**Strategy type**	**Mean**	
Mood derivable (imperative)	1.5	Mood derivable (imperative)	1.6	**Direct**
Want statements	1.6	Obligation statements	1.9	
Obligation statements	1.8	Performatives	2.5	
Performatives	2.17	Want statements	2.5	
Suggestory	2.5	Hedged performative	2.6	
Hedged performatives	2.8	Query preparatory	2.7	
Query preparatory	3.01	Suggestory	2.8	
Hints (A)	5.6	Hints (A)	5.12	
Hints (B)	7.1	Hints (B)	6.40	**Indirect**

(from Blum-Kulka 1987:133)

such as hedges or politeness markers ('please') and reason justifications. We suggest that this creates a somewhat non-representative sample because *Would/Could you please . . .* is probably more frequent in English usage than *Would/Could you . . .*

Table 4.3. Politeness scales in Hebrew and English for the nine request types

HEBREW		ENGLISH		
Strategy type	Mean	Strategy type	Mean	
Mood derivable (imperative)	2.3	Mood derivable (imperative)	2.09	**Least polite**
Want statements	3.2	Obligation statements	2.84	
Obligation statements	3.36	Want statements	3.54	
Suggestory	4.18	Performatives	4.0	
Hints (A)	4.38	Suggestory	4.25	
Hints (B)	4.47	Hedged performative	5.09	
Performatives	6.06	Hints (A)	5.23	
Hedged performative	6.34	Hints (B)	5.33	**Most polite**
Query preparatory	7.08	Query preparatory	7.10	

(from Blum-Kulka 1987:133)

Despite this slight drawback, this methodology has resulted in some interesting cross-cultural comparisons.

House and Kasper (1981) report on research involving German and British subjects using a similar methodology to that reported in Blum-Kulka (1987), but with a focus on requests with a **low degree of imposition** between equals.

House and Kasper found that the most preferred request type for English speakers was the Query Preparatory type, for example *Can you close the window?*, while the most preferred type for German speakers was the Locution Derivable (= Obligation Statement) type, for example *You should close the window* (*Du solltest das Fenster zumachen*). Thus, they concluded that, on the whole, German students selected more direct requests than did their English counterparts.

House and Kasper (1981) also include a section examining the use of hedges of various kinds, which they called **Modality Markers**. Such an inclusion acknowledges the fact that although *Come here, Please come here* and *Come here will you*, are all **Mood Derivables** (Imperatives), the addition of *please* and *will you* (and their German counterparts *komm doch bitte mal her, ja*) also affect the directness of the utterance.

House and Kasper (1981:166–70) further identify two types of modality markers, which they call Downgraders and Upgraders. **Downgraders**, which include *please* and *will you*, play down the impact that the Speaker's utterance is likely to have on the Hearer, whereas **upgraders**, such as *absolutely, really, certainly,* increase the force or the impact an utterance is likely to have on the addressee.

4.2   COMPLAINTS

House and Kasper's 1981 paper also reports on the cross-cultural research of complaints. **Complaints** typically occur when the addressee has done an action (P) which the Speaker interprets as bad for him or her, and House and Kasper suggest that a complaint may include the following components:

- the action is referred to explicitly
- the speaker's negative evaluation of the action is expressed explicitly
- the addressee's agentive involvement is implicitly or explicitly expressed
- the negative evaluation of both the addressee's action and of the addressee himself/herself are implicitly or explicitly stated.

House and Kasper (1981:159–62) characterise eight **levels of directness** by using a single situational context in which the addressee (Y), who is well known to the speaker (X) and often borrows X's things, has stained X's new blouse.

Progressing from the least direct to the most direct, House and Kasper exemplify the range of levels of directness as follows:

1. By performing the utterance in the presence of Y, X implies that he knows that the P has happened and he implies that Y did P.
   Odd, my blouse was perfectly clean last night.
   Seltsam, gestern war meine Bluse doch noch ganz sauber.
2. By explicitly asserting that P, X implies that Y did P.
   There's a stain on my blouse.
   Das ist ein Fleck auf meiner Bluse.
3. By explicitly asserting that P is bad for him, X implies that Y did P.
   Terrible, this stain won't come off.
   Schrecklich, dieser Fleck wird wohl nie wieder rausgehn.
4. By explicitly asking Y about conditions for the execution of P, or stating that Y was in some way connected with the conditions for the doing of P, X implies that Y did P.
   Did you wear my blouse by any chance?
   Hast du etwa meine Bluse angehabt?
5. X explicitly asserts that Y did P.
   You've stained my blouse.
   Du hast den Fleck draufgemacht.
6. By explicitly stating that the action P for which Y is agentively responsible is bad, or explicitly stating a preference for an alternative action not chosen by Y, X implies that Y is bad/or X asserts explicitly

that Y did P and that P is bad for X, thus also implying that Y is bad.

You shouldn't have taken my blouse without asking my permission/You have ruined my blouse.

Du hättest die Bluse nicht ohne meine Erlaubnis nehmen sollen/Du hast meine ganze Bluse ruiniert.

7. X asserts explicitly that Y's doing of P is bad.

I think it's mean that you just take my things.

Ich finde es gemein von dir, dass du einfach mein Sachen nimmst.

8. X asserts explicitly that Y is bad.

You are really mean.

Du bist wirklich unverschämt.

House and Kasper (1981:159–60) point out that 'on all the lower levels the addressee Y must perform an **inference process** on the basis of the **situational context**, especially the **relationship** holding between the interlocutors X and Y and the **social norms** recognized by both X and Y'. They suggest that 'through this inference process Y is enabled to work out for himself both an adequate **propositional content** and the intended **illocutionary force** of X's utterance'.

Table 4.4 is taken directly from House and Kasper (1981) which outlines their findings relating to 80 **complaints** in English and 107 complaints in German.[2]

Table 4.4. Directness levels: Complaints

Directness level	1	2	3	4	5	6	7	8	9
GERMAN									
Number of instances	7	8	18	10	19	36	8	1	107
Relative frequency	0.065	0.075	0.168	0.093	0.178	0.336	0.075	0.009	1
ENGLISH									
Number of instances	11	5	14	17	15	18	–	–	80
Relative frequency	0.138	0.063	0.175	0.213	0.188	0.225	–	–	1

(from House & Kasper 1981: Table 1)

House and Kasper (1981:161) found that in the English data, levels 7 and 8, the most direct levels, did not occur at all in a total of 80 complaints, whereas in the German data, level 8 occurred once (0.9 per cent) and level 7, eight times (7.5 per cent) out of a total of 107 complaints.

Level 6 was by far the most frequently used complaint level in the German data (36 instances out of a total of 107, i.e. 33.6 per cent). In English, Level 6 was also the most frequently used, but by only a small margin (18 instances out of a total of 80, i.e. 22.5 per cent) compared with 17 instances for Level 4. House and Kasper comment that whereas Level 6 is the 'standard complaint form' for German, that level was most frequently used in English in contexts of familiarity and equality.[3]

4.3 APOLOGIES

Apologies are speech acts which come under the broad category of **Expressives**, along with thanking, forgiving, blaming, complaining and apologising. Searle characterises **apologies** as speech acts in which the speaker (S) makes known his/her attitude about a proposition to the hearer (H).

Searle (1969) does not provide detailed conditions for apologies; however Clyne (1994) examines apologies in some detail, and illustrates how these may vary across cultures. Clyne (1994:77) notes that the definition of an apology in the *Concise Oxford Dictionary* (1976) refers to three components of an apology:

- regretful acknowledgement of failure or fault
- assurance of no offence intended
- explanation or vindication.

Cohen and Olshtain (1981:113–34) (also Olshtain & Cohen 1983: 22–3; Blum-Kulka, House & Kasper 1989:289) actually identify six major components of apologies, as follows:

1. Illocutionary Force Indicating Devices (IFIDs)
   An expression of regret, e.g. *I'm sorry*
   An offer of apology, e.g. *I apologize*
   A request for forgiveness, e.g. *Excuse me/Forgive me/Pardon me.*
2. Explanation of Account
   Any external mitigating circumstances, 'objective' reasons for the violation, e.g. *The traffic was terrible.*
3. Taking on Responsibility
   a. Explicit self-blame, e.g. *It is my fault/my mistake*
   b. Lack of intent, e.g. *I didn't mean it*

c. Expression of self-deficiency, e.g. *I was confused/I didn't see you/I forgot*

d. Expression of embarrassment, e.g. *I feel awful about it*

e. Self-dispraise, e.g. *I'm such a dimwit!*

f. Justify hearer, e.g. *You're right to be angry*

g. Refusal to acknowledge guilt

Denial of responsibility, e.g. *It wasn't my fault*

Blame the hearer, e.g. *It's your own fault*

Pretend to be offended, e.g. *I'm the one to be offended.*

4. Concern for the Hearer, e.g. *I hope I didn't upset you/Are you all right?*

5. Offer of Repair, e.g. *I'll pay for the damage.*

6. Promise of Forbearance, *e.g. It won't happen again.*

Suszczyńska (1999) used a discourse completion test based on the above categories of apologies to compare the types of apologies provided by 110 subjects – 14 American, 20 Hungarian, and 76 Polish native speaking students. The test comprised eight situations with varying degrees of offence.

Table 4.5 provides a summary of the different types of apologies reported by Suszczyńska (1999) for the three groups. Here, Suszczyńska focuses on four subtypes of Blum-Kulka, Olshtain and Cohen's type (1) apologies (IFIDs).

Table 4.5. Speech act formulas for apologies in English, Hungarian and Polish

English (14 subjects)			
Sorry	*Excuse*	*Forgive*	*Apologize*
89	14	1	1
Hungarian (20 subjects)			
Sjanálom	*Elnézést*	*Bocsánat*	*Ne haragudjon*
(Sorry)	(Excuse)	(Forgive)	(Don't be angry)
26	34	37	58
Polish (76 subjects)			
Przepraszam	*Przykro mi*	*Wybacz*	*Nie gniewaj się*
(I apologize)	(Sorry)	(Forgive)	(Don't be angry)
291	47	27	6

(from Suszczyńska 1999:1057, Table 1)

Suszczyńska (1999:1058) points out that the three IFID sets cannot be perfectly mapped onto one another because, for example, Hungarian lacks a true performative verb; English does not seem to use the expression 'don't be angry' as an apologetic formula; and Polish, unlike English or Hungarian, has no equivalent of 'excuse me' for smaller offences but simply uses *Przepraszam* (*I apologize*) in all such situations. Yet, more generally, there are obvious similarities to be observed. In all three languages, there are IFID formulas expressing regret, asking forgiveness, or pleading to withhold anger, which reflect common human experience. Suszczyńska makes the point that what is important from the perspective of cross-cultural comparison is which of these expressions have been routinised in a particular language group.

In English, the overwhelming expression is one of regret *I'm sorry*, with few cases of *excuse me*, and sporadic cases of *forgive me* or *I apologise*, the latter being used more in written apologies. However, Suszczyńska shows that this is not the case for the Hungarian and Polish data.

In the Hungarian data all four strategies are well represented and routinised. There is a preference for *Ne haragudjon* ('Don't be angry'), then comes *Bocsánat* ('Forgive me'), followed by *Elnézést* ('Excuse me') and *Sjanálom* ('Sorry') which is used least of all.

In Polish, the performative verb *Przepraszam* is used most often (literally translated as 'I apologise'). There are fewer cases of *Przykro mi* ('I am sorry') and *Wybacz mi* ('Forgive me'), and just a handful of *Nie gniewaj się* ('Don't be angry').

While Suszczyńska notes the limitations of this research (it is based on three unequal corpora of elicited (not natural) data and no correlations with situational variables have been shown), it does demonstrate certain important and non-arbitrary preferences. This is an interesting illustration that a speech act, such as apologising, may be achieved using a different set of strategies in different cultures, and that certain strategies may be preferred over others.

In an earlier role-play study of apology strategies used by Chilean Spanish and Australian English speakers to their 'bosses' (workplace superiors), Cordella (1990) found that Chilean and Australian cultural values were reflected in the act of apologising. While Chileans made less use of the 'explicit expression of apology' they did, however, appear to give more explanations than the Australians. Cordella also found that for some strategies the addressee's gender played an important role in both languages.

Sugimoto (1998) investigated norms of apologies depicted in American and Japanese literature on manners and etiquette and found that not only did the recommended forms of apologies differ, but that the range of people to whom apologies are considered appropriate differed greatly. In general, American etiquette texts focused on apologies for individual behaviour in public contexts (including the acts of the individual's small children and pets). In contrast, the Japanese manuals dealt mainly with apologies in situations involving people who know each other (e.g. friends, neighbours, colleagues) rather than strangers. Sugimoto (1998:258) observes that in general, the Japanese indicate sincerity and respect by conforming to cultural norms involving formulaic expressions appropriate to different social relationships, while United States Americans strive for spontaneous and original messages of apology because it is felt that originality is indicative of sincerity.

Clyne (1994) provides the following example of an apology, and the eventual acceptance of the apology from his multicultural workplace data. In this apology, Krysztina, a Polish operator, is 'apologizing' to Jennifer (her workplace supervisor of Malaysian–Chinese background) in a self-initiated stretch of discourse. Clyne (1994:78) observes that ostensibly Krysztina wants to be 'freed from her guilt' for she fears the consequences of an error she committed at work. Clyne suggests that in actual fact, she is 'fishing' for an assurance that nothing will happen to her, or rather, that Jennifer will support her if necessary. Clyne represents the apology by the following schema:

a. admission of guilt
   It was . . . probably it was my fault.
b. doubts about her guilt
   I don't know whose fault but I take my . . . I blame myself for it.
c. explanation of 'what went wrong'
d. anxiety about the reactions of another worker
e. appeal for compassion
f. an assurance that the delay in reporting the matter to Jennifer is not the result of antipathy (or prejudice?)
g. seeking a reassurance.

Clyne makes the point that Krysztina continues to elaborate her apology until her superior explicitly 'accepts' the apology.

4.4   ACCEPTANCE OF AN APOLOGY

Acceptance of an apology deserves examination because individuals and groups may have different expectations about what a suitable response to an apology is. Clyne (1994:82–3) indicates that although his workplace data on apologies relates to a relatively small number of individuals, it does support the generalisation that Central Europeans tend to expect that an apology will be elaborate and that it be explicitly accepted; whereas South-east Asians tend not to require a great deal of fuss. Clyne (1994:84) suggests that 'this puts both Europeans and South-East Asians at variance with Anglo-Australians, who occupy the middle ground in that they tend to apologise as a formality, according to conventions of politeness, but do not make a "big deal" out of it'.

This is illustrated in the interaction between Krysztina, the Polish operator and Jennifer, her Malaysian–Chinese superior. Clyne (1994:78) observes that for most of the interaction, Jennifer does not understand the nature of Krysztina's concerns and responds by:

a. multiple use of *don't worry*
b. expressing her sympathy, e.g.
   I understand these things, these things happen
c. advising Krysztina to forget it
d. diverting her
   Is your husband back from Atlantic?
e. advising her to *take it as it comes.*

The interaction does not terminate until Jennifer overtly acknowledges the apology. In Clyne's workplace data a high percentage of the apologies are offered by Central Europeans of both genders with a much smaller representation from other groups. Clyne (1994:82) points out that Central Europeans seem to put enormous effort into the appropriate choice of apology schema to save face.

We may note that Australian English speakers have more in common with the approach taken by Jennifer, Krysztina's Malaysian–Chinese superior, in that the expression 'No worries' is often used in the context of apologies in Australia.

4.5   THE GENDER FACTOR

Some sociolinguistic research suggests that women are more likely than men to use politeness strategies in their speech, and that the extent of the differences between men's and women's speech may vary from culture to culture. Hobbs (2003:244) points out that such research suggests that women pay more compliments than men (Herbert 1990; Holmes 1988, 1998; Johnson & Roen 1992), and that women in talk with same-sex peers use a large number of positive-politeness strategies while men in analogous situations do not (Pilkington 1998). He also indicates that research has shown that women are more likely to apologise, soften criticism or express thanks than men (Tannen 1994:56–7). Similar findings have been observed in other cultures, for example Brown (1998) studying Tzeltal (Mayan) speakers in Chiapas, Mexico, where it was found that there was a greater use of both positive and negative politeness by women than men. Smith (1992:67), discussing research which has identified a distinct women's speech style in Japan, reports that such quantitative work has repeatedly demonstrated that women use polite and honorific forms more than men in standard Japanese and in other urban dialects. Smith (1992:79), however, suggests that this may only be typical of the speech of women in traditional roles and that the changing roles of some women are leading to innovative ways to express the 'voice of female power and authority'.

Hobbs (2003) argues that it is important that studies in gender variation examine the relationship between situation and language use. Hobbs cites Ochs (1992:340–1), who pointed out that while a culture may associate the use of particular forms with 'masculine' or 'feminine' speech, such forms do not typically appear exclusively in the speech of members of that sex alone; instead, such 'gendered' forms are associated with the coding of social information such as activity and stance. Hobbs (2003) shows that male attorneys, involved in legal settings where negotiation and settlement is advantageous, use a variety of politeness strategies (as evidenced in the voice mail data on which her study was based). Hobbs found that the use of negative politeness by male and female speakers was roughly equal, while the use of positive politeness did not appear to be related to status or gender, but rather to role, since positive politeness was used only by attorneys (Hobbs 2003:260).

There is a growing body of research on the gendered use of politeness strategies in different cultures which is showing that, as Smith (1992:79) points out, '. . . men's and women's approaches to politeness are not simply binary approaches in which cultural stereotypes of male power and female powerlessness reflect social reality and in which politeness forms are selected accordingly. Rather, a more complex, multistrategy phenomenon is at work'.

4.6   SUMMARY

In this chapter we have examined research on requests, complaints and apologies to exemplify the types of cultural variation that can occur in relation to speech acts, and taken account of some of the social context that contributes to this variation. While there seems to be a 'universal' set of features that tend to be found in requests, complaints and apologies, a particular subset may be preferred by members of particular cultures.

4.7 REVIEW

1. Key Terms: Speech acts (direct and indirect), request, directive, apology, complaint, hint, conventionally indirect request, discourse completion test.

2. Key Ideas

Having read this chapter you should:

a. understand the structure of speech acts, particularly requests, directives, apologies and complaints

b. understand the differences between direct and indirect directives and requests

c. appreciate why speakers from different cultures and backgrounds may have different expectations in relation to particular speech acts

d. appreciate the significance of these different expectations for intercultural communication.

3. Focus Questions

a. Requests

(i) Which of the Blum-Kulka Request Categories given in Table 4.1 are you least likely to use in English?

(ii) Does this differ if you are using another language?

b. Complaints

(i) Which of the House and Kasper (1981) complaint forms would you be most likely to use if you suspected that a room mate/family member had borrowed a piece of your clothing and got it dirty?

(ii) What components does this complaint include?

c. Apologies

(i) How would you apologise to a classmate for having forgotten to return a book you had borrowed?

(ii) How would you classify your apology in terms of Cohen and Olshtain's characterisation of apologies?

4. Research Analysis

Consider the following extracts from the screenplay of the *Titanic* (Cameron 1996:94–5).

In these two extracts the screenwriter represents interactions between a steward on the Upper Decks with his passengers and stewards in Steerage with their passengers.

Extract 1: Upper Deck

There is a loud knock on the door and an urgent voice. The door opens and their steward puts his head in.

Steward Barnes: Sir, I've been told to ask you to please put on your lifebelt, and come up to the boat deck.

Cal: Get out. We're busy.

The steward persists, coming in to get the lifebelts down from the top of a dresser.

Steward Barnes: I'm sorry about the inconvenience, Mr Hockley, but it's Captain's orders. Please dress warmly, it's quite cold tonight.

(He hands a lifebelt to Rose)

Not to worry Miss, I'm sure it's just a precaution.

Extract 2: Steerage
BLACKNESS. Then BANG! The door is thrown open and the light snapped on by a steward. The Cartmell family rouse from a sound sleep.

Steward #2: Everybody up. Let's go. Put your lifebelts on.
IN THE CORRIDOR outside, another steward is going from door to door along the hall pounding and yelling.

Steward #3: Lifebelts on. Lifebelts on. Everybody up, come on. Lifebelts on.
People come out of the doors behind the steward, perplexed. In the foreground a SYRIAN WOMAN asks her husband what was said. He shrugs.

a. Compare the ways in which the three stewards ask their respective passengers to put on their life jackets and go upstairs; using the categories of requests defined by Blum-Kulka (1987) (see Table 4.1).

b. Considering TV dramas with which you are familiar, select and describe one character/context in which formal/polite language (similar to that used by Steward Barnes to the Upper Deck passengers) is used and give some approximate examples.

c. Select and describe one character/context in which extremely informal language (such as that used in Extract 2) is used. Give some approximate examples.

d. Note the reference to the Syrian woman in the last stage note. This represents a typical case of non-communication often experienced by international travellers. How is it possible to avoid potentially dangerous situations such as this? What obligations does a tourist operator have to issue warnings that can be understood?

5. Research Exercise

Construct three discourse completion tests to elicit forms of Apology – varying P, D and R (see also Chapter 3, Brown & Levinson 1987).

NOTES

1 The languages studied as part of the CCSARP project were Hebrew (Blum-Kulka & Olshtain), Danish (Faerch & Kasper), British English (Thomas), American English (Wolfson & Rintell), German (House-Edmonson & Vollmer), Canadian French (Weizman), Argentinian Spanish (Blum-Kulka & House) and Australian English (Ventola). Publications from this study include House and Kasper (1981), Blum-Kulka and Olshtain (1984), Blum-Kulka (1987), Cohen and Olshtain (1981) and the volume edited by Blum-Kulka, House and Kasper (1989).
2 The data on which this table is based included examples ± social distance and ± authority relationships.
3 We have replaced House and Kasper's phrase 'minus social distance and minus authority constellations' with 'contexts of familiarity and equality'.

SUGGESTED FURTHER READING

Blum-Kulka, S. 1989 *Cross-cultural Pragmatics: Requests and Apologies*. Norwood, New Jersey: Ablex.

Cordella, M. 1991 'Apologizing in Chilean Spanish and Australian English: A cross-cultural perspective'. *Australian Review of Applied Linguistics*, Series S, vol. 7, pp. 66–92.

Herbert, R. K. 1990 'Sex based differences in compliment behaviour'. *Language in Society*, vol. 19, pp. 201–24.

House, J. & Kasper, G. 1981 'Politeness markers in English and German'. In Coulmas F. (ed.) *Conversational Routines*. The Hague: Mouton, pp. 157–85.

Lee-Wong, S. M. 1994b 'Qing/Please: A polite or requestive marker? Observations from Chinese'. *Multilingua*, vol. 13, no. 4, pp. 343–60.

Smith, Janet. S. 1992 'Women in change: Politeness and directives in the speech of Japanese women'. *Language in Society*, vol. 21, pp. 59–82.

Suszczyńska, M. 1999 'Apologizing in English, Polish and Hungarian: Different languages, different strategies'. *Journal of Pragmatics*, vol. 31, pp. 1053–65.

Trosborg, A. (ed.) 1994 *Interlanguage Pragmatics: Requests, Complaints and Apologies* (Studies in Anthropological Linguistics 7). Berlin/New York: Mouton de Gruyter.

5 | The analysis of conversation

GREETINGS AND LEAVE-TAKINGS are aspects of conversation that we may never think about because they are such an integral part of our everyday lives, yet they can be quite complex. In this chapter we will look at some of the complexity inherent in greetings and leave-takings, and examine some cultural variation.

Humour and laughter are widely used to establish and maintain rapport, yet these are also aspects of communication which are often not contemplated. Some of the similarities and differences between cultures in the way they incorporate humour and laughter will be discussed in this chapter.

We will begin by examining some of the features of turn-taking in conversation, drawing on the field of research known as Conversational Analysis and provide some examples of how turn-taking can be managed by speakers from different cultures.

5.1   TURN-TAKING IN CONVERSATION

Sacks, Schegloff and Jefferson (1974), in their seminal work on turn-taking, observed the following three key features in the organisation of **turn-taking** in conversation:

- one party talks at a time
- transitions are finely coordinated for speaker change
- utterances are constructed in such a way as to show coordination of turn transfer and speakership.

Sacks, Schegloff and Jefferson identified **adjacency pairs** as a key feature of conversation. They pointed out that most conversation is composed of pairs of utterances, with the prototypical example being a **question–answer** sequence. There is a sense in which the question 'requires' the answer as the second part of the adjacency pair.

Clark (1996:196–7) provides an excellent summary of some of the key principles of conversational analysis. He gives the following five essential properties of adjacency pairs identified by Schegloff and Sacks (1973), exemplifying them with an extract from the London-Lund corpus of British English (Svartvik & Quirk 1980):

- Adjacency pairs consist of two ordered utterances – the *first pair part* and the *second pair part.*
- The two parts are uttered by different speakers.
- The two parts come in types that specify which part is to come first and which second.
- The form and content of the second part depends on the type of the first part.
- Given a first pair part, the second pair part is *conditionally relevant* – that is, relevant and expectable – as the next utterance.

Clark (1996:196–7) provides the following example of a brief telephone conversation from the London-Lund corpus which contains a number of adjacency pairs:

Jane: (rings C's telephone)

Kate: Miss Pink's office, hello
Jane: hello, is Miss Pink in?
Kate: well, she's in, but she's engaged at the moment, who is it?
Jane: oh it's Professor Worth's secretary, from Pan-American College
Kate: m,
Jane: could you give her a message *for me?*
Kate: *certainly*
Jane: u:m Professor Worth said that, if Miss Pink runs into difficulties on Monday afternoon . . . with the standing subcommittee . . . over the item of Miss Panoff . . .
Kate: Miss Panoff?
Jane: Yes
Jane: that Professor Worth would be with Mr Miles all afternoon – so she only had to go round and collect him if she needs him . . .
Kate: ah . . . thank you very much indeed, right
Jane: right
Kate: Panoff, right *you are*
Jane: *right*
Kate: I'll tell her*. . .*

Jane: *thank you*
Kate: bye bye
Jane: bye

[*marks the beginning and end of overlapping words or phrases]

Jane and Kate's conversation illustrates the following types of adjacency pairs:

Adjacency pair		Example
1. Summons	Jane:	(rings)
2. Response	Kate:	Miss Pink's office
1. Greeting	Kate:	hello
2. Greeting	Jane:	hello
1. Question	Kate:	who is it?
2. Answer	Jane:	oh it's Professor Worth's secretary . . .
1. Assertion	Jane:	oh it's Professor Worth's secretary . . .
2. Assent	Kate:	m,
1. Request	Jane:	could you give her a message *for me?*
2. Promise	Kate:	*certainly*
1. Promise	Kate:	I'll tell her
2. Acknowledgment	Jane:	thank you
1. Thanks	Kate:	thank you very much indeed
2. Acknowledgment	Kate:	right
1. Goodbye	Kate:	bye bye
2. Goodbye	Jane:	bye

In each case, the second pair part (2) is regarded as **conditionally relevant** upon the first pair part (1). For example, in the question–answer sequence, Jane's question is the first pair part, and Kate's answer, the second.

1. Question	Kate:	who is it?
2. Answer	Jane:	oh it's Professor Worth's secretary . . .

Given Jane's question, Kate's answer is conditionally relevant as the next utterance. Clark (1996:200–1) suggests that **adjacency pairs** may be seen as a type of action–response pair, or the proposal and uptake of a joint project. On one level, the entire conversation is one type of joint project. However, he argues that the **minimal joint project** is the **adjacency pair** – a proposal plus its uptake.

We can see that the above question–answer sequence (in italics in the sequence below) is in fact a side sequence, associated with the answer to the question immediately preceding it.

Q	Jane:	is Miss Pink in?
A	Kate:	well, she's in, but she's engaged at the moment,
Q	*who is it?*	
A	*Jane*:	*oh it's Professor Worth's secretary, from Pan-American College*
Q	*Jane*:	*could you give her a message*for me?**
A	Kate:	*certainly*

In fact, Kate's first turn contains both the answer to Jane's question, as well as the initiation of the question in the side sequence.

Sacks, Schegloff and Jefferson (1974) suggest that a formal model of the details of turn-taking needs to account for the following:

1. speaker-change occurs and recurs often
2. overwhelmingly, one party speaks at a time
3. occurrences of more than one speaker at a time are common but brief
4. transitions (from one turn to a next) with no gap and no overlap are common
5. turn order is not fixed, but varies
6. turn size is not fixed but varies
7. length of conversation is not specified in advance
8. what parties say is not specified in advance
9. relative distribution of turns is not specified in advance.

Sacks, Schegloff and Jefferson (1974), in discussing when it is appropriate for a new speaker to take a turn, identify the importance of a Transition-Relevance Place (TRP):

> . . . any syntactically defined turn-constructional unit of speech is followed by a transition-relevance place (TRP). At these TRPs, turn allocation takes place, and a transition to a new speaker may occur. At every TRP, a set of rules for turn allocation is applied by the participants: the current speaker may select the next; the next speaker may self select; or, if neither of these possibilities is taken, the current speaker may continue his or her turn.

In certain circumstances, a speaker may want to have a longer turn than usual, for example if the speaker wants to tell a story. To do this, the speaker usually foreshadows this with what Sacks (1992) calls a **story preface**. Such a story preface could be 'Something awful happened to me today' and would be perceived as a request to undertake the activity of telling a story. It might therefore be responded to in the next turn by an acceptance such as 'what?' In such contexts, the primary speaker has the right to talk until the completion of his or her speech, and the recipient can respond with continuers, but they will not generally take over the floor.

Kjaerbeck (1998), in an article on the organisation of discourse units in Mexican and Danish business negotiations, suggests that business negotiation often includes a metalinguistic formulation akin to the story preface previously identified by Sacks (1992) which is used to introduce a new discourse unit. The Mexican example Kjaerbeck (1998:349) provides is the following:

A: *hm m* (clearing his throat) (.)
sí claro me permiten que yo intervenga (0.80)
yes of course if I may intervene
E: ***e en apoyo aquí de mi compañero*** (1.1)
uh: uh in support here of my colleague
creo que este producto: como ya lo mencionó Chucho
es la Revolución
I believe this product: as Chucho already mentioned is a revolution.

Kjaerbeck (1998:356–7) observed that similar metalinguistic brackets were used as a preface in both Mexican and Danish negotiation sequences. However, a key difference between the Mexican and Danish material was that in the Danish material, a response was typically employed after a preface, and interpreted as the recipient's acceptance of the announced intention to produce a long stretch of talk. In the Mexican material, such a response could not be found. Based on these findings and other details outlined in her paper, Kjaerbeck (1998:348) concludes that:

> there might be certain basic common features in the way Mexican and Danish participants construct the argumentational discourse unit; still certain organizational differences can be observed.

5.2   SOME DIFFERENCES IN TURN-TAKING IN INTERCULTURAL CONTEXTS

Clyne (1994:188) identifies the following differences in turn maintenance and appropriation procedures evident in his Melbourne intercultural workplace data:

> Content-based cultures such as Central and Southern Europeans (and to a lesser extent South Asians) use an increase in tempo or simultaneous speech to indicate that the speaker wants to say all s/he needs to say.

The harmony value is reflected in the turn-taking procedures of Vietnamese, ethnic Chinese and generally South-east Asians who do not 'fight' to maintain their turns and certainly do not increase the speed to do so. They also generally back down rather than engage in simultaneous speech.

5.3   THE ROLE OF BACK-CHANNELLING

It is usual in conversation for the participant not holding the floor to provide acknowledgment that they are continuing to follow what the speaker is saying. In English, this is typically done by utterances such as *mm-m* and *uh-uh*. Kjaerbeck's (1998) Mexican data shows similar uses of *uh-uh*. It has been suggested that Japanese speakers may use the word *hai* 'yes' as a **back-channel** device, not necessarily indicating agreement, but rather indicating 'I am listening'. Kjaerbeck's Danish examples contain several instances of *ja ja* 'yes', more as a positive back-channel device than as a clear marker of agreement.

5.4   REPETITION AS BACK-CHANNELLING IN SUCCESSFUL INTERCULTURAL COMMUNICATION

Bowe (1995), reporting research examining discourse between recently arrived migrants and their supervisors in an industrial environment, found that there was a considerable difference in the style of discourse adopted by supervisors who had an Anglo–Australian background and those that had been from non-Anglo backgrounds and migrants themselves.

A prominent feature of the English discourse of supervisors who were of non-Anglo backgrounds and migrants themselves, was the use of **repetition** for a range of discourse functions including agreement, assent, affirmation, acknowledgment and passive recipiency. These are precisely the types of functions which researchers such as Duncan (1973, 1974), Sacks, Schegloff and Jefferson (1974), Schegloff (1982) and Levinson (1983) have identified for the use of minimal responses such as *m-hm*, and *uh-huh* and other phrases including repetition.

Duncan (1974) lists the following five types of auditor **back-channel** communication:

1. 'm-hm, yeah, right'
2. sentence completions

3. requests for clarification 'you mean?'
4. brief restatement (repetition)
5. head nods and shakes.

It is not clear from the literature whether a back-channel response should be taken as constituting a turn or not. Perhaps it is best analysed as a type of side sequence. Duncan notes that early auditor back-channels have the effect of significantly increasing the probability of display of a subsequent speaker continuation signal whereas a between unit auditor back-channel does not.

Early auditor back-channels not only signal that the auditor is following the speaker's message, but also that the auditor is ahead of it. Accordingly, it would be appropriate for the speaker to proceed directly to the next unit regardless of whether or not he had displayed a within-turn signal.

Late auditor back-channels, however, indicate that the auditor is not quite following the speaker's message.

The use of **repetition** (Duncan's type (4) **back-channel** communication) rather than the more **minimal responses** such as *m-hm* and *uh-huh* ensures not only communication of the intended feedback, but that the propositions on which the feedback is based are able to be checked.

In cases where the proposition was correctly restated, the repetition functions as the response; that is, agreement, assent, query, and so on. In cases where the proposition was misunderstood, the response in the form of repetition can expose the source of the misunderstanding and hence, the proposition can be corrected.

Bowe (1995) reports that **repetition** can be used in the following range of functions:

- as a means of acknowledging receipt of information
- as a means of confirming information
- as an expression of solidarity
- as a means of confirmation of speaker's hypothesis
- as a means of answering a negative question
- as a query
- as a means of acknowledging the correction of a wrong hypothesis
- as a means of framing a question.

Bowe suggests that the multi-functionality of repetition renders it a useful discourse strategy for intercultural communication. This research is presented in more detail in section 11.1.

5.5   GREETINGS AND LEAVE-TAKING

In Chapter 3 we briefly considered the following set of greetings:

Hi, What's up? How's it going? G'day (Australian English), How are you? Hello, How do you do?

All of these expressions might be used by certain people in certain contexts. The choice of form would be governed to some extent by the consideration of social relationships and features of the context, which might dictate different levels of formality or informality.

Each of the above expressions is only the first part of the greeting, and is conventionally followed by at least a response, and more often, by a series of exchanges. Thus, the response to *How do you do?* might be *Very well thank you* and the response to *Hi* might be *Hello,* or vice versa, but to simply leave it at that would be unusual except if you are passing someone, perhaps on the stairs.

The convention in English is to follow the greeting exchange with at least one further exchange, which may take a number of forms including:

- a question regarding health: *How are you? How are you doing?*
- a comment on the weather: *Terribly hot, isn't it?*
- a comment regarding length of time between contact, for example: *Haven't seen you for ages*
- a question relating to activities: *What have you been up to?*

The almost obligatory nature of at least a second exchange is obvious on talk-back radio where we have noticed that many callers feel the need to enquire about the radio host's health and he or she feels obliged to reply, even though they may have given the same reply several times in the last hour. In such contexts, a question regarding health seems to be the default, and this is probably the case in most of the English-speaking world.

A further example of the conventional nature of the health enquiry is that, at the beginning of a medical consultation, if the doctor, asks *How are you?*, an English-speaking patient invariably feels the need to reply *Fine thanks* and it is sometimes then necessary to add a qualification such as *Well actually, I haven't been feeling quite so well . . .* and then the health issue that is the reason for the visit can be raised.

The topic of health and wellbeing is not restricted to Anglo–Celtic cultures. In Chapter 3 we referred to de Kadt's (1998) findings that for Zulu speakers, greeting rituals are viewed as being compulsory and are generally initiated by the subordinate person in the interaction and then followed by enquiries into the status of one's health and wellbeing by the person of higher status. A colleague from Kenya[1] once reported that greeting rituals in her culture are so elaborate that if you happen to see a friend or relative approaching and you are in a hurry, it is better to avoid the person by crossing the road, than to cut short the greeting ritual, which would of necessity include enquiries into the health and wellbeing of all family members in turn.

Farewells can be even more lengthy and complex, though perhaps this is changing to some extent by the pressures of the modern world. In general, a short farewell, particularly after a special occasion, can seem strange unless some reason for an abrupt departure has been foreshadowed or a compelling reason develops. A short and abrupt farewell seems to devalue the interaction in some way. Ferguson (1976) suggests that the form of a farewell is influenced by factors such as degree of intimacy between the two participants, relative status, and length of contact or expected time apart.

Clark and French (1981), in a paper describing their research on telephone goodbyes offered to operators in routine enquiries to a university switchboard, identified three components of the closing sequence: The first is *topic termination*, the second is *leave-taking*, and the third is *contact termination* (accomplished by the closing clicks of the telephone being hung up).

The **topic termination** component typically involves the parties agreeing that they have nothing more to add, and is generally followed by an exchange of confirmations such as *Okay*. In certain cases, the topic termination is not a simple matter, as one or the other of the participants may think of additional issues to raise. (Users of public telephones may recall waiting patiently as a previous user seems to be involved in a topic termination, only to find that one of the parties comes up with another item of unfinished business, and this may happen several times over. It is almost possible from the body language of a telephone user to tell when the topic termination phase begins.)

The **leave-taking** phase has been referred to as the *reaffirmation of acquaintance* and typically includes a goodbye exchange. Clark and French (1981:4) following Goffman (1971) observe that:

> . . . people from different cultures have different ways of breaking contact with each other. In small close-knit societies in which continuing relations among individuals are taken for granted, people may not need an elaborate form of leave-taking. In urban America, however, people generally need to reassure each other that the break in social contact is only temporary – that they are still acquainted and will resume contact at some time in the future.

Clark and French, drawing on Albert and Kessler (1976, 1978) and Knapp, Hart, Friedrich and Shulman (1973), report that in **leave-taking**, people may:

1. summarise the content of the contact they have just had
2. justify ending their contact at this time
3. express pleasure about each other
4. indicate continuity in their relationship by planning, specifically or vaguely, for future contact
5. wish each other well.

Albert and Kessler (1978) found, in fact, that statements of these five kinds occurred precisely in the above order. In most languages, the common terminal expressions incorporate one or the other of the last two functions, at least historically. *See you, auf wiedersehen, au revoir,* and *hasta la vista* are all derived from expressions of well-wishing. Thus, at least part of the reaffirmation process is generally expressed in the **terminal exchange** itself (Clark & French 1981).

Given that routine enquiries do not typically involve any type of acquaintance, either past acquaintance, or acquaintance arising from the interaction, Clark and French (1981:5) predicted that such conversations would not end in a *goodbye* sequence but instead would conclude with a *thank you – you're welcome* sequence. In fact, they did find that the majority of simple requests ended as they predicted.

When they examined conversations which contained other than minimal exchanges of one telephone number, they found that the likelihood of a goodbye exchange taking place increased with the complexity of the information requested and expressions of gratitude for the assistance. Significantly, a goodbye exchange was also initiated by female callers in conversations in which an 'operator mistake' occurred. Such mistakes included misspelled names, and misquoted numbers, and would usually be followed by the correction and a short apology by the operator, such as *I'm sorry* or *My fault.*

Clark and French provide the insightful suggestion that complex requests on the part of caller and operator mistakes have in common a degree of **personalisation** of the encounter, and argue that the personalisation results in a feeling that callers have become acquainted enough with the operator to warrant a **closing section** and a *goodbye* exchange.

Telephone **opening sequences** have been studied by researchers beginning with Schegloff (1968) in the United States, and others such as Goddard (1977) who compared telephone conversations in France and the United

States, and Sifianou (1989) who compared telephone behaviour in England and Greece.

Schegloff saw **telephone openings** as part of a broader category of summons–answer sequences: the telephone ring being the summons and the person picking up the telephone providing the answer, typically with *hello*. Schegloff commented on the fact that the typical sequence of exchanges for telephone openings (in the United States) does not provide for the identification of the caller, and that the caller's identity is usually deduced speculatively by the answerer (1968:351).

Goddard's (1977:211) account of the expected sequence of a French telephone opening can be summarised as follows:

Caller: Dials number
Answerer: Allo?
Caller: Checks number
Answerer: Oui (yes)
Caller: Identifies himself and either:
             1. Answerer: recognises and interrupts Caller
             2. Caller: excuses himself and asks for addressee.

Goddard (1977:212) comments that this sequence is explicitly taught and children are instructed that when they ring to speak to a friend they should:

1. check number
2. excuse yourself
3. name yourself
4. ask for your friend.

Goddard reports that with the exception of calls between intimate friends, where both the caller and the answerer would recognise each other's voice, the most common telephone beginning is a question *Is this X?* or *X*. He noted that on one occasion, when he was renting a house, a caller, hearing a foreign voice when expecting to hear her friend (the owner of the house), initiated the exchange with *Who are you?* which he regarded quite negatively.

Sifianou (1989) further reports that telephone callers in England use somewhat of a mixture of the strategies identified by Goddard for French, depending on the context. For example, verification of the telephone number would only take place if there was something unexpected about the answerer. Sifianou (1989:534) reports that Greeks, however, never answer their telephone by reciting their telephone number or giving their name. She offers the explanation that:

Giving too much unnecessary information flouts Grice's maxim of quantity and can be interpreted as being insulting or even rude; identifying one-self on the phone in Greece seems to be interpreted in a similar way and, consequently, it is omitted. Callers presume that the answerer will recognize them from clues.

Sifianou suggests (1989:529) that telephone callers in England are more likely to use negative politeness strategies as characterised by Brown and Levinson (1978), using indirectness, whereas Greek callers prefer to use positive politeness strategies such as in-group markers and more direct constructions.

Both Goddard (1977:218) for the United States, and Sifianou (1989:539) for Greece report that the use of the telephone is an expected and almost obligatory means of **maintaining social contact** among family and friends who rarely see each other. Sifianou further observes that in Greece, 'such calls are customary even among friends and relatives who see each other quite frequently' and notes that 'a rough Greek equivalent to the English farewell formula *See you* is δα tilefoniδume "We'll ring each other"'. Sifianou sees the enthusiastic use of the telephone as a logical extension of the Greek predisposition to **closeness** as well as their eagerness to share views and opinions and for frequent contact. She suggests that in England, the primary function (of telephone conversations) seems to be **transactional**, whereas in Greece, the primary function seems to be **interactional** (Sifianou 1989:527).

5.6   SOME FUNCTIONS OF LAUGHTER

Laughter can be seen to play an important role in conversation. Research on laughter has shown that laughter has a range of functions both as a response and as a self-initiated comment.

Responsive laughter is laughter initiated by the hearer, which can fulfil the following functions:

- to acknowledge humour, wit
- to signal friendly support (solidarity)
- to minimise disagreement
- to show politeness (respect)
- to ridicule, to laugh at (conflict).

Self-initiated laughter (laughter by the speaker) on the other hand, can serve:

- to invite others to join in the conversation (managing social rela tionships)
- to encourage and support others
- to frame or modify an utterance
- to indicate:
  - irony
  - humour
  - modesty
  - uncertainty
  - anxiety.

Research by Gavioli (1995), using the methodology of conversational analysis, focuses on the use of laughter to **mitigate** a hearer's frustration or disappointment when unexpected negative news is communicated. Gavioli examined the use of turn-initial versus turn-final laughter for **initiating remedy** in English and Italian bookshop service encounters to illustrate how laughter can be used differently in quite similar situations in different cultures. The contexts involved instances where the assistant had to supply a **dispreferred response**, such as a book required by the customer was not available, or the customer was not in the correct department.

Gavioli (1995:374) found that in the English encounters, 75 per cent of the instances of laughter occurred at or near the beginning of the turn and were accompanied or preceded by hesitations like *well* or *um*, as exemplified in example 5.6.1. Thus, it served to introduce the explanation about to be offered by the assistant.

EXAMPLE 5.6.1: FROM ENGLISH BOOKSHOP ENCOUNTER

Assistant:	Well. LAUGHTER yeah, there isn't anything in here at all! There's the 'Basic writings on phenomenology', but there is no – no S – I'm getting mixed up with Hegel I'm afraid
Customer:	Ah: yeah (that's it)
Assistant:	We haven't even got anything listed as no longer stocked, or out of print or anything
Customer:	Aha. It might actually be more than a year ago then I suppose
Assistant:	Yeah. I think you can forget that one altogether quite frankly, and I don't think it'd be worth looking even in *SLOV*

> Customer: Oh: could you tell me where it is anyway, just so I can have a look through it?

In contrast, in the Italian encounters, 90 per cent of the laughter occurred at the very end of a turn as illustrated in example 5.6.2.

EXAMPLE 5.6.2: FROM ITALIAN BOOKSHOP ENCOUNTER

> Assistant: No. I haven't got it then. Nothing doing LAUGHS
> Customer: Because it was in the newspaper that –
> Assistant: that it had been published
> Customer: That it is on sale on the . . .
> Assistant: Yes erm but we don't stock all the newest books so actually it is unlikely that we LAUGHS stock it.
> If you want to try either at Muratori or perhaps at the Rinascita also.

Gavioli (1995:378) concludes that:

> . . . there are different preferred ways in which this mechanism works in the two languages. Whereas laughter in English usually prefaces some forthcoming excuse or account within the same turn, in Italian it marks the point where turn transition takes place, and it is left to the customer to elicit the remedy. So, the meaning of laughter in English could be considered something like 'excuse me, I am not doing very well but let me explain'. In Italian it signals that the current speaker cannot do any better and that he or she needs some help from his or her interlocutor.

5.7   ANOTHER FUNCTION OF HUMOUR: JOKING

Brown and Levinson (1978) regard joking as one of the **positive politeness** techniques, that is, as a strategy used to minimise the threat to one's positive face. Positive politeness realisations are ways of minimising social distance. Joking may serve this purpose, for example when S is joking in order to 'put H at ease'. Joking then is meant to generate feelings of familiarity and friendship by alluding to S's and H's shared background knowledge and values. Another kind of humorous expressions aiming at maintaining both S's and H's positive faces are 'inside jokes', which claim common attitudes and empathy between S and H, with an additional touch of superiority feeling in both towards the uninitiated.

5.8 CULTURAL DIFFERENCES IN CONVERSATIONAL ROUTINES

Social relations are advanced by a variety of **conversational routines** related to various topics in different societies. The following illustration from Béal (1992) shows that even simple questions contain a variety of assumptions ranging from whom it is suitable to ask, to the kind of answer or the amount of detail expected.

Béal (1992) describes the **role** of the question *Did you have a good weekend?* in workplace interaction in a French company operating in Australia, and indicates how such a simple question evokes quite different responses from Australian and French co-workers. Béal reports that Australian workers generally use the routine quite widely and view the question as a **general expression of friendliness**, and she further notes that the exchange is expected to be relatively short. By contrast, French co-workers tend only to ask such a question of individuals with whom they feel they have a good rapport, and treat the question as a **sincere enquiry** offering detailed responses, including the expression of opinions and feelings. Béal (1992:25) observes that this difference of expectations results in tension as:

> The Australians mentioned it as proof of the French tendency to be self-centred, forceful and insensitive to other people. The French in turn, mentioned it as a good example of what they perceived as the indifference and lack of sincerity of Australians.

Béal's research on workplace interaction in a French company operating in Australia (see also Béal 1990) is an excellent study based on naturally collected intercultural communication data, and follow-up interviews.

5.9 SUMMARY

In this chapter, we have considered a number of features of conversation including greeting and leave-taking routines, some ways in which laughter can be used in conversation, function and use of humour, and examined some features of turn-taking including adjacency pairs, back-channelling and repetition. We have attempted to show the variety of dimensions along which cultural preferences can be found when communicating within and across cultures.

5.10   REVIEW

1. **Key Terms:** Conversational routine, turn-taking, topic termination, leave-taking, contact termination, turn change, back-channelling, conversation openings, conversation closings, preferred and dispreferred turn structure.

2. **Key Ideas**

   Having read this chapter you should:

   a. appreciate the ways in which routine conversations (such as answering the telephone and taking leave from someone) display conventionally determined patterns across different cultures

   b. appreciate the role of turn-taking in both intra- and cross-cultural contexts

   c. be able to analyse a stretch of recorded dialogue with reference to both turn-taking and the patterning of interruptions

   d. be familiar with the concept preferred and dispreferred turn structure

   e. appreciate the reason why feelings of ease or discord about an interaction are often related to the use (or non-use) of expected norms

   f. be aware of the significance of different norms and conventions for intercultural communication.

3. **Focus Questions**

   a. Greetings and leave-takings

   (i) As part of your daily routine, what kinds of greetings and leave-takings do you use? Describe the factors which affect the use of such aspects of conversation, including the social context, age differences, frequency of use, language factors, formality vs informality of context, and so on.

   (ii) If you know more than one language, how do the greetings and leave-takings and their usage differ from one language to the other?

   b. Telephone conversations

   The following extract is taken from the above text (section 5.5). Consider the extract and answer the questions:

   > Schegloff saw telephone openings as part of a broader category of summons–answer sequences: the telephone ring being the summons and the person picking up the telephone providing the answer, typically with *hello*.

(i) While Schegloff (1968) was describing the use of a fixed telephone, do you think the same can be said for the telephone behaviour when using a mobile phone? Provide reasons for your answer.

(ii) Sifianou (1989:527) suggests that, in England, telephone behaviour appears to be *transactional* (serving to convey information) whereas in Greece it is *interactional* (serving to establish and maintain social relationships). In your own culture, which is the preferred telephone behaviour and is this the same for the fixed telephone and the mobile phone? Give examples and reasons.

(iii) Goddard (1977:212) comments that this sequence is explicitly taught and children are instructed that when they ring to speak to a friend they should:
   (1) check number
   (2) excuse yourself
   (3) name yourself
   (4) ask for your friend.
   When you were a child, did you learn the above sequence of answering the telephone? If so, do you continue to use this sequence in your daily life? If not, what sequence were you taught? How has it changed over time?

c. **Repetition in intercultural communication**
Using Bowe's (1995) range of functions for repetition as a guide (see section 5.4), identify how you use repetition as a strategy in your daily interactions and whether it is or has been useful as a strategy in intercultural communication. Provide examples for your answer.

4. **Research Analysis**
Laughter

Consider the following extracts taken from Gavioli (1995:374).

From English bookshop encounter:

Assistant: Well. LAUGHTER yeah, there isn't anything in here at all! There's the 'Basic writings on phenomenology', but there is no – no S – I'm getting mixed up with Hegel I'm afraid

Customer: Ah: yeah (that's it)

Assistant: We haven't even got anything listed as no longer stocked, or out of print or anything

Customer: Aha. It might actually be more than a year ago then I suppose

Assistant: Yeah. I think you can forget that one altogether quite frankly, and I don't think it'd be worth looking even in *SLOV*

Customer: Oh: could you tell me where it is anyway, just so I can have a look through it?

a. What is the function of this turn-initial laughter in the above example?

From Italian bookshop encounter:

Assistant: No. I haven't got it then. Nothing doing LAUGHS

Customer: Because it was in the newspaper that –

Assistant: that it had been published

Customer: That it is on sale on the . . .

Assistant: Yes erm but we don't stock all the newest books so actually it is unlikely that we LAUGHS stock it.

If you want to try either at Muratori or perhaps at the Rinascita also.

b. What is the function of the turn-final laughter in the above example?

c. In your own language, is turn-initial or turn-final laughter the preferred response in initiating a remedy? Give an example and reasons for this preferred response.

d. What do you think the consequences might be in an intercultural context when a person uses turn-initial laughter to initiate a remedy in a language where turn-final laughter is the preferred response?

e. Have you ever been in or know of a situation in which you (or another) have laughed at an inappropriate moment? What were the consequences of such a dispreferred response? How was the situation remedied?

5. Research Exercise
Adjacency pairs

Record a conversation between yourself and another person, which lasts for approximately 30 seconds. Transcribe and analyse the conversation to identify the adjacency pairs. Identify the adjacency pairs using the examples given for Jane and Kate's conversation in section 5.1 (e.g. *summon–response, question–answer*).

NOTE

1 Personal communication, Dr Angelina Nduku Kioko.

SUGGESTED FURTHER READING

Béal, C. 1992 'Did you have a good weekend? Or why is there no such thing as a simple question in cross-cultural encounters?' *Australian Review of Applied Linguistics*, vol. 15, no. 1, pp. 23–52.

Clark H. & French, J. 1981 'Telephone goodbyes'. *Language in Society*, vol. 10, no. 1, April.

Coulmas, F. (ed.) 1981 *Conversational Routines*. The Hague: Mouton.

Goddard, D. 1977 'Same setting, different norms: Phone call beginnings in France and in the United States'. *Language in Society*, vol. 6, pp. 209–19.

Gumperz, J. 1992 'Interviewing in intercultural situations'. In Drew P. & Heritage J. (eds) *Talk at Work*. Cambridge: Cambridge University Press, pp. 302–27.

Sacks, H., Schegloff, E. A. & Jefferson, G. 1974 'A simplest systematic for the organization of turn-taking in conversations'. *Language*, vol. 59, pp. 941–2.

Schegloff, E. A. 1968 'Sequencing in conversational openings'. In Gumperz J. & Hymes D. (eds) *Directions in Sociolinguistics: The Ethnography of Communication*. New York: Holt, Rinehart & Winston, pp. 346–80.

Sifianou M. 1989 'On the telephone again! Differences in telephone behaviour: England versus Greece'. *Language in Society*, vol. 18, pp. 527–44.

6

Power relations and stereotyping

CULTURAL DIFFERENCES IN THE CONCEPT OF **self and others**, and related perceptions of power are important in understanding the social expectations and conventions which underlie language use and are used to interpret linguistic meaning in a given interaction.

Important intercultural communication research in this area has focused on the notions of **power relations** (e.g. Searle 1995; Fairclough 1989; Foucault 1978, 1980; Giddens 1982, 1993), **stereotyping and group marking** (Scollon & Scollon 2001; Tajfel 1982) and includes Hofstede's work on the characterisation of national cultural differences (e.g. Hofstede 1980, 1983, 1991).

Hofstede (1991:5)defines culture as 'the collective programming of the mind which distinguishes the members of one group or category of people from another'. He further suggests that this collective programming can be manifested in a variety of different ways when people interact with each other (Hofstede 1998:10).

However, as El-Dash and Busnardo (2001) point out, any categorisation of a group results in some level of stereotyping. Thus, while linking certain characteristics to different cultures serves as a useful guide in understanding power relations and linguistic communication, such categorisations may lead to some level of overgeneralisation.

6.1   HOFSTEDE AND THE DIMENSIONS OF CULTURE

Hofstede's work (1980, 1983, 1991, 1998) has been highly influential in the study of **national cultural differences**. Hofstede's research is based on information gained from studies of a multinational corporation (IBM) in 64 countries. He has also conducted subsequent studies concerning students in over 20 countries and 'elites' in 19 countries (Hofstede 1998:11). Hofstede proposes that five independent dimensions of national cultural differences can be identified:

- power distance
- uncertainty avoidance
- individualism/collectivism
- masculinity/femininity
- long-term/short-term orientation.[1]

The first dimension, **power distance**, relates to the degree to which members of a culture accept institutions and organisations having power. Hofstede's second dimension, **uncertainty avoidance**, is the degree to which members feel uncomfortable with ambiguity and uncertainty. With regard to **individualism/collectivism**, Hofstede suggests that individualist cultures place a higher emphasis on individual goals in comparison to group achievements in collectivist cultures. Hofstede (1983:336) characterises an individualist culture as preferring a 'loosely knit social framework in which individuals are supposed to take care of themselves and their immediate families only'. With regard to the **masculinity/femininity** dimension, Hofstede (1983:337) defines a masculine culture as that which has a 'preference for achievement, heroism, assertiveness, and material success', whereas a feminine society is viewed as having a 'preference for relationships, modesty, caring for the weak, and the quality of life'. Therefore we see that **masculinity** is more achievement-oriented and **femininity** has a greater focus on relationships and maintaining a balance among people.

Table 6.1 highlights the characteristics of Hofstede's dimensions, excluding the long-term orientation. In this table, Hofstede indicates that a **high Power Distance index** (PDI) reflects an acceptance of inequality and an asymmetrical relationship in interactions. In such cultures, the powerless are often blamed for society's problems or any conflict between the powerful and the powerless. Hofstede (1998:14) classes 'Latin', Asian and African countries as examples of those with a high PDI. A **low Power Distance index**, however, illustrates the interdependence and equality between members of a society and focuses on developing a harmonious relationship between the powerful and the underdog. In these cultures, the blame is placed on the 'system' and not any one particular group. Examples include Germanic countries.

A **high Individualism index** reflects a society in which the working life is seen as secondary to a personal life outside work. In such cultures,

Table 6.1. Hofstede's cultural dimensions

Small Power Distance societies (PDI)	Large Power Distance societies (PDI)
• Hierarchy means an inequality of roles established for convenience	• Hierarchy means existential inequality
• Subordinates expect to be consulted	• Subordinates expect to be told what to do
• Ideal boss is resourceful and democratic	• Ideal boss is benevolent and autocratic

Collectivist societies	Individualist societies
• Value standards differ for in-group and out-group	• Same value standards apply to all
• Other people are seen as members of their group	• Other people seen as potential resources
• Relationship prevails over task	• Task prevails over relationship
• Moral model of employer–employee relationship	• Calculative model of employer–employee relationship

Feminine societies	Masculine societies
• Assertiveness ridiculed	• Assertiveness appreciated
• Understate yourself	• Oversell yourself
• Stress on life quality	• Stress on careers
• Intuition	• Decisiveness

Weak Uncertainty Avoidance societies (UAI)	Strong Uncertainty Avoidance societies (UAI)
• Dislike of rules – written or unwritten	• Emotional need for rules – written or unwritten
• Less formalisation and standardisation	• More formalisation and standardisation
• Tolerance of deviant persons and ideas	• Intolerance of deviant persons and ideas

(from Hofstede 1998:12)

there is less importance placed on duty, expertness and prestige at work. Hofstede (1998:14) claims that 'Individualism prevails in developed and Western countries, while Collectivism prevails in less developed and Eastern countries; Japan takes a middle position on this dimension'.

A **high Masculinity index** indicates a society which favours aggressive and ambitious behaviour, which contrasts with a low index emphasising compassionate and friendly behaviour as well as valuing negotiation. Masculine cultures, according to Hofstede, include Japan and some European nations like Germany, Austria and Switzerland, whereas those countries with a low Masculinity index are Nordic countries and the Netherlands.

A **high level of Uncertainty Avoidance** (UAI) characterises a culture in which there is a high level of anxiety and job stress, fear of failure, low risk-taking, need for security, reduction of ambiguity as well as dependence on experts and authority figures. A **low Uncertainty Avoidance index**, in contrast, shows a society in which there is a low level of anxiety and few rules are followed or instigated. Uncertainty avoidance is high in 'Latin' countries, Japan and German-speaking nations, while it is lower in Anglo, Nordic and Chinese cultures.

Hofstede (1991, 1998) suggests that these scores illustrate the sources of cultural differences. He suggests that higher UAI cultures include Catholic nations which deal with uncertainty through ritualistic ways in contrast to the Protestant ones, and include such countries as Israel as well as Muslim nations. Nations with a low UAI, on the other hand, are India and the Philippines. Cultures with a low PDI and UAI are English-speaking and Northern European cultures, whereas those with a low PDI but high UAI include German-speaking nations. 'Latin' and Japanese both reflect cultures with a high PDI and UAI.

The qualities Hofstede identifies seem to be of value in understanding potentially different patterns of thinking, feeling and acting. However, we are concerned about the **appropriateness** of the terms *Masculinity* and *Femininity* as labels for describing cultural variation. The use of these terms to denote a distinction between cultures in which individual achievement is highly valued, compared to cultures in which relationships are highly valued, is perpetuating an **overgeneralisation** regarding gender. Also, Hofstede's choice of words to describe those cultures and nations according to his dimensions can be viewed as containing **Western bias** and value judgment. This can be seen in his description of those countries with a high Power Distance index as having such positive characteristics as interdependence and equality between members of society, as well as a **harmonious relationship** between the powerful and underdog (European countries); in comparison to those with a low Power Distance index in which there is a gap between the powerful and powerless, thus, according to Hofstede (1998:14) being characterised by inequality (e.g. 'Latin' and some Asian countries). However, Hofstede's observations are none the less of interest as a standing point for identifying some relevant cultural parameters.

In his analysis of workplace communication data in terms of cultural value systems, Clyne (1994:179–86) finds some of the features of

Hofstede's model to be useful in understanding the cultural varieties in his corpus. Clyne largely avoids using the terms 'masculinity' and 'femininity' and instead uses such words as *harmony*, and *degrees of negotiation* as well as *assertiveness* and *weakness*. Wierzbicka (1991) also draws attention to the extreme polarities inherent in Hofstede's framework. In spite of the limitations of Hofstede's model, it does contain a useful inventory of parameters along which cultural value systems and the concept of power relations within cultures can be analysed. However, it needs to be understood that such categorisations, while useful, are based on general national cultural differences and may not be relevant to all members of that cultural grouping.

6.2 POWER RELATIONS IN INTERACTIONS

Hofstede's cultural dimensions also are beneficial in helping to explain the social, cultural, political and economic factors which influence power relations in given interactions – both within cultures and between cultures. Searle (1969) pointed out that the **social expectations and conventions**, which underlie communication, are critical to the interpretation of linguistics meaning in a given interaction. This means that linguistic communication can be regarded as a form of social action. Brown and Levinson (1987:77) define 'power'as follows:

> P (power) is an asymmetric social dimension of relative power, roughly in Weber's sense. That is, P is the degree to which . . . H (Hearer) can impose his own plans and his own self-evaluation (face) at the expense of . . . S's (Speaker's) plans of self-evaluation.

This conceptualisation of power is based on the Weberian perception in which power is seen to negatively influence others' behaviour or force people to perform acts which they wouldn't undertake by themselves.

Searle (1969, 1995) and Foucault (1980), however, argue that power relations exist as part of the social fabric of communication and should not be solely regarded as being the negative forces of domination by those in powerful positions (e.g. the state, the police, etc.). Power should not only be seen in terms of inequity and domination, because 'power comes from below; that is, there is no binary and all-encompassing opposition between rulers and ruled at the root of power relations' (Foucault 1978:94). Foucault emphasises that **power** is something which is not imposed 'from above', but is **created through people interacting in a certain social context.**

Giddens (1993:116) further suggests that the concept of social action is 'logically tied to that of power'. He also conceives **power** as being **contextually determined** as it is regarded as a component of the discourse. Giddens suggests that the act of participation in an interaction can be sufficient to enable a person to acquire some level of control over the conversation. Giddens (1993) provides examples of extreme forms of social control which include an interaction between a prison guard and a prisoner. For example, a prisoner can still maintain some level of social control even when in solitary confinement, by going on a hunger strike. Thus, even though there is an asymmetrical power relationship in favour of the prison guard, the prisoner can still exert some level of power within the interaction (see Giddens' 'dialectic of control').

Davidson (1986:226) takes a similar perspective and suggests that power needs to be viewed 'as a netlike, circulating organization'. Power exists within the fabric of language and not outside of it, and is part of the interactional process. Therefore, the concept of power is not socially predetermined, but is dependent upon the context of the interaction.

Access to information and resources can directly influence the power relations between participants. Those who have access to information have more powerful positions in interactions. The differing degrees of symmetry in power relations and the relationship between power and discourse are the foci of research by critical discourse analysts. Such researchers as Fairclough (1989), van Dijk (1987, 1996), Wodak (1996), Fairclough and Wodak (1997), Teo (2000) and Eades (2000) have attempted to identify and determine how access to information differs as a result of the socioeconomic, educational and cultural backgrounds of the participants and how this in turn impacts on the power relations in a given interaction and/or institution.

The access to information is central in an institutional context. The person with the greater access to information and resources is sometimes referred to as the **gatekeeper**, meaning that they possess more power and thus control the information flow in a given interaction (see Sarangi 1996; Sarangi & Roberts 1999). 'Institutions' or 'organisations' can be viewed as 'cultures with an emphasis on discourse and power' (Wodak 1996:10). Sarangi and Roberts (1999) suggest that it is the setting (e.g. legal, educational, medical) that is important when studying institutional interactions. The roles of the participants and their access to information are continuously changing which means that the power relations do not remain static. Given that, the power relations between participants depend on the particular context of the interaction, whether that be in a legal, educational, medical or media setting.

The aims of a **Critical Discourse Analysis** approach (CDA) can be said to include understanding and analysing the influence of **ideological loading** in certain words and phrases in languages and the relations of power which underlie such linguistic forms which are often not apparent to language-users. CDA can also be applied to examine **racist ideologies, discriminatory language** or **stereotyping in discourse** (van Dijk 1987, 1996; Eades 2000; Teo 2000). It is used to address the different levels of access that members of a society may have to such resources based on their social class, education and cultural background. Fairclough and Wodak (1997) identify eight such principles:

1. CDA addresses social problems
2. power relations are discursive
3. discourse constitutes society and culture
4. discourse does ideological work
5. discourse is historical
6. the link between text and society, between the micro and the macro, is mediated
7. discourse analysis is interpretative and explanatory
8. discourse is a form of social action.

These principles highlight the need to view power relations within and between societies in relation to a given interaction and in the context of social, political, historical, economic and linguistic ideologies and social practice. While Hofstede's dimensions are useful in identifying the ideologies and social practice, Fairclough (1989) and Pennycook (2001) have both investigated the concept of ideology and power from the perspective of CDA. Fairclough proposes that language and power are affected by 'ideologies' that are 'implicit in the conventions according to which people interact linguistically, and of which people are generally not consciously aware' (1989:2). Thus, when examining how power is used and manipulated, it needs to be analysed in terms of '**the ideological workings of language**' (Heydon 2005). Pennycook (2001:7) further suggests that 'turning a sceptical eye towards assumptions, ideas that have become "naturalized", notions that are no longer questioned' needs to be addressed when considering these 'ideological workings of language'.

The concept of **social practice** is also important in understanding the relationship between language and power. Fairclough (2000:156) defines **social practice** as 'a particular area of social life which is structured in a distinctive way involving particular groups of people in particular relations with each other'. This means that language is identified as just one factor influencing the manifestation of power and ideologies in a given interaction. Language can be regarded as 'internalised' in discourse which exists as part of and is interrelated with the physical, sociological and psychological elements which also affect power relations in interactions, such as in institutional encounters (Heydon 2005).

Foucault (1980:99) provides a succinct summary to the study of the relationship between power and language in that such a relationship should be analysed by:

> starting . . . from the infinitesimal mechanisms, which each have their own history, their own trajectory, their own techniques and tactics, and then see how these mechanisms of power have been – and continue to be – invested, colonised, utilised, involuted, transformed, displaced, extended, etc., by ever more general mechanisms.

6.3   STEREOTYPING AND IDEOLOGY

Ideologies or an **ideological statement** can be referred to as **stereotypes** which often result from the belief that any two cultures or social groups are polar opposites (Scollon & Scollon 2001). Stereotyping often involves **overgeneralisation**. According to Scollon and Scollon (2001:168) it is 'the process by which all members of a group are asserted to have the characteristics attributed to the whole group'. Any classification or grouping of people involves stereotypes. Tajfel (1982) suggests that people often categorise themselves positively at the centre (in-group) to create and promote self-esteem and pride and classify others negatively on the outside (out-group). According to Hofstede (1998), such differentiation between in-group and out-group members is more characteristic of collectivist societies. Positive in-group stereotypes are utilised to develop self-esteem to mark oneself as being different from the out-group.

Hogg and Abrams (1988), who have further developed Tajfel's approach, suggest that the **in-group members** impose their **dominant** value system and ideology on the **out-group** to advantage themselves and legitimise the status quo. In contrast to such positive self-stereotyping, the out-group (or the people in a subordinate position) are made to believe that they themselves and their culture are somehow inferior to the dominant in-group. As van Dijk (1987:111) emphasises:

> Dominant group members regularly engage in conversations about ethnic minority groups in society, and thus express and persuasively communicate their attitudes to other in-group members.

Such **stereotypes** perpetuate the differences between the culturally, socially, politically, historically and economically dominant in-group and the subordinate out-group.

Scollon and Scollon (2001) also use the terms 'negative' and 'positive' stereotyping. **Negative stereotyping** is seen as a method of reiterating a binaristic contrast as a negative group difference. Scollon and Scollon (2001:171) identify four major steps in negative stereotyping:

- Contrast two cultures or two groups on the basis of a single dimension.
- Focus on this artificial and ideological difference as a problem for communication.
- Assign a positive value to one strategy or one group and a negative value to the other strategy or group.
- Regeneralise this process to the entire group.

A final step can also be added and refers to viewing negative stereotyping in terms of genetic and racial characteristics.

Such binary contrasts are used both within a society and between different societies. For example, the in-group may be Westerners (taken from their perspective) and the out-group Asians. Of course, placing all people of 'Western' nations in one category and 'Asian' nations in another creates a stereotype already. However, here all Westerners may contrast themselves with all Asians and state that the out-group 'refuse(s) to introduce their topics so that we [the Westerners] can understand them' in business encounters (Scollon & Scollon 2001:171). Scollon and Scollon emphasise that such negative stereotyping 'leads to the idea that somehow members of the other group are actively trying to make it difficult to understand them' (2001:171).

Positive stereotyping, in contrast, can be divided into two main strategies:

- solidarity fallacy and
- lumping fallacy.

The **solidarity fallacy** relates to falsely combining one's own group with some other group in order to establish common ground on one single dimension (Scollon & Scollon 2001). Scollon and Scollon compare Tannen's (1994) research concerning the perceptions of American men and women with respect to Chinese men and women. Tannen observes that American men have a tendency to stress information over relationship, while American women favour relationship over information (see also Hofstede's dimensions). The solidarity fallacy develops when American women group themselves with Chinese people in general in contrast to American men to emphasise both the similarities between themselves and the Chinese, and the difference from American men. While such groupings may assist in understanding the similarities between American women and the Chinese in general, it can lead to the misconception that all cultural characteristics of the two groups are similar or the same.

The second type of positive stereotyping is the **lumping fallacy**. This occurs when a person makes a false grouping in reference to two other groups (Scollon & Scollon 2001:173). An example of this would be the statement that Westerners consider all Asians to be members of the same group, thus ignoring the contrasts between the groups and that such groupings include a diversity of different cultures and languages.

In summary, the major problem of **negative stereotyping** involves regarding members of a group as being **polar opposites**, whereas with **positive stereotyping** the members of different groups are **viewed as being identical** (Scollon & Scollon 2001:173).

Stereotypes, whether positive or negative, like group markings, limit our understanding of human behaviour and can lead to **miscommunication** in intercultural discourse because, as Scollon and Scollon (2001:169) conclude, 'they **limit our view of human activity** to just one or two salient dimensions and consider those to be the whole picture'. People need to consider the differences and similarities which exist between people and cultures. In other words, no individual member of a group encompasses or displays all of the characteristics of their group. Individuals belong to a variety of different groups and thus their identity and characteristics can be asserted differently, depending upon the situation. This is especially so for those who relate to more than one ethnic or cultural group.

6.4   SUMMARY

The relationship between power and language use can be studied from a variety of approaches. Hofstede's (1980, 1983, 1991, 1998) categorisation of national cultural differences provides one framework for understanding communication across cultures. The social, cultural, historical, political and economic characteristics identified by Hofstede can be used to examine and analyse those factors which influence the manifestation and development of power relations and group markings in a given interaction. Power is not predetermined, nor intrinsically associated with oppression or inequity, but is determined by the participants' own experiences, status and backgrounds

(Giddens 1982, 1993; Davidson 1986; Searle 1995). Power relations are also affected by the underlying assumptions and ideologies embedded in people's beliefs and perceptions in language. Stereotypes develop when overgeneralisations are made by applying one individual characteristic to an entire group. Thus, any categorisation of a group leads to a stereotype, and therefore influences the power relations in a given context. This can occur through group markings such as in-group and out-group, or even through the categorisation of national cultural dimensions.

An awareness of such contrasts and classifications can assist in helping to understand how power evolves in different cultures and may reduce the possibility of communication breakdown. Such understanding can also be beneficial to better comprehend the social expectations and conventions underlying language use in different cultures in order to more successfully interpret linguistic meaning in a given interaction.

6.5   REVIEW

1. **Key Terms:** Stereotyping: positive stereotyping, negative stereotyping, overgeneralisation, group marking, in-group, out-group, interactional context, uncertainty avoidance, individualism, collectivism, masculinity, femininity, harmony, power: power relations, institutions, gatekeepers, ideology, critical discourse analysis.

2. **Key Ideas**
   Having read this chapter you should:
   a. understand some of the factors that contribute to the formation of stereotypes
   b. be aware of the contribution of Hofstede to the analysis of cultural difference
   c. be aware of the potential role of ideology, institutions, gatekeepers in the creation and perpetuation of perceptions of power
   d. be aware of the perspective of critical discourse analysis in the discussion of power stereotyping and cultural differences
   e. appreciate the importance of interactional context to discourse power.

3. **Focus Questions**
   a. **Stereotyping: in-group and out-group**

   Consider the following quote about in-group and out-group stereotypes: 'Dominant group members regularly engage in conversations about ethnic minority groups in society, and thus express and persuasively communicate their attitudes to other in-group members' (van Dijk 1987:111).

(i) Based on the discussion in section 6.3 Stereotyping and ideology, why is the dominant group referred to as the 'in-group'? In the above statement, which group is regarded as the 'out-group'? Give reasons.

(ii) Based on what is current news in the mass media in your country, at a global level, who (person or group) is regarded as the 'dominant group' and thus the 'in-group', and who is often negatively described as being on the outside, or the 'out-group'? Give reasons.

(iii) In your own society, who (which group of people) would you describe as being part of the 'in-group', and who would be classified as being part of the 'out-group'? What do you think are the political, social, cultural, etc. reasons for such a grouping? What words or phrases are used to describe the 'in-group' and 'out-group' members?

b. Institutional power

Based on your own experience and language background, provide an institutional context, indicating the 'gatekeeper', the role of the participants and the setting (e.g. legal, educational, medical). Describe the power relations between the 'gatekeeper' and other participants in the context, and provide reasons as to whether the access to information changed or continues to change over time.

c. Power and meaning in newspapers

(i) How do the newspapers in your country or another with which you are familiar promote certain ideological constructions or stereotyping through the use of headlines, leads and generalisations (e.g. sexism, racism, relations between the in-group and out-group, etc.)?

(ii) What other examples of ideological bias or stereotyping have you read and/or heard about in newspapers and on the online news sites using such linguistic mechanisms (e.g. use of quotes, the types of people and their occupations quoted, use of adjectives and other words to describe events and/or people, etc.)?

4. Research Analysis
a. Discriminatory language

Consider the following extract by Gottlieb (2006):

Discriminatory language, and whether it should be regulated or not, have been hot topics in Japanese social debate for many years. The 1970s and 1980s in Japan saw an upsurge of protest from marginalised groups about the terms and stereotypes used to describe them in the language of public life, most often in the mass print and visual media. The Buraku Liberation League [the descendants of outcasts who were (and are still now) heavily discriminated against in Japan] and its forerunners had been active since the 1920s in rooting out and confronting any reported instance of derogatory language, subjecting offenders to a process of denunciation aimed at extracting both an apology for that particular instance and a promise of a more educated and serious approach in the future. Following their lead, disability activist groups, ethnic Korean resident groups and, to a lesser extent, women's groups mounted similar protests in the 1980s, energised by a wave of moral support offered by both international and domestic social changes occurring at the time. The International Year of Disabled Persons (1981) for example, provided the impetus for a change of terminology relating to disability in Japanese laws and statutes and for pressure to be brought to bear on media organisations about their use of language in this area.

As a result of vocal protests from those groups affected, the Japanese media during this period drew up lists of words not to be used on any account [*kinkushū*] and lists of suggested substitute terms [*iikaeshū*]. Many of these lists were in-house only and were not made public, although that of Japan's major public broadcaster, N.H.K., was. Other early ones may be found included as appendices in Japanese books on the subject. The motivation behind the lists and the consequent self-censorship of contentious terms was simple: to avoid the embarrassment of public protest (which could be very vocal indeed and occasionally spilled over into violence) and consequent loss of face.

(i) In the above extract, Gottlieb discusses numerous groups in Japanese society which have been subjected to discrimination and linguistic stereotyping. Using these groups as a basis, provide examples of discriminatory language which you have encountered in similar groups in your own social environment (e.g. sexist language, discriminatory language against people with disabilities or from certain cultural and ethnic groups, or people from certain socio-economic groups). How has the usage of such discriminatory language changed over the last two decades and why has it?

(ii) Do you think that the substitutions of certain words and phrases can be effective in overcoming discriminatory language in the mass media? What strategies do you think could be successful in overcoming discriminatory language and linguistic stereotyping in your own country?

b. Hofstede's cultural dimensions

Consider Table 6.1 from Hofstede (1998:12).

  (i) Based on this table, what dimensions would best describe your own national culture?

  (ii) Provide an example for each dimension and indicate the reasons for your choice.

  (iii) Do you believe that national cultures which are characterised by Hofstede as having a high level of uncertainty avoidance (UAI) (e.g. Japan, 'Latin' and German-speaking nations) would encounter communication difficulties with those of a lower UAI (e.g. Nordic, Anglo and Chinese cultures)? Provide reasons and examples of communication success/failure for your choice.

  (iv) Hofstede's model has been criticised by some linguists in the past due to its Western bias and extreme polarities (Wierzbicka 1991). Do you agree with such criticisms? Depending on your answer, how does Hofstede's model enhance or limit our understanding of cultural value systems and cultural groupings in the world?

5. Research Exercise

As more and more people from different linguistic and cultural backgrounds are coming into contact with each other, how can people address and overcome differing power relations and cultural and linguistic stereotypes to successfully communicate in an intercultural context? Give three examples of strategies to ensure successful intercultural communication.

NOTE

1 For this final dimension, Hofstede (1998:13) writes that 'there has been insufficient research as yet on the implications of differences along this dimension'. Hofstede does not elaborate on this dimension and we will not mention it further here.

SUGGESTED FURTHER READING

El-Dash, L.G. & Busnardo, J. 2001 'Perceived in-group and out-group stereotypes among Brazilian foreign language students'. *International Journal of Applied Linguistics*, vol. 11, no. 2, pp. 224–37.

Fairclough, N. 1989 *Language and Power*. Harlow: Longman Group.

Gottlieb, N. 1998 'Discriminatory language in Japan: Burakumin, the disabled and women'. *Asian Studies Review*, vol. 22, no. 2, pp. 157–73.

Hofstede, G. 1983 'Dimensions of national cultures in fifty countries and three regions'. In Deregowski J. B. & Dziurawiec S. et al. (eds) *Explications in Cross-cultural Psychology*. Netherlands: Swets & Zeitlinger, pp. 335–55.

Sarangi, S. & Roberts, C. (eds) 1999 *Talk, Work and Institutional Order: Discourse in Medical, Mediation and Management Settings*. Berlin: Mouton de Gruyter.

Sarangi, S. 1996 'Conflation of institutional and cultural stereotyping in Asian migrants' discourse'. *Discourse & Society*, vol. 7, pp. 359–87.

Scollon, R. & Scollon, S. Wong 2001 *Intercultural Communication: A Discourse Approach*, 2nd edn. Oxford: Blackwell.

Teo, P. 2000 'Racism in the news: A critical discourse analysis of news reporting in two Australian newspapers'. *Discourse & Society*, vol. 11, no. 1, pp. 7–49.

Van Dijk, T. 1987 *Communicating Racism: Ethnic Prejudice in Thought and Talk*. Newbury Park, California: Sage Publications.

Wodak, R. 1996 *Disorders of Discourse*. London: Addison Wesley Longman.

7

Naming and addressing: Expressing deference, respect, and solidarity

FIRST NAMES, MIDDLE NAMES, LAST NAMES, nicknames, pronouns and other terms of address all identify individuals in a society. Such address forms can contribute to a person's sense of identity and can characterise 'an individual's position in his family and in society at large; it defines his social personality' (Mauss 1974:134). Kinship and other terms indicating relationships are also important as terms of address in certain cultures. Appel and Muysken (1987:13) suggest that personal identity can be defined as 'the self feeling in relation to the group'.

Braun (1988) outlines some basic concepts in his theory of terms of address. According to Braun, **address** denotes a speaker's linguistic reference to his/her collocutors (1988:7).

Words and phrases such as second-person pronouns, names, kinship terms and titles, reflect the relationship between the individual and their social context. Braun (1988:13) suggests that:

> . . . address behavior is the way individual speakers or groups of speakers use the repertory of address variants available to them. From a sociolinguistic point of view, address behavior is meaningful whenever speakers have to choose between several variants . . . Address behavior is further influenced by a speaker's social and linguistic background.

7.1   PRONOUNS OF ADDRESS

Pronouns are markers of personal identity in relation to the group. Thus, **pronouns of address** serve to identify individuals within a given society and their daily usage reinforces **personal and social identity**. Pronouns are usually regarded as being primarily anaphoric devices, creating cohesion with grammatical structures and their behaviour is believed to be governed by rules that specify which pronouns can 'replace' which other nominal constructions.

Mühlhäusler (1996:300) points out that in addition to their grammatical and discourse cohesive functions, pronouns are important in the social context. He suggests that pronouns establish the divisions of personal space and the relations between one person and another. Therefore, pronominal systems portray the '**culture-specific organisations of people**, space and its limits within which speakers can create speech situations'.

In most languages, the pronoun form of address has at least two second-person pronouns, such as *thou* and *ye* in early English. Examples of these second-person pronouns in contemporary languages include:

Italian   *tu* and *voi* (*lei* replacing *voi*)
French   *tu* and *vous*
Spanish   *tu* and *vos* (later *usted*)
German   *du* and *ihr* and then also *sie* (third-person plural as a 'polite' form of 'you')

In many of these languages, the earlier second-person plural forms, for example *vous, vos,* and *sie* were also used as polite second-person forms, regardless of plurality. Some third-person plural forms, such as *Sie* (German) and *usted* (Spanish) are now used as polite forms of address.

Brown and Gilman (1960) and Brown and Ford (1961) argue that the use of **pronouns of address** is primarily determined by the relationship between the Speaker and the Hearer, and that this relationship can be interpreted in terms of two semantic dimensions – **power** (or 'status') and **solidarity** (or 'intimacy').[1] Brown and Gilman (1960) introduce the symbols *T* and *V* (Latin *tu* and *vos*) to differentiate the second-person pronouns which denote the 'familiar' (*T, tu*) and the 'polite' (*V, vos*). They suggest that in Western societies, during the nineteenth century, there was a shift in the 'power semantic' (i.e. hierarchical address system) towards the 'solidarity semantic' (i.e. greater equality between interactants).

T and V have now become generic symbols to designate a familiar (T) and a polite (V) pronoun in any language. In this sense address can be **reciprocal or non-reciprocal** and **symmetrical or asymmetrical**.

Braun (1988:13) explains that:

> Address is reciprocal when two speakers exchange the same form of address (or equivalent ones) . . . Correspondingly, address is non-reciprocal when the forms used by the two speakers in a dyad are different (or non-equivalent)

. . . All forms of address in a given dyad (interaction) being used reciprocally, the address relationship is symmetrical. When different forms are used, the address relationship is asymmetrical.

The **power semantic** is characterised by a non-reciprocal, asymmetrical relationship between the Speaker and the Hearer. Brown and Gilman (1960:255) argue that 'power is a relationship between at least two persons, and it is **nonreciprocal** in the sense that both cannot have power in the same area of behavior'. The meaning of non-reciprocal V could be *older than, parent of, employer of, richer than, stronger than,* and *nobler than,* implying a relation of '**more powerful than**'.

Brown and Gilman (1960:257) also outline how the shift from a power semantic to a **solidarity** semantic may have occurred:

For many centuries French, English, Italian, Spanish, and German pronoun usage followed the rule of nonreciprocal *T-V* between persons of unequal power and the rule of mutual *V* or *T* (according to social-class membership) between persons of roughly equivalent power. There was at first no rule differentiating address among equals but, very gradually, a distinction developed which is sometimes called the *T* of intimacy and the *V* of formality. We name this second dimension *solidarity* . . .

Brown and Gilman provide the schemas shown in Figure 7.1 to illustrate the power and solidarity dimensions.

In these schemas, Brown and Gilman distinguish three levels of power - superior, equal and inferior. In schema (a) the solidary dimension is shown as only relevant between equals, whereas in scheme (b) solidary is shown as relevant at each of the three levels of power, creating six categories of relationships:

1. a. Superior and solidary: T (e.g. parent to child)
   b. Superior and not solidary: T/V (e.g. employer to employee)

2. a. Equal and solidary: T
   b. Equal and not solidary: V

3. a. Inferior and solidary: T/V (e.g. child to parent)
   b. Inferior and not solidary: V (e.g. employee to employee)

Moreno (2002:18) points out, with reference to the distinctions drawn by Brown and Gilman, that the T pronoun of solidarity 'can be produced by frequency of contact (if contact results in the creation or discovery of "like-mindedness", behaviour similarities, or affection), as well as by objective similarities of class, political membership, family, religion, profession, sex, or birthplace.'

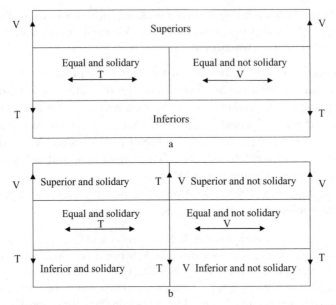

Figure 7.1. Use of T/V in relation to equality/inferiority/solidarity
(Brown & Gilman 1960:259)

Pronouns of address reflect the relationship between the Speaker and Hearer. The V form (*vos, voi, vous, ihr*) is generally said to indicate **formality**, whereas the T form (*tu, du*) embodies **intimacy**. According to this two-dimensional semantic, T is a pronoun of **condescension or intimacy** and V is used for **reverence or formality**. Figure 7.2 illustrates the accepted directions of use of these pronouns of address between pairs of speakers in particular relationships.

The first row of dyads in Figure 7.2 exemplify relationships that allow both T and V alternatives to be used to inferior addressees but not vice versa, whereas the second three dyads exemplify relationships which allow both alternatives to superior addressees only. The final six dyads allow only one form, either formal or informal, depending on the relationship between members of the dyad.

The choice of pronouns in those languages with the T and V distinction may be sensitive to salient features of relationships including respect, deference, intimacy and/or familiarity. In **English**, however, the distinction between the T and V forms has been lost and **other features of the grammar** need to be used to code deference and intimacy.

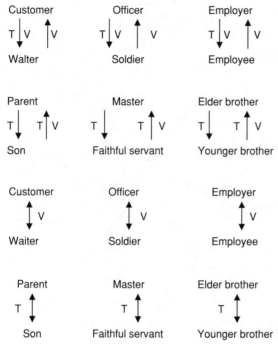

Figure 7.2. Use of pronouns of solidarity
(Brown & Gilman 1960:260)

DIFFERING USAGE OF PERSONAL PRONOUNS

The above examples of the use of T and V forms illustrate how speakers of English, Italian, French and German may address each other by using second-person pronouns. In a given conversation, the Speaker and Hearer change roles according to whose turn it is to speak, that is, who 'has the floor'. Such changes entail a shift in the use of the first- and second-person pronouns. At the beginning of the interaction, the Speaker uses the first-person pronoun to denote himself/herself; however, when the turn changes and the Hearer becomes the Speaker, the original speaker becomes the second person. Suzuki (1976:261) suggests that this transfer between first- and second-person pronouns is a clear demonstration that the use of the first-person pronoun at root entails that 'The person who is speaking now is myself', that is, it is the linguistic expression of the speaker's role, while the second-person pronoun says to the addressee, 'You are the listener at this point in the conversation'. While this change in personal pronouns

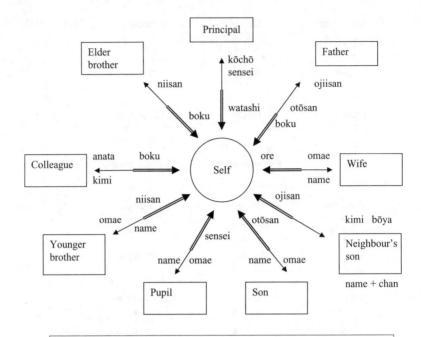

Terms used in Figure 7.3:

Self-specifiers

watakushi (I, formal), *boku* (I, informal), *ore* (I, intimate and vulgar), *ojisan* (uncle), *otōsan* (father), *sensei* (teacher), and *niisan* (elder brother).

Other-specifiers

Besides the second-person pronouns *anata* (*you*, formal), *kimi* (*you*, informal), *omae* (*you*, intimate and vulgar), we find as other-specifiers the person's name, *ojiisan* (grandfather/old man), *otōsan*, and *niisan*, among others.

Figure 7.3. Interaction, communication and grouping
(from Suzuki 1976:257)

and perceived roles seems obvious to speakers of such languages as English, French and German, in Japanese the roles in a conversation and, therefore, the use of pronouns and forms of address, are often fixed. Suzuki (1976:261) argues that:

> In fact, the reason why this class of words is called *personal* pronouns in European languages is that they are pronouns which possess the characteristics of a *persona,* or a player's mask. The interpersonal relationship visible in the interchangeable Latin 'ego' 'tu' transformation, or the English 'I' – 'you' transformation is correspondingly symmetrical.

Suzuki (1976) discusses ways in which formality and familiarity in the pronominal system can be expressed differently. She describes the Japanese method of address using a mixture of what she terms **self-specifiers** and **other-specifiers** (personal pronouns and kinship terms). We have observed that such variety in the terms of address is still actively used in present-day Japanese society. Figure 7.3 is a description of certain specifiers in Japanese which are more complex than the T and V distinction. This figure is written from the perspective of a 40-year-old male teacher. What we see is that there is a variety of relationship terms that are typically used as an alternative to the use of pronouns.

Brown and Gilman's features of formality and intimacy are still very relevant in more complex systems of address, such as the Japanese system exemplified above. However, there are many ways to indicate personal and group identities besides the use of pronouns of address.

TERMS OF ADDRESS IN THE VIRTUAL WORLD

Usami (2002), de Oliveira (2003) and Kretzenbacher (2005) argue that in the world of computer-mediated communication (CMC), the use of an incorrect or inappropriate address form can cause great offence and need redress. Kretzenbacher (2005:6) suggests that 'neither the T nor the V form *per se* can be said to be the "polite form", but only the form which is **agreed upon** to be the **unmarked** form in a particular situation by all participants in that situation'. Kretzenbacher (2005:5) provides the following example taken from a newsgroup in which the administrator *Christof* admonishes a newcomer *werbefrust* for his/her use of the V form *Sie* instead of T form *du*:

> *Zum Thema duzen: Im täglichen Leben im Internet ist es KEINE Unsitte sich zu duzen. Es ist sogar gänzlich normal.*
>
> *Andere Länder, andere Sitten, und das Internetist definitiv ein 'eigenes Land' [. . .] In Anlehnung an das englische 'you' hat sich im Laufe der Zeit im deutschsprachigem Internet durchgesetzt "Du" zu sagen, unabhängig davon, mit wem man es zu tun hat.*
>
> [Regarding *du*-ing: In daily life on the Internet it is NOT bad manners to address each other as *du*. Rather, this is completely normal.]

When in Rome, do as the Romans do, and the Internet definitely is 'a different country' [. . .] Following the model of English *you*, in the German speaking Internet it has become customary over time to address everybody as *du*, no matter who you are dealing with.]

Kretzenbacher (2005) points out that much literature dealing with address in German on the internet, such as Schulze (1999), Bader (2002), Hess-Lüttich and Wilde (2003), consider *du* as the universal form of address in CMC. However, Kretzenbacher's research illustrates that both *du* and *Sie* are used, depending upon the chat rooms and newsgroup. Based on the above example, the newcomer *werbefrust* did not accept *Christof's* argument posting that in other newsgroups '*Sie* address is customary' (Kretzenbacher 2005:5). Kretzenbacher (2005:6) reaches the conclusion based on the research conducted with focus groups and network interviews that:

in the case of the Usenet, we find a parallel to off-line communication in the coexistence of two systems, one tending towards unmarked *du*, the other towards unmarked *Sie*. These two possible situations have to be negotiated by newcomers, and often this is done on the basis of perceived degree of social distance.

It will remain to be seen, whether, as internet use increases, the use of formal *Sie* stabilises or decreases over time, marking internet chat as a distinct genre.

7.2   NOUNS OF ADDRESS

Nouns of address are another means of indicating identity and personal relationships with others. Such forms of address can include:

- names   William
- kinship terms   Father
- titles (Honorifics) Mr, Dr
- abstract nouns   Your Honour.

NAMES

Each culture has its own naming system. Names and other terms of address may have different functions across societies. Wilson (1998:xii) suggests that in contemporary European and North American societies, the family name (or surname) attached to an individual indicates that he/she belongs to that particular family as a legitimate child, whereas the full name shows the 'place and roles within a family'. In contrast, in the languages of the Pacific region, calling a person by their name used to be viewed as giving power and/or possessing power over the named person (Mühlhäusler 1996:56). This is also the case in Kyrgyz culture in which it was believed that a first name was 'loaded with power' (Hvoslef 2001:87). Hvoslef also suggests that particular shamans could 'tell the future of an individual only by knowing his or her personal name'. In interviews with Javanese people, we have observed that in Javanese (as in other languages, i.e. Kyrgyz) the choosing of a name was very important to ensure the prosperity of the name bearer. The importance of naming practices is highlighted by Bateson (1980:228) in the following quote concerning the Iatmul of New Guinea:

> The naming system is indeed a theoretical image of the whole culture and in it every formulated aspect of culture is reflected. Conversely, we may say that the system has its branches in every aspect of the culture and gives its support to every cultural activity. Every spell, every song . . . contains lists of names. The utterances of shamans are couched in terms of names . . . Marriages are often arranged in order to gain names. Reincarnation and succession are based upon the naming system. Land tenure is based on clan membership and clan.

Names may change as an individual progresses through life. For example, changes in names may occur at puberty, marriage, death of father or mother, or when there is a change in job. An individual may also be addressed differently depending on the context – such as the name employed by a close relative, a business associate, an acquaintance, by friends, in public, by spouses, and the list continues. Last names can also vary according to whether the referent is a female or male. For example, in Russian, a man might have the last name of *Petrov*, while the woman would have the feminine *Petrova*. Another example of gender differences is found among Sikh Indians where men and women may have similar 'given' names, but their gender is marked by the use of 'Singh' for males and 'Kaur' for females. In Australia, however, 'Singh' is often adopted as a surname by Sikh Indians (males) and the general population view this as the last name of both the females and males.

The following example from Hvoslef (2001:86) shows how the use of personal names can vary according to the culture and context. This example comes from the Kyrgyz Republic, one of the fifteen new states after the dissolution of the Soviet Union:

> Dinara and Anara Khasanbaeva are, together with the driver, Asan Sartbai, heading towards the small village of Ensjilesj where the two girls were born and raised some thirty years ago . . . [They are] meeting *tai ake* Toktobai ('mother's brother') and *tai ene* Burulusj ('mother's mother') . . . Toktobai turns toward Asan and asks him who he is and where his relatives come from. Asan . . . presents himself as *Kanat uulu Asanbek Sartbai* (*Kanat* = the personal name of his father, *uulu* = son, *Asan* = his own first name, *Sartbai* = the personal name of one of his ancestors). He continues telling that his relatives have their place of origin in a village near Naryn and that the name of his clan is 'Suksur' and the tribe 'Sajak'.
>
> From the boy's name Toktobai can read that Asan is son of Kanat and that one of his forefathers probably had the personal name Sartbai.

In Kyrgyz society the personal name described a person's relationships with others and some other qualities. Traditionally, the Kyrgyz language didn't have a last name/surname as such, but in recent times the naming practices have changed under the influence of Russian, and the equivalent of a surname has now been adopted.

It is obvious from the above discussion, that naming practices differ widely across cultures. The incorrect usage of a particular name or not being aware of differing naming systems could lead to miscommunication and ultimately insult and hurt.

USE OF FIRST NAMES

In an intercultural context, the inappropriate use of first names can cause great harm and offence. Bargiela et al. (2002:1) argue that 'for many British and American (English) speakers informality is taken to be an indicator of ease of communication with strangers'. However in other cultures (Russian, Chinese, Italian and Arabic), such informality is seen as being overfamiliar and thus impolite, and instead, distancing strategies in naming and addressing are employed to show politeness (e.g. use of first name plus an honorific). While Bargiela et al. (2002:4) acknowledge that naming practices in different English-speaking countries such as Australia, Britain and America do differ, they indicate that 'the general rule in English speaking cultures is that you move to first name terms as soon as possible'.

Scollon and Scollon (2001) provide an example of how this English-speaking strategy of first name usage can cause problems when interacting with people from a Chinese language background. In the anecdote, an American, Andrew Richardson, introduces himself to a Chinese person by saying 'Call me Andy'. In response, the Chinese person gives his business card upon which the first name on this card is 'Hon-fai'. Andrew Richardson decides to call the man Hon-fai, based on his own English naming strategy of using the 'first name'. However, Scollon and Scollon (2001) observe that in this situation, the use of the name 'Hon-fai' is only for intimates, and not strangers. Consequently, the use of such a 'first name' instead of establishing a sense of rapport and friendliness caused great embarrassment and discomfort due to the inappropriate use of an intimate form of address where distance, and not familiarity (non-reciprocal form), was regarded as a polite naming strategy.

Bargiela et al. (2002) further contrast Georgian and Russian naming practices and the use of first names and/or diminutive forms when addressing a person for the first time. The example given to illustrate this point is between a Georgian female patient and a young Russian female doctor in Moscow (in Russian). The Georgian female wants to show her familiarity and friendliness to the Russian doctor who is substituting for the professor/consultant at the hospital, so she asks whether she can address the doctor using a diminutive form of her first name (Bargiela et al. 2002:5):

G. female: *mèzna j? vas budu nazivat? galicka?*
(May I call you 'Galichka'?)[2]
R. doctor: *net, pèzaluísta*
(No, please, don't)

In Georgian, the use of this informal diminutive would have been appropriate; in Russian, however, such usage is regarded as not showing sufficient deference or respect. In Russian, the appropriate form of address would have been the first name plus a patronymic (Bargiela et al. 2002:5). In this particular example, the rejection of the diminutive first name usage shows a conflict in the cultural values associated with the meaning of using the first name.

As can be seen in the above examples, Georgians, like British and Americans, regard the **reciprocal first name** usage as indicating **familiarity** and **friendliness**, however in other languages such usage can be interpreted as being **overfamiliar** and **impolite**. This is because in those languages (i.e. Russian), a level of deference is appropriate due to the asymmetrical power and status differences.

NICKNAMES

Nicknames serve numerous functions over and above that of the merely referential one of first names. Their usage can portray physical and personal characteristics of the name holders (e.g. *porky* or *dumbo*), or a person's hobbies and interests, or their role in society (e.g. *smithie*). In general, nicknames develop spontaneously among people who know each other intimately and there is a high degree of familiarity between the interactants. Nicknames can be signs of endearment as well as of friendship and often signal a person's social and cultural position within a group. Affectionate nicknames can be diminutive forms of names such as *Che* for *Cheryl* or *Billy* for *William*.

Some nicknames, especially in English-speaking countries, are referred to as 'inevitable nicknames' in that individuals having certain last names are given a pre-existing nickname. These include *Thompson* becoming *Tommo* and *Webb* becoming *Spider* (Beale 1990).

De Klerk and Bosch (1997:298) observe that diminutive forms with /i:/ for female nicknames are more frequent in English than for male nicknames (e.g. *Katy, Lizzie* versus *Tommo* or *Dave*). In Australia name puns are an important source of nicknames. Heather Bowe recalls that her sister, Olwen, was called *Oboe* by close school friends, who then called Heather *Clarinet* ('sister of oboe'). Furthermore, in Australia the acquisition of a nickname and its acceptance by people of non-English-speaking backgrounds (e.g. of German, Chinese backgrounds) creates a greater level of familiarity and solidarity between people of differing language backgrounds and can help to more readily establish new identities within the wider Australian community.

Nicknames and their associated identities, in the emerging medium of computer-mediated communication (CMC), have also become an important means in identifying the participants in online chat rooms and newsgroups. Bays (1998:11) observes that online, a nickname or *nick* 'can be anything from numbers and punctuation to a highly personal and/or evocative name' and potentially contains numerous sociological cues (i.e. gender, approximate age, music and sports interests). Examples may include *camel66, musiclover33, Iamsohot1, Birdie_sunneyman*. She further points out that 'the nickname is the first sign of individuality when one encounters another participant. It serves as a first impression and shows the aspect of *face* that the participant wants to present on-line' (1998:11). In addition, a nickname has the function of beginning a person's *line*, which is followed by other verification process attempts to discover the authenticity of the nickname adopted and the information contained in the *line*.

Bays (1998:11) comments on the relationship between the virtual and physical world of nicknaming practices:

> The criteria for the construction of the online identity diverges from that of the physical person . . . with each successive nickname one can assert a new individuality and recreate the limits of his 'self', whereas in the physical world one is technically less able to change his identity with such malleability . . . the (online) participant technically can question his identity on a physical, superficial, social level each time he connects. In contrast, because the referent is less changeable, in the physical world the connection between one's name and one's physical identity is much stronger.

However, while it may appear that in a virtual world, there is no end to the great diversity and flexibility in the adoption of nicknames, Schiano (1997) argues that as the majority of online users develop a sense of 'CMC maturity', 'the perceived anonymity of early days develops into pseudonymy, where participants reciprocally recognize each other' and a more stable and set identity is adopted (Bays 1998). Consequently, nicknames used in cyberspace act as a marker or representative that individualises its name holder or, in this case the online participant, just as in the physical world.

KINSHIP TERMS

These forms of address relate to blood relations or are extensions of these blood ties. For example, in English a male friend of one's parents' generation may be called *uncle*. Kinship relationships are of great importance to intercultural communication. In some cultures such as Japanese, Korean, Vietnamese and Chinese, kinship relationships reflect the hierarchical social structure. The use of **kinship terms** reinforces the importance of the relationships they code. Suzuki (1976) uses the concept of kinship as the basis of her description of forms of address in Japanese society. She characterises terms of address in terms of distinctions between **self and other**, and **intra- and extra-familial:**

> **Self-specifiers:** terms used to denote the speaker (personal pronouns) (see above discussion). The choice of self-specifier is determined by the relationship between the Speaker and the Hearer. A choice of self-specifiers reflects power differences and gradations of social distance.

> **Other-specifiers:** terms used to denote the hearer or third person.

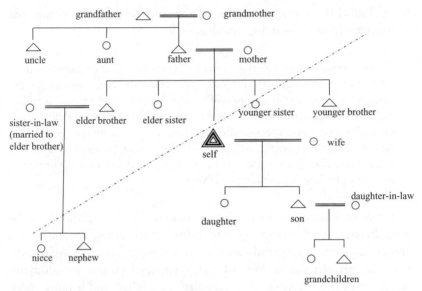

Figure 7.4. Superior vs inferior/equal status
(Suzuki 1976:257)

> **Intra-familial self and other specifiers:** Suzuki proposes five princi-
> ples to account for the ways in which a speaker may refer to self and
> others, according to whether the 'other' is in the group of superiors
> or inferiors (see below for details).

> **Extra-familial self-specifiers:** Japanese speakers expand the five prin-
> ciples of intra-familial specifiers to the community at large. **Societal
> specifiers** are used in place of the familial terms but the superior–
> inferior relationship is maintained.

Suzuki (1976) argues that these self- and other-specifiers are similar to
personal pronouns (see above discussion of T and V forms). However,
unlike pronouns, these terms are based on kinship relationships. As a result
of the hierarchical nature of kinship relations, the use of these terms can
be reciprocal or non-reciprocal and symmetrical or asymmetrical, similar
to that of the use of T and V pronouns. Suzuki provides an example of the
intra-familial self-specifiers and other-specifiers to explain the address system in Japanese. Figure 7.4 is taken from Suzuki (1976), and is used in her
explanation of the five principles which relate to the 'boundaries of superior
and inferior relations ... among members of a family or relationship group'.

The relationships in Figure 7.4 are shown from the perspective of a
40-year-old teacher. Those above the diagonal broken line are treated as

superiors and those below are regarded as either being inferior or equal in relation to self. Suzuki's five principles are:

A. The speaker (self) cannot address other relatives above his locus in the family by means of personal pronouns. He is not permitted, for example, to address his father as *anata* (you formal) or *kimi* (you informal), and the same strictures apply when he addresses, say, his elder brother.

B. The speaker addresses people above his station in the family, as a rule, by use of terms denoting their relationship to him. But he does not address people below himself by the terms for those relationships. He would not, for example, call his younger brother vocatively with a phrase like, 'Hey! Ototo (younger brother)!' nor would he ask pronominally his daughter, 'Where is Musume (daughter) going?'[3]

C. The speaker may not address people located above himself by their names alone (unless suffixed by an appropriate kin term), but may so address those located below him.

D. Speakers, especially female speakers, may, in addressing people above themselves, use their own names as self-specifiers, but may not do so in conversation with people located below them. Thus, Yoshiko (daughter) may say to her mother, 'Momma, Yoshiko hates that,' but her mother may not use her own name in a similar situation in conversation with her daughter.

E. In conversation with relations below himself the speaker may use as a self-specifier the term indicating his own relationship to the addressee, but a junior speaker may not do this in speaking to a senior one. In a conversation between brothers, for example, then, the brother may specify himself by saying 'niisan', but the younger brother may not use 'ototochan' to indicate himself.

(Suzuki 1976:257–8)

Such kinship terms can also be expanded to be used in an extra-familial context to refer to people of the older generation or younger generation even though there are no blood relations between the interactants. Other nouns of address can also be used to denote numerous asymmetrical relationships.

7.3   HONORIFICS

Titles and forms of address such as what Braun (1988:10) calls 'abstract nouns' can also be referred to as *honorifics* (e.g. Your Honour). Titles themselves can be prefixed or suffixed to names, terms of occupation or they can just be free (e.g. *Mrs and Mr* in English). The honorific registers in languages are traditionally viewed as a means of showing respect and deference or to convey honour. However, Agha (1998:153) argues that honorific speech also serves other roles such as 'control and domination, irony, innuendo, and masked aggression'. Honorific discourse is usually associated with both linguistic and non-linguistic elements (e.g. gesture, dress, or bodily posture of the interactants). Agha (1998:153) suggests that 'every language contains some items that conventionally possess honorific value; for example, every language contains honorific titles'. Examples include *Herr/Frau/Fräulein* in German, first name and patronymic in Russian, and *Mr/Mrs/Miss/Ms* in English. In Japanese, the equivalents of such titles are suffixes attached to an individual's first or last name, such as *-sama, -san, -kun* and *-chan*:

-sama:	the formal version of -san, and is used primarily in addressing persons of much higher rank and in commercial and business settings to address customers. It is also used to address or speak of persons or things for which the speaker wishes to show deference, kami-sama (spirits or deities). It is also found following a person's name in addresses on envelopes and frequently appears in business emails.
-san (Yoshida-*san*):	used for both single and married people and when attached to the last name/family name conveys a greater degree of formality. (Never used as a self-specifier)
-kun (Takahiro-*kun*):	used when addressing people of equal or lower status. It is also commonly used for boys of primary and secondary school ages, whereas -san is the equivalent for girls
-chan (Yoko-*chan*):	used to express intimacy and familiarity between close friends and for children.

Agha (1998:153) points out that different languages use different methods to indicate honorific language. These may consist of the use of titles and terms of address as well as honorific forms including pronouns, nouns, verbs and adverbs. The use of the honorific register often marks a social relationship of respect among the interactants.

Honorific abstract nouns in English include *Your Honour, Your Grace, Your Majesty, Your Highness* and *Your Excellency*, and all occur with possessive pronouns. English also contains such nouns of address as *Ladies and Gentlemen* to address a group and the nouns *Sir* and *Madam* to address individuals. Occupational terms, such as *doctor*, can also be used in English either as an **honorific title** such as *Dr Murphy*, or as an **honorific** *Doctor, could you please* . . . In Japanese, other occupational terms such as *sensei* 'teacher' are also used in these two ways – *Yoshida sensei* or just *sensei*. Koyama (1992:46) points out that the term *sensei* 'is often employed as a general term to refer to a person of higher status – a teacher, a doctor or even a politician'.

HONORIFIC LANGUAGE USE

Respect for either the speaker or the hearer can be shown not only in the terms by which they are addressed or by nouns and adjectives, but by choices relating to other **word classes**, that is verbs, adverbs and verbal auxiliaries. In the Javanese language, pronouns, nouns, adjectives and verbs are all used to signal the **honorific register**. Javanese is comprised of an elaborate system of at least nine different speech levels. In order to understand these speech levels, Geertz (1976:173) uses the metaphor of a protective barrier to explain the levels of politeness and formality in behaviour in traditional Javanese. The features of this barrier depend on the people involved in a given language context. These levels differ as a result of obligatory distinctions according to differences in status, rank, seniority and degree of regular acquaintance between the addresser and addressee (Errington 1985:10–11). Each speech level is a metonym for social situations in traditional Javanese society. If a Javanese person fails to use a speech level correctly in a given situation, they may be called *durung nJawani* ('not yet Javanese') which implies a level of immaturity or being 'less than fully human'. The proper behaviour of Javanese firstly depends on the control of the proper forms of linguistic expression, and secondly on the ability to choose the appropriate etiquette pattern by properly determining the social relations.

The most basic distinction is between high (*krama*) and low (*ngoko*) speech levels. *Ngoko* is the 'basic' language in which people speak to intimates or inferiors, express anger and humiliate their superiors. *Krama*, the honorific register, is employed to show a level of respect and honour when addressing people who are older, unfamiliar and superior (Koentjaraningrat 1989:16–18). Some examples of the differences between these two registers are the synonyms *wôs* (*krama*) and *beras* (*ngoko*) meaning 'uncooked rice', and *awrat* (*krama*) and *abôt* (*ngoko*), which means 'heavy'. Koentjaraningrat (1989:139–40) observes that these synonyms are related phonemically. Where the phoneme /w/ occurs in *krama*, the /b/ phoneme is found in *ngoko*.

Geertz (1976) employs the 'barrier' metaphor to highlight the use of particular speech levels in Javanese. Figure 7.5 displays Geertz's representation of the relationship between two individuals who are close friends of equal status and will consequently use the *ngoko* speech level when speaking to each other. The solid circle represents the inner core and the one 'layer' surrounding this circle symbolises the low speech style.

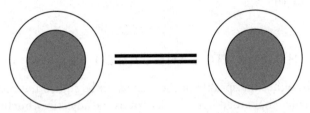

Figure 7.5. Individuals who are close friends use* Ngoko *(basic) speech level (Geertz 1976:174)

Figure 7.6 shows the connection between a high official and an ordinary educated person from an urban region. The high official should speak in *antya-basa* (middle *ngoko*), whereas the educated man should use *krama inggil* to address his superior. The larger circle is the high official and the three solid outer rings represent the third speech level, *krama* or High Javanese. These rings show the appropriate speech level which is used to refer to the high official.

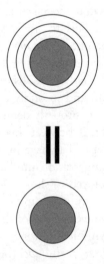

Figure 7.6. High official (*Antya-basa*) and educated person (*Krama inggil*) (Geertz 1976:174–5)

The final diagram (Figure 7.7) depicts two ordinary village people, who are not intimate friends. They should, therefore use *krama madya* (middle speech level) with each other. The two outer circles represent the second or middle basic speech level.

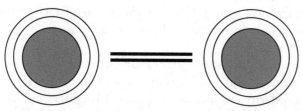

Figure 7.7. Village people who are not intimate friends will use* Krama madya *(middle speech level)
(from Geertz 1976:175)

In traditional Javanese, every person needs to be aware of their position in society and act accordingly. If the social behaviour, and the use of the correct speech level are inappropriate, the addresser or addressee is thus not at all well regarded.

Japanese is another language example which uses honorific forms of verbs and adverbs. Koyama (1992) gives the example of Tom, an exchange student who has been living with a Japanese host family for nearly one year. One day, Tom gives his host sister Yoko a birthday present. However, Yoko appears to become quite angry when Tom uses the verb *yarimasu* ('to give') when addressing her. Her response is *So you think I'm inferior to you, do you? After all, you're younger than me* (in English). According to Koyama, this example illustrates the problems using the appropriate language register in Japanese society.

The use of particular word forms depends on the age and status (**power** vs **solidarity**) of the interactants – that is, the superior–inferior relationship. In Japanese 'to give' could be expressed using *yarimasu, agemasu* and *sashiagemasu.* The use and meaning of these verbs are as follows:

yarimasu:	used from a superior to an inferior
agemasu:	a neutral form used to a Hearer of equal status (i.e. between friends)
sashiagemasu:	an honorific form used with a Hearer of equal status in a distant social relationship or from an inferior to a superior

(Koyama 1992:33)

The appropriate use of such forms is essential in successfully communicating in the Japanese context. In Japanese the roles between interactants are generally fixed and dependent on age, social distance and the status between the people in a given conversation. We have observed while living and researching in Japan that the strict usage of honorific forms is changing in modern Japanese society. However, the misuse of such forms can still lead to offence and discomfort, and result in the addresser or the addressee being poorly regarded.

Thus, honorific discourse is part of a complex interactional system which uses both linguistic and non-linguistic elements to convey **respect, deference** and **solidarity**. As illustrated above, all languages and cultures use honorific forms whether they be honorific titles or a more complex system of pronouns, nouns, verbs and adverbs.

7.4   SUMMARY

Names and terms of address are important for identifying individuals and their role in society and their use serves to maintain social cohesion. Names and terms of address can also influence the individual's perception of self and relationships. The linguistic choice of forms of address can be sensitive to the age of the Speaker and Hearer, the medium of communication (physical and virtual worlds), social status (i.e. power vs solidarity), social distance (superior/inferior relationships or equals) and even someone's physical and personal attributes (especially for nicknames). Each culture and language has its own differing norms as to the correct usage of forms of address. Clyne and Platt (1990:46) suggest that when dealing with differing forms of address across cultures:

> . . . the most appropriate strategy is to be alert, to enquire and not to be surprised about differences from the English language system.

7.5   REVIEW

1. **Key Terms:** forms of address, pronouns of address, semantics of pronouns of address, T and V, honorifics, speaker, addressee, power, solidarity, superiors and inferiors, group styles, nicknames, self-specifiers, other-specifiers, intra- and extra-familial, roles.

2. **Key Ideas**
Having read this chapter you should:

a. understand the significance of the (unspoken) rules that lie behind such practices as the assignment of nicknames, the employment of special forms of address, and the ascription of honorific titles
b. understand, and be able to critique, in the light of inter- and cross-cultural evidence, the 'universality' claims relating to systems of address
c. appreciate how naming practices are employed in particular cultures.

3. Focus Questions
a. Pronouns of address
(i) Using Brown and Gilman's (1960) dyads in Figure 7.2 to identify the T and/or V distinctions, describe what would be the appropriate pronouns of address in the following situations:
 – between a second-year undergraduate student and the Head of the Department at university
 – between fellow classmates in a Mathematics class at high school
 – between a customer and a customer service person at a big department store (e.g. Wal-Mart or Kmart)
 – between an undergraduate student and an administrative officer at university.

If you speak a language other than English as your first language, or if you are very familiar with another language, then also consider your answer using that language.

(ii) What are the salient features which influence that choice of such T and V forms of address? As in the above question, if you speak a language other than English as your first language, or if you are very familiar with another language, then also consider your answer using that language.

b. Nicknames
Nicknames serve numerous functions over and above that of the merely referential one of first names.
(i) What nicknames, if any, have you personally acquired? What are the functions of these nicknames?
(ii) What is the meaning associated with these nicknames and the social contexts of their use?

c. Nicknames online
In computer-mediated communication the use of a nickname and/or *nick* can be used to provide anonymity and pseudonymy.
(i) What examples of a nickname have you encountered in your experience in online chat rooms and newsgroups?

    (ii) Does the use of such nicknames online differ from those used in the physical world?

d. Use of first names

Do you agree with the statement by Bargiela et al. (2002) that 'the general rule in English speaking cultures is that you move to first name terms as soon as possible'? Provide two examples to illustrate your opinion. Try to use examples in which the interactants are from different language backgrounds. If you speak a language other than English as your first language, or if you are very familiar with another language, then consider your answer from the perspective of that language and cultural group.

4. Research Analysis

a. Avoidance of naming

Consider the following extract taken from Bargiela et al. (2002:12) describing a naming strategy employed by British people.

> Many British people have adopted the strategy of not using names at all in certain circumstances to avoid the difficulty of finding the appropriate form of address. For example, it used to be relatively acceptable to summon a waiter in a restaurant by calling out 'Waiter', however this is a very rare practice now, and saying 'Excuse me', gesturing or trying to catch the waiter's eye, are now far more common. This avoidance of naming is also made more complicated by not knowing what is the correct name for someone because of changes in the way that women, in particular, name themselves. Thus, it is not self-evident that the wife of Mr Jones will be called Mrs Jones. Nor will it be clear whether a woman wishes to be called Mrs, Miss or Ms. First name use for women has been identified as problematic, since it is far more frequently used in relation to women than to men and may be considered demeaning, overly familiar and even infantilising (Mills 1997). Thus, a frequent strategy in Britain, when meeting someone for the first time, is either to wait until they have introduced themselves or have been introduced, before using a name, or to use no name at all.

    (i) Have you ever encountered a naming practice, such as that described in the above quote, or employed it yourself in order to avoid any offence or misunderstanding? Besides the example contexts given, in what other contexts do you think such a naming practice would be acceptable in the English-speaking world?

(ii) In cultures where the preferred naming strategy is to use a name or an honorific to show deference and respect, what would be the consequences of avoidance of naming in an intercultural context? To illustrate your opinion, provide three examples of cultures in which such a naming practice might be considered impolite.

(iii) If a person intends to show solidarity and friendship with their interlocutor, what would be the most appropriate naming strategy to use? However, if a person wants to show deference, how do these naming strategies differ? How do social differences such as age, education and job status affect such naming practices? If you speak a language other than English as your first language, or if you are very familiar with another language, then also consider your answer using that language. Provide at least two different language examples.

b. Use of T and V forms

Consider the following consumer opinions of the use of the German T and V forms of address in corporate/business situations reported by Kretzenbacher (2005:10, 12) in response to the questions: Have you ever been addressed with a form you didn't expect? When, by whom?

Consumer 1:

Wenn es förmlich ist, wenn es um einen Vertrag geht, kann ich es überhaupt nicht leiden, wenn man sich mit du anspricht, weil man dann in so eine unformale Ebene fällt, wo es immer ganz schwer ist, seine Interessen durchzusetzen. Ein Beispiel ist, ich wollte ein Auto kaufen, da kam der Mann zu mir und sagte, was für ein tolles Auto es war und du . . . und so . . . das war in diesem Moment extrem unpassend. Das war ein seriöses Geschäft, da möchte man sich nicht duzen . . . ich hab ihn zurückgesiezt, aber er hat mich geduzt. Das war ein eigenartiger Mensch. Das war unangenehm.

[In a formal situation, if it is about a contract, I don't appreciate it at all if one is on a *du* basis, because it moves one to such an informal level at which it is always very difficult to see to one's own interests. One example is, I wanted to buy a car, and this man approached me and told me what a brilliant car it was . . . and addressed me as *du* . . . and so . . . that was extremely inappropriate at that moment. That was a serious business transaction, one does not want to be on a *du* basis there . . .I returned a *Sie* address, but he addressed me as *du*. That was an odd person. It was unpleasant.]

Consumer 2:

Sogar im aktuellen ikea-katalog wird man neuerdings geduzt, und das obwohl die seit jahren ihr studi-image erfolgreich hinter sich gelassen haben. Befremdlich.

[Even in the new IKEA catalogue one is addressed as du now; even though they have succeeded in leaving behind their student image for years. Disconcerting.]

(i) In the above examples, why do you think the use of the T form of address du caused such annoyance? Give reasons.

(ii) Based on the above consumer responses, why is there such reluctance in accepting the du form by consumers in consumer advertising in German? From the consumer's perspective, what is the meaning associated with the use of the T form du, instead of the V form Sie?

(iii) Why do you believe that IKEA has adopted the use of the T form in its advertising? What advantage is there for IKEA to use the T form instead of the V form in their marketing strategy?

(iv) From the perspective of the customer what would have been the most appropriate form of address for the car salesman to use to consumer 1? Why do you think the salesperson used the reciprocal pronoun of address (T form), even after the customer used the non-reciprocal Sie form?

5. Research Exercise

Within your own extended family, what names, pronouns and other forms of address are used to address your family members from an intergeneration perspective (e.g. those forms of address used between a grandchild and grandparent, child and parent, between siblings, between husband and wife).

NOTES

1 Brown and Gilman (1960:253) define 'semantics' as the 'covariation between the pronoun used and the objective relationship existing between speaker and addressee'.

2 *Galichka* is the informal short form for *Galina*.

3 A parent doesn't refer to a child as 'daughter' but would either use a pronoun or the child's name.

SUGGESTED FURTHER READING

Banks, S. P. 1989 'Power pronouns and the language of intercultural understanding'. In Ting-Toomey S. & Korzenny F. (eds) *Language Communication and Culture*. Newbury Park: Sage Publications, pp. 180–98.

Blum-Kulka, S. & Katriel, T. 1991 'Nicknaming practices in families: A cross-cultural perspective'. In Ting-Toomey S. & Korzenny F. (eds) *Cross-Cultural Interpersonal Communication*. Newbury Park: Sage Publications, pp. 58–78.

Braun, F. 1988 *Terms of address: Problems of Patterns and Usage in Various Languages and Cultures*. Berlin: Mouton de Gruyter.

Brown, R. & Gilman, A. 1960 'The pronouns of power and solidarity'. In Sebeok T. A. (ed.) *Style in Language*. New York: Technology Press of MIT.

Koyama, T. 1992 *Japan: A Handbook in Intercultural Communication*. Australia: Macquarie University Press.

Suzuki, T. 1976 'Language and behavior in Japan: The conceptualization of personal relations'. *Japan Quarterly*, vol. 23, no. 3, pp. 255–66.

8

Cultural differences in writing

VARIATION IN THE ORGANISATION OF WRITING across cultures has been studied from a cross-linguistic perspective, particularly over the last two decades. Some key work in this area includes the work of Givón (1983), who developed a quantitative model for cross-language discourse analysis to measure topic continuity (thematic, action and topics/participants continuity) in discourse; and the pioneering work of Kaplan (1972; see also Kaplan 1988; Connor & Kaplan 1987) in the area known as contrastive discourse analysis (also known as contrastive rhetoric).

In this chapter, we will examine some of the research based on Kaplan's approach, including Hinds (1980) on Japanese, Eggington (1987) on Korean, and some of Clyne's work on academic texts with specific reference to English and German (Clyne 1980, 1987; Clyne & Kreutz 1987).

8.1 LINEARITY: A KEY PRINCIPLE OF ENGLISH WRITTEN DISCOURSE

Kaplan (1972) contrasted various discourse types with the **linear** structure of English writing, most typically exemplified in English expository prose.

Clyne (1987) reports on a small study he conducted on the expectations of expository discourse patterns in English and German based on (a) English and German essay-writing manuals, and (b) one set of upper secondary school assignments, each (in three subjects) from different Australian and West German schools, together with marks and teachers' comments. He reports that the following expectations of discourse could be deduced for English but *not* for German:

1. Essay form is essential for most upper secondary school assignments. (This does not apply to the United States, where the big composition thrust is in the first year of tertiary education.)
2. The aim of an essay should be deduced strictly from the wording of the topic or question, which needs to be defined at the beginning. (In German-speaking countries, the wording of the topic or question is usually more general and does not need to be considered carefully by the student.)
3. Relevance is advocated as the primary virtue to be striven for in the construction of an essay. In German there appear to be few limitations on the inclusion of material, as the emphasis is almost entirely on the extent and correctness of the content.
4. The end of one paragraph should lead to the beginning of the next, which (especially in the United States) should be a topic sentence.
5. Repetition is deemed undesirable. (In German, where digressions are tolerated more, a logical development may entail more recapitulation.)

Clyne (1987:212) points out that expectations 3, 4 and 5 are all tantamount to requiring a linear development in English texts, and that although these expectations do play some part in German-speaking countries, they are certainly not so important as, for instance, in Australia, where essay-writing techniques are drilled for years. In most American universities, expectations of expository prose, including linearity, are focused on through a required first-year subject.

The following comments made by Australian final-year secondary school examiners in the state of Victoria, reported in Clyne (1994:162), exemplify the above findings:

- Clearly many candidates had either a general knowledge of the topic . . . or a thorough specific knowledge . . . But just having such information is not what is required by most . . . essays . . . those who write controlled relevant essays will always be appropriately advantaged (Eighteenth Century History 1978)
- Lack of relevance remains the major cause of failure (Politics 1987)
- Rather than answer in structural terms, many resorted to circular arguments (Biology 1972)

Clyne (1980:14–15) found a direct link between marks gained and discourse structure in an analysis of 400 History exam papers and examiners' comments.

8.2   NON-LINEAR DISCOURSE STRUCTURES

Based on an analysis of English essays written by foreign students in the United States, Kaplan (1972) reported four kinds of discourse structures that contrast in different ways with the English ideal of 'linear texts'.

These can be summarised with some typical exemplars as follows:[1]

1. Parallel constructions, in which the first idea is completed in the second part (*Semitic*, Arabic).
2. Circling organisation/Multiple perspectives approaches ('indirection' in Kaplan's terms), in which the topic is looked at from a variety of different tangents, but the subject is never looked at directly (*Oriental*, e.g. Indonesian, Indian, Chinese, Japanese, Korean).
3. Freedom to digress and to introduce 'extraneous' material (*Romance*, Central European – German, Italian, Spanish, Latin American (less of French)).
4. Similar to 3, but with different lengths, parenthetical amplifications of subordinate elements, and no 'rounding off' (*Russian*, Eastern European variant of 3).

PARALLEL CONSTRUCTIONS: EXAMPLES FROM ARABIC

Arabic discourse is influenced by the ancient Semitic oral tradition which Kaplan (1972:250) suggests is based on a complex set of parallel constructions, both positive and negative. This kind of parallelism can be demonstrated in English by reference to the King James version of the Old Testament of the Bible, as for example in the extracts below. Clyne (1994:172) points out that this ancient Semitic rhetorical tradition is also evident in the Koran, and in the New Testament verses of the Lord's Prayer and the Beatitudes.

We exemplify this parallelism from the first part of the Beatitudes (Matthew 5, 3–5):

> *Blessed are the poor in spirit; for theirs is the kingdom of heaven.*
> *Blessed are they that mourn; for they shall be comforted.*
> *Blessed are the meek; for they shall inherit the earth.*
> *Blessed are they which do hunger and thirst after righteousness for they shall be filled.*

Parallelism in the above example is illustrated by the two-part structure of each sentence *'Blessed are . . . , for . . .'* and by the four-line structure, the last line of which is longer than the others.

Clyne (1991a:213) provides the following examples of such parallelism from a letter of inquiry from an Egyptian university student:

My Dear respected Master xxx University
'Good morning or after Good Night'

We can see the parallelism in the double greeting structure, and also in the complementarity of the second line *Good morning or after Good Night*. Some of these features are also found in the letters discussed in section 8.6.

8.3   MULTIPLE PERSPECTIVES: THE EXAMPLE OF JAPANESE

Japanese is one of the Oriental languages identified by Kaplan (1972) as having a discourse structure he characterised as 'an approach by indirection', with the topic being looked at from different tangents. Other languages described as having this structure include Indonesian, Indian (Pandhari-pande 1983; Kachru 1988), Chinese, and Korean (Eggington 1987).

Hinds (1980) reviews two expository prose styles in frequent use in Japan. Hinds (1980:132) briefly discusses one style which reflects the classical Chinese organisation of poetry. Hinds (following Takemata 1976), describes this style of prose in terms of the four characters: *ki, shoo, ten*, and *ketsu* (here represented in Pin Ying, the Chinese adopted use of the Roman alphabet). These characters describe the development of a classical Chinese poem. Hinds provides their respective meanings as defined by Takemata (1976:26):

(*ki*)	First, begin one's argument
(*shoo*)	Next, develop that
(*ten*)	At the point where this development is finished, turn the idea into a sub-theme where there is a connection, but not a directly connected association (to the major theme)
(*ketsu*)	Last, bring all of this together and reach a conclusion.

Hinds comments that while this style is common, it is not the sole means of organisation afforded to the Japanese author.

In the body of his article, Hinds (1980) goes on to illustrate a second style of discourse organisation he calls *Return to Baseline Theme*. He examines two articles from a Japanese–English bilingual fan magazine published in Honolulu, Hawaii, each written in English and in Japanese.

Hinds (1980:148–50) identifies the characteristics of Japanese expository prose as follows:

1. Paragraphs are organized by means of the return to a theme at the initiation of each perspective.
2. The theme of an article is continually reinforced, although the theme may never be explicitly stated.
3. Information in each perspective frequently maintains a loose semantic cohesiveness, although this cohesiveness is subordinated to the reinforcement of the theme.
4. Perspectives are structured paratactically: there will be (a) an introduction which reinforces the theme, (b) directly or indirectly related comments, and (c) an optional generalization, a summation, or both.
5. Grammatical reflexes of paragraph structuring are weak, but suggestive.

These features can be seen in the following literal translation of one of the Japanese texts presented by Hinds (1980:138–40). (Hinds also provides the Japanese text in Roman script with morpheme glosses (1980:141–4), although this is not reproduced here.)

The article about May Yokomoto is from the magazine *Kokiku*, published in Hawaii, which contains articles about popular television, movie and recording stars. Typically, two articles appear on the same page, one in Japanese, and the other in English. Some of these articles are translations from one language to the other, and some are original compositions in each language based on the same set of notes. (The English article on May Yokomoto is presented below so that the difference between the Japanese discourse style and the English discourse style can be seen.)

May Yokomoto (literal translation of the Japanese text)

(1) 'I hosted a program called "World Circus" with Masai Sakai. The film of the show came from London, and I had to do things like dress up like clowns, and fly on a trapeze in a large studio. I'm happy.'

(2) The parents of May Yokomoto keep a close eye on this modern girl who speaks Japanese fluently.

(3) She is fresh as a young sweet-fish splashing on the water.

(4) When she speaks of Japan, she continually uses the word *tamoshi* (happy).

(5) Some examples of her happiness are: When she appeared twice on Sanshi Katsura's program 'Let's Get Married,' she was paired with two of her fans, and she ended up winning both times; and now she has two tickets for a Hawaiian vacation.

(6) She now lives in an apartment near Tokyo Metropolitan University by herself, and since she cannot read Japanese, she has difficulty with the trains.

(7) However, many strangers recognize her on the street and help her.

(8) She has traveled in her work from Hokkaido to Kyushu, and has been able to sample a variety of local foods etc.

(9) 'Well, there are bad things too, but I forgot those.'

(10) She is perfectly open and friendly.

(11) Because of this she is loved by everyone.

(12) 'However, when I don't grasp the meaning of the songs I sing it's terrible. There are lots of words that don't appear in the dictionary. At those times I think back on all the help with the language I used to get from Mr Urata when I was in Hawaii.'

(13) She began hula lessons at five, and at seven she began singing lessons with Harry Urata.

(14) She began with a song something like 'The Doll with Blue Eyes.'

(15) The TV programs she appears on frequently are singing shows like Star-Tanjo.

(16) Last year she had a 2.5 hour radio program on Radio Kanto called 'Teach Japanese to May'.

(17) The last program at the end of March was done via international telephone from Hawaii.

(18) This time she has returned home in conjunction with an appearance on Star-Tanjo in Waikiki, and for a magazine frontispiece picture session with Sakiko Itoh.

(19) May Yokomoto, who was elected two years ago as Hawaii's new star on Star-Tanjo is a lucky girl whose looks and talents were noticed, and who has been sought after for commercials for leading companies, for magazines, and for TV after her debut in May of last year.

(20) She has released her third record called 'Anata chance yo'.

(21) Her real name is Cid Akemi Yokomoto.

(22) She graduated from Roosevelt High School.

(23) She is a pure Hawaiian product, and was runner-up in the Miss Teenage Hawaii contest in 1974.

(from Hinds 1980:138–40)

Hinds represents the structure of this Japanese text as in Figure 8.1.

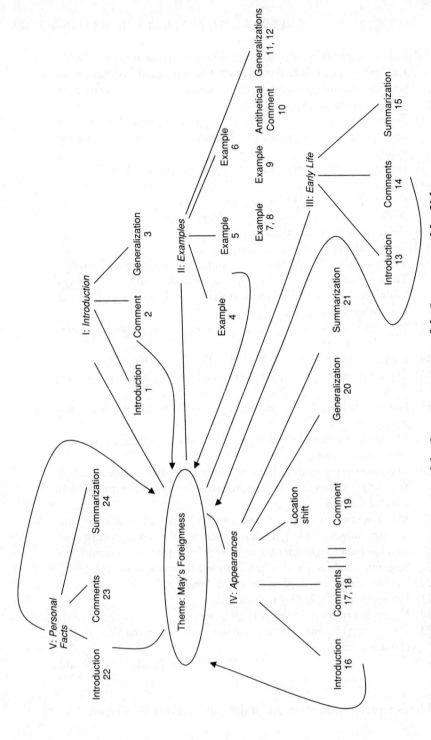

Figure 8.1. Diagrammatic representation of the discourse structure of the Japanese text May Yokomoto (from Hinds 1980:149)

May Yokomoto (English text)

Hinds (1980:124) provides a parallel text, written in English from the same bilingual magazine. The more linear discourse structure of this article will be more familiar to English readers.

> May Yokomoto returned to Hawaii recently to appear in the Star Tanjo. In addition, the friendly eighteen year old was kept busy by photo sessions with Sakiko Ito. They had numerous pictures taken of them on the beach for *Myojo* magazine in Japan.
>
> She is having a good time in Japan doing commercials, television and radio work. For example, she appeared on the TV game show 'Kekkonshimashoo' (Let's Get Married), where she won two trips to Hawaii, which she is saving for future use. May also appears on 'Sekai no Circus' with her favourite actor, Masai Sakai. On this program, May had to dress up like a clown and even swung on a trapeze. She also had a radio program on Radio KANTO called 'Teach Japanese to May'.
>
> May has her own apartment in Tokyo, but still has a hard time getting around on trains. Recently, though, people have begun to recognize 'May-chan' and help her find her destination. She says living in Japan is not easy, but is fun most of the time.
>
> May's parents are pleased that her Japanese has improved so much, but says she still has a hard time understanding some of the songs.
>
> May says 'While in Hawaii, my teacher Harry Urata always explained everything to me. He made it seem easy.'
>
> May has travelled all over, from Hokkaido to Kyushu. In the process, she has learned all about Japanese gourmet foods.
>
> Two years ago May was the winner of the 'Star Tanjo'. Last year, she made her debut in Japan and is already a popular talent.
>
> May began studying hula at the age of five, and started music lessons with Harry Urata at the age of seven. She was runner up in the Miss Teenage Hawaii contest in 1974. Her real name is Cid Akemi Yokomoto. She is a graduate of Roosevelt High School.
>
> (from *Kokiku*, May 1977)

In these two texts from Hinds (1980) we can see how the same content can be presented using different methods of textual organisation depending on the cultural preference. The Japanese text is a clear example of the Circling organisation (indirection in Kaplan's terms) identified above.

8.4 'DIGRESSIVENESS': A FEATURE OF GERMAN ACADEMIC REGISTER

Clyne (1987:213) lists the following four features of the German academic register, which have been observed by various researchers, and which students entering German universities are in the process of acquiring (e.g. papers in Bungarten 1981; Clyne 1991b). Clyne (1994:164) further exemplifies the first two of these observed features.

1. Agentless passives and impersonal reflexive constructions, e.g. 'Selection error <u>must be regarded</u> as a defect'
'<u>One</u> can assume that there was competition for the best job.'
'There <u>it is obvious</u> that returnees are underprivileged.'
es zeigt sich 'it shows itself'
es fragt sich eben, ob nicht 'it asks itself if not . . .'
2. Hedged performatives using modals *kann* 'can', *muss* 'may' and *darf,* parenthetical verbs, the equivalent of 'seem, appear, guess' and passive infinitives 'it is to be hoped . . .' e.g. 'Thus it seems unnecessary to discuss a new model here.'
3. A large number of nominalisations and compound nouns.
4. Syntactic complexity.

Clyne's (1987) research also identifies a fifth feature, 'digressiveness', which had not been previously described in the literature. 'Digressiveness' may include a separately labelled section called the *Exkurs* ('excursus' or 'excursion'). Clyne (1994:163) provides the following summation of 'digressions':

'Digressions' generally fulfil particular functions in German academic texts. In our corpus, 'digressions' enable writers to add a theoretical component in an empirical text, a historical overview, ideological dimension, or simply more content, or engage in a continuing polemic with members of a competing school . . . these are all crucial aspects of German intellectual style and German culture. The presence of one or more sections labelled *Exkurs* (excursion 'digression') in most good dissertations in German speaking universities confirm that linearity is not a prerequisite of academic writing in German.

8.5   THE FORM/CONTENT DISTINCTION

The linear/non-linear distinction proposed above may be better understood as a form/content distinction. Clyne (1994:186) suggests that although all cultures could be expected to apply a combination of formal and content criteria to determine the structure and progression of a piece of discourse, some cultures, such as English-based ones, more strongly foreground form while others are more content-oriented. The following points illustrate this distinction.

- Content orientation often appears to be associated with a cultural idealisation of knowledge and the authority of the academic or intellectual work. For example, if a text can be readily understood, then, from a German perspective, it may be seen to be dubious and unprofessional.
- From the perspective of content-oriented cultures, the English linear structure might be considered simplistic, due to its high usage of advance organisers and its emphasis on the careful presentation of thought structures and strategies of expression.
- In Japanese and Central European cultures, the onus falls on the reader to make the effort to understand the text produced by the knowledgeable, and therefore, authoritative person; rather than the writer seeing it as his/her job to present the material in a well organised and understandable way, as is the case for English-based cultures.

These differences are likely to cause difficulties for readers and writers with different expectations of written discourse and may pose particular challenges for international students (see also Connor 2003; Noor 2001).

8.6   LETTER WRITING

Although there are many differences between spoken and written language, letter writing sits somewhere between the two, because a letter is typically part of an expected exchange.

Letters are distinct from other forms of writing in that they typically contain a greeting and a goodbye sequence. Here, we will examine some of the features of letters, and present some research on preferred ways of writing in different cultures.

In addition to *greetings* and *closings*, business letters usually contain at least one of the following 'speech acts' (see Chapter 3 for definitions):

- requests for information
- directives
- complaints
- threats
- promises
- social comments.

In a study of letters of request by Mandarin speakers from China to the China Section of Radio Australia, Kirkpatrick (1991) found that native speakers of Chinese prefer to place requests towards the end of letters, and that a typical scheme for a Chinese letter of request includes: salutation, preamble (facework), reasons, and then the request (Kirkpatrick 1991:183). Kirkpatrick reports that while the request and the reason can potentially occur in either order in both Mandarin and English, his research shows that there is a strong preference by Mandarin writers to put the reason before the request, rather than the reverse, which he suggests is more typical in English. Kirkpatrick sees the reason–request sequence as an instance of the more general *because–therefore* sequence.

In a sample of 20 letters of request from South Asian students requesting university application information comprising eleven letters from Indians, seven from Pakistanis, and one each from a Bangladeshi and a Sri Lankan, Clyne (1991a:209) found that the main speech acts performed were request, introduction and expression of interest. Clyne found that nine out of the 20 letters followed the sequence: introduction + expression of interest + request, while seven went directly to the expression of interest followed by the request. Clyne notes that many of these letters were in a formal register and contained honorific formulas (see below). We note that the preference for the request to come towards the end of the letter is similar to what Kirkpatrick reports for Mandarin.

In a sample of 20 similar letters of request from Arabic-speaking students, consisting of eleven letters from Egyptians, two from Syrians and one each from a Jordanian, a Kuwaiti, a Lebanese, a Libyan, an Omanian, a Moroccan and a Saudi Arabian, Clyne (1991a:211) found far more individual variation and creativity. However, in most cases the request tended to be towards the end of the letter.

The following three business letters written in English from writers from different cultural backgrounds illustrate some of the possible variation.

LETTER 1

Origin: Japan

Dear Mr *SURNAME*,

Re: Shipping advice for your order.

We are very happy to inform you that we have already shipped your order of wrapping papers 20,000 sheets as per enclosed shipping documents.

Enclosed please find a copy of shipping documents herein.

We hope, it will be received safely in your hand and we will be able to get your valuable reorders in a very near future.

Mr *SURNAME,* regarding with Paper napkins, would you kindly please study carefully about our best prices and if you want to import directly from us, please let us have your valuable order without hesitation.

We are waiting for your nice letter about this matter, with much expectation.

We were very sorry we could not see you at Tokyo during your staying at Tokyo. When you come to Japan in future, please let us know Flight number. We would like to welcome you at Tokyo air port.

It was very regrettable we could not talk about future business plans with you, in this time.

Looking forward to your early good news, we are,

Yours very truly,

Company name

Division

By: *signature*

Branch Manager: *FIRST NAME, SURNAME*

P.S.: Regarding with business of paper napkins, would you kindly please let us know your frank opinion by return mail. Thank you very much!

LETTER 2

Origin: India

Dated: 4th Month, Year

Mr *FIRST NAME, SURNAME*

Address

Australia

Ref No. *XXXXXXX*

Dear Mr *SURNAME,*

I recall with nostalgia our meeting in India as well as in Australia. In recent issue of *RETAILER*, I find you have entered hockey market and I would certainly like to be assistance to you.

May I therefore request you to foreward to me any special specifications, weights, Lengths and any other relevant detail which you think will be proper enebling me to forward you samples of my sticks which you will find excellent from all aspects. I can also supply nude sticks, on which you can do the meke up at your end. I can also supply you excellent quality of plastic and cork composition balls.

Concluding I look foreward to hear from you and wish you bumper christmas and new-year sales.

Best personal regards,

Sincerely yours,

FIRST NAME, SURNAME

Managing Director.

LETTER 3

Origin: Italy

Company

Address

Australia

00.00. Year

Re: New order *(PRODUCT NAME).*

referring your request for a discount of 10% P.L.S. Note that, notwithstanding a great italian inflation, we have maintained our price of *PRODUCT NAME* like the past year and besides you have a better change in the money about 10%. You remember the change of the past year was I.T.L. 902,150, this year is 1044,93.

If you consider these factory you understand that we cannot gave a discount!

We believe in your necessity and for this reason we confirm the discount of the last year, 8%, with no plasticised labels or 4% with plasticised labels, for a good packing we prefer this second possibility.

Do it like this, if you consider the better change, the usual price of the past year and the discount, you will have a reduction in the cost of the product about 20% referring the past years.

We cannot go any further and BELIEVE us in this condition we not have profit.

For the delivery terms we can organise a shipment for the first week of march.

P.L.S. send again the order with our conditions.

Best regards

Signature

INITIAL, SURNAME

The following summary of features of business letters has been drawn from the letters (provided in English translation from Mandarin) quoted in Kirkpatrick (1991), and from the three sample letters above, from a corpus of international business letters available to the writers, and incorporates features identified by Clyne (1991a) from letters from South Asian and Middle Eastern students requesting university application information.

SALUTATIONS AND OPENING SEQUENCES

The standard English business letter form of address: *Dear Mr SURNAME,* is used in both Letter 1 from Japan and Letter 2 from India, whereas Letter 3 from Italy does not include a salutation at all (perhaps assuming that the company name and address identifies the addressee).

In many instances the initial salutation is followed by an expression of good health or wellbeing, which can be seen as a way of engaging with the addressee:

> *Dear Sir,*
> *I hope that you are in good health*
> *Good morning or after Good Night* (Egyptian)
> *Dear Sir:*
> *Hello, hope you are well* (Jordanian)
> *Dear Sir*
> *I hope you are well and enjoying your self* (Egyptian)
>
> (Clyne 1991a)

Clyne (1991a) identifies the following forms of address in his corpus and notes that many of these greetings contained honorific expressions:

- *Dear Sir*
- *Sir(s)*
- *(My dear) Registrar in xxx University*
- *(Dear) Registrar,*
- *(My dear) Respected Master (cf. Arabic syadi 'master' used to address people of high status)*
- *Your Lordship*

We note that two out of the four Mandarin letters quoted by Kirkpatrick (1991:194) also begin with honorific forms of address:

Respected Radio Australia producers;
Respected Mr –

The letters include the standard English address *Dear XXX* which is also a type of honorific, although it is being replaced by less formal greetings such as *Hi*, or other expressions such as *Good morning* by some writers.

While greetings/salutations are almost always found at the beginning of a letter, they can also be repeated to focus attention on a crucial part of the letter. For example, in Letter 1 above, from Japan, the writer begins the fourth paragraph with the vocative, *Mr SURNAME*, . . .

HONORIFIC FEATURES

In addition to expressions of deference in the greeting, Clyne (1991a) noted that in the letters from East Asian and Middle Eastern students, deferent and honorific expressions were evident throughout the letters:

Expressions of deference, e.g. *I beg to say* (Pakistani); *I beg to state* (Bangladeshi); *I have the honour to intimate* (Indian).

Honouring Addressee, e.g. *With due respect* (Pakistani and Bangladeshi).

Vocative of address, e.g. *Respected Sir* (Pakistani); *Please Sir* (Pakistani); *Your Honour* (Pakistani).

Adjectival/adverbial honorific, e.g. *Your esteemed university* (Indian); *May I again request you to kindly look into this matter* (Indian).

Clyne (1991a:210) points out that although the addressee is clearly given the greatest benefits at the expense of the writer, the East Asian and Middle Eastern students do also present their own status in a positive light:

Reference to the writer's family status, e.g. *My family background too is excellent* (Indian).

Reference to the writer's academic status, e.g. *I possess a very good academic career* (Pakistani).

Reference to the writer's financial status, e.g. *I can transfer appropriate amounts of currency exchange* (Pakistani).

EXPRESSIONS OF DEFERENCE

Clyne reports that deference is expressed by the Middle Eastern writers in the following way:

> *It is a great honour that I ask you to help me subscribe in your university* (Moroccan)
> *I have the honour to introduce myself* (Egyptian)
> *I have the honour to inform you* (Egyptian)
> *I begged you to accept my application* (Egyptian).

PARALLEL CONSTRUCTIONS

At the beginning of this chapter we noted the examples of parallel constructions from letters of inquiry from writers from the Middle East (Clyne 1991a:213). One such example from a letter of an Egyptian university student is repeated here:

> *My Dear respected Master xxx University*
> *'Good morning or after Good Night'*

Parallel constructions appear to be used widely by writers from the Middle East.

CLOSINGS

Clyne (1991a) identifies the following (pre-) closing sequences:

> Awaiting to hear from you soon, accept, Sir, the assurance of my highest consideration (Egyptian).

> I asked my professor about the best universities to enter to it and my professor recommended your university to me (Saudi Arabian).

> Traveling to Australia is my dream. I want to live in Australia and marry and constituate a small family and spend all My age in Australia (Egyptian).

Clyne also notes that several letters included flattering remarks about Australia in the pre-closing part of the letter.

The following closings are typically found in English business and professional letters:

- Yours faithfully, FIRST NAME, SURNAME
- Yours sincerely, FIRST NAME, SURNAME
- With best wishes, FIRST NAME, SURNAME.

These closings are usually preceded by a reiteration of the main business of the letter, a pre-closing remark and/or an expression of well-wishing.

Kirkpatrick (1991) reports a variety of closing sequences in the translation of the Mandarin letters of request written to Radio Australia that are more specific to the purpose of the letter than the more general English closings:

- *Wishing you happiness at work,*
    Loyal Listener –;
- *Wishing Radio Australia's mandarin programs even more interest,*
    Listener –;
- *End*
    Best wishes, ADDRESS, NAME
- *This time I'll stop here.*
    Wishing everyone happiness at work and best wishes! NAME

The closing sequence in Letter 2 (above) from India also makes reference to the context of the reader.

Concluding I look foreward to hear from you and wish you bumper christmas
and new-year sales.
Best personal regards,
Sincerely yours,
FIRST NAME, SURNAME
Managing Director

What we have seen from this study of letters is that although there are common themes expressed within letters from different cultures, it is the relative ordering of different segments of the letters that may differ cross-culturally. Other cultural specific features, such as the Middle Eastern preference for parallelism, are also examples of cross-cultural differences found in letters.

8.7   SUMMARY

In this chapter we have examined research on variation in the organisation of written discourse from a cross-linguistic perspective. This has included academic writing and other forms of expository prose as well as a section on letters. We have found that, as with spoken discourse, the organisation of writing is influenced by culture-specific norms, which could give rise to negative evaluations in intercultural contexts.

8.8   REVIEW

1. **Key Terms:** Discourse patterns, linearity, digression, circling, parallelism, textual symmetry, hedging, advance organisers, return to baseline theme, honorific, salutation, vocative.

2. **Key Ideas**
   Having read this chapter you should:
   a. appreciate that different preferences for the organisation of written texts are culturally determined conventions
   b. be aware of the significance of written discourse conventions for international cultural interaction.

3. **Focus Questions**
   a. Analysis of written discourse
      (i) Based on Kaplan's (1972) analysis of discourse, categorise your own language's written discourse (e.g. linearity, digressive, etc.). Give at least three reasons for your choice.
      (ii) Which discourse structure do you feel the most comfortable with in writing essays? Give reasons for this.
   b. Japanese
      (i) Based on the description and analysis of Hinds (1980) of an article about May Yokomoto, do you think that such phrases as *multiple perspectives* and *circular* accurately describe the Japanese written discourse?
      (ii) How does this discourse structure differ from the linear written style (i.e. English)? Provide at least four examples.
   c. Content-oriented and form-oriented cultures
      Consider the following extract from section 8.5:
      'From the perspective of content-oriented cultures, the English linear structure might be considered simplistic due to its high usage of

advance organisers and its emphasis on the careful presentation of thought structures and strategies of expression.'

(i) Based on your own language background, do you agree or disagree with the above statement? Give reasons for your choice.

4. Research Analysis
Regional discourse patterns

Consider the following table taken from Precht (1998:260) in which Letters of Recommendation (LRs) were analysed. The table below summarises some of the features of LRs:

American	German	British	Eastern European
Linear	Linear	Linear	Digressive tendency
Symmetrical	Asymmetrical	Symmetrical	Symmetrical
Integration of data	Data not integrated	Integration of data	Integration of data
Early advance organisers	Few advance organisers	Some advance organisers	Some advance organisers

a. How does Precht's research on digressiveness/linearity, textual symmetry and advance organisers agree or disagree with Clyne's (1987, 1994) categorisation of German and English academic written discourse? Analyse the above table.

b. What do you think the reasons are for these different findings?

c. Do you think that an American employer would negatively or positively regard a letter of recommendation with a digressive tendency instead of a linear writing style (i.e. Eastern European)? Give reasons for your answer.

d. What interpretation do you think a German employer would have of a letter of recommendation using advance organisers at the beginning of the text (i.e. American English)?

e. In your own experience, how have your own letters of recommendation (those written for you) been structured and organised? Have the structure and organisation of information differed according to the language used and/or the language background of the writer? Use the above table as a guide for your description and analysis.

5. Research Exercise
Letters and emails
Find 6 examples of written letters (3 samples) and emails (3 samples) which cover the same topic and serve the same purpose (e.g. personal communication to a friend, business correspondence) and compare and contrast their contents and form. In your analysis address such questions as:

a. How has the advent of email affected the style of letter writing (i.e. salutations and opening sequences, honorific features)?

b. Using the discussion of the differences in letter writing styles across cultures, describe and analyse the similarities and differences between letter writing and emails in the same language.

NOTE

1 This listing largely follows Clyne (1994:161). Kaplan's language types are given in italics and Clyne's cultural grouping, giving more specific language exemplification, is given as well.

SUGGESTED FURTHER READING

Clyne, M. 1987 'Cultural differences in the organisation of academic discourse'. *Journal of Pragmatics*, vol. 11, pp. 211–47.

Clyne, M. 1994 *Inter-cultural Communication at Work: Cultural Values in Discourse*. Cambridge: Cambridge University Press, Chapter 5, pp. 160–74.

Connor, U. & Kaplan, R. B. (eds) 1987 *Writing Across Cultures*. Reading, Massachusetts: Addison-Wesley.

Eggington, W. 1987 'Written academic discourse in Korean'. In Connor U. & Kaplan R. B. *Writing Across Cultures*. Reading, Massachusetts: Addison-Wesley, pp. 153–68.

Hinds, J. 1980 'Japanese expository prose'. *Papers in Linguistics: International Journal of Human Cognition*, vol. 131, no. 1, pp. 117–58.

Kirkpatrick, A. 1991 'Information sequencing in Mandarin letters of request'. *Anthropological Linguistics*, vol. 33, no. 2, pp. 183–203.

Precht, K. 1998 'A cross-cultural comparison of letters of recommendation'. *English for Specific Purposes*, vol. 17, no. 3, pp. 241–65.

9 | Interpreting and translating

INTERPRETING AND TRANSLATING involves rendering information and ideas from one language to another. **Interpreters** are concerned with the spoken word. **Translators** are concerned with the written word.

9.1   TYPES OF INTERPRETING

There are three main types of interpreting used in the world:

- **Simultaneous interpreting**, typically used at international conferences where personal headphones are used, and interpreting is conducted into numbers of languages simultaneously, each with a different interpreter. In such circumstances, delegates often present prepared papers and these can sometimes be made available to the interpreters ahead of time to assist in their preparation. However this is not always the case. Simultaneous translation is not used very often in Australia.
- **Chuchotage**, a term used to refer to the kind of interpretation where an interpreter 'whispers' simultaneous translation to a single client.
- **Sequential translation**, the type of translation most widely used for community and business purposes.

In all types of interpreting, the interpreter is expected to represent what the speaker says and to speak in the first person, for example *I went to the city*, not *He says that he went to the city*.

9.2   PRIMACY OF THE MOTHER TONGUE

Best practice suggests that translators and interpreters should preferably translate into their mother tongue. For example, if you want something translated from English to Mandarin, a native speaker of Mandarin would probably be better for the job, whereas if you wanted something translated from Mandarin to English a native English speaker would probably be better; all other things being equal. It is generally possible to make such choices for translating and for simultaneous conference interpreting. However, interpreting often involves conversation between two parties, and would therefore require two interpreters to be present if an interpreter worked into the mother tongue only. In contexts such as that in Australia, where most interpreting is between individuals or small groups, then interpreters are typically required to work into both languages, and are expected to act with impartiality so as not to prejudice either party to the conversation.

9.3   DIFFICULTIES IN ACHIEVING A BALANCE BETWEEN PRAGMATIC EQUIVALENCE AND IMPARTIALITY

The tradition of translation theory identifies the complexity of the task facing translators (and interpreters). Translation theorists have identified 'dynamic equivalence' (Nida & Taber 1974:200) or 'pragmatic equivalence' (Widdowson 1978:54) as being the key objective of successful translation. Widdowson emphasises the point that translation not only involves correspondence between formal pattern and cognitive meaning, but also correspondence in the situation of use.

Larson (1984:33) claims that to be faithful to the original a translator must communicate not only the same information, but must also attempt to evoke the same emotional response as the original text:

> In many ways, the *emotional tone* of a passage is the key to real communication effectiveness. The author may wish to create a feeling of urgency, persuasiveness, tentativeness, exuberance or despondency. Whatever the *tone* of the source text, built into it by choices of tense, mood, voice and choice of the main action verbs, it is important that this same emotion be communicated in the translation. For an effective transfer of the text, the translator must be well acquainted with both the source and receptor language and culture.
>
> (Larson 1984:425)

We are concerned that the re-creation of the *emotional tone* of the source is particularly difficult for interpreters who are asked to interpret *impartially* for two parties. Given that *pragmatic equivalence* involves re-creating a new utterance with all the nuances of the source utterance, this must surely involve unpacking any implications that could conventionally be intended by the first party and rendering the complete message to the second party. Unless an interpreter is a consummate actor, and has outstanding pragmatic competence in both languages, it may be difficult for interpreters to convey the *emotional tone* or *pragmatic equivalence* of the spoken word for both sides of a negotiation in an ongoing way.

For business negotiation, therefore, it might be more reasonable to engage an interpreter or bilingual professional to act as a dedicated advocate for a single party rather than expect a single interpreter to serve both parties.

9.4   INTERPRETERS ASSUMING THE ROLE OF INSTITUTIONAL GATEKEEPER: A CASE STUDY

Davidson (2000) reports a study conducted in the outpatients unit of the Riverview General Hospital in Northern California where about 40 per cent of outpatients requested an interpreter.

Davidson (2000:385) approached the study as a political, social and linguistic enterprise with an eye towards answering the following questions:

- What is the role of the interpreter within the goal-oriented, learned form of interaction known as the 'medical interview'?
- What is the 'interpretive habit', and how does one engage in the practice of interpreting?
- If interpreters are *not* neutral, do they challenge the authority of the 'physician-judge' (cf. Foucault 1979), and act as patient 'ambassadors' or 'advocates' (as Haffner 1992; Juhe 1982 and Kaufert & Koolage 1984 suggest) . . . or do they reinforce the institutional authority of the physician and health-care establishment, and should we create a model for the 'interpreter-judge'? (cf. Foucault 1979)

From the analysis of interactions recorded in 1996, Davidson found that the interpreters in the study tended to adopt the role of 'institutional gatekeeper' by selective non-reporting of aspects of the patients' discourse, partly as a consequence of perceived time constraints, and partly due to their own sense of the relevance of the patient's input. Out of 33 patient-generated questions (from 10 interpreted visits) only 15 were passed on to the doctor, while 18 were not passed on at all. Seventeen out of the 18 not passed on to the doctor by the interpreter were actually answered by the interpreter with no reference to the doctor (2000:391). A qualitative analysis of the data suggested that some material that was not passed on was in fact relevant to the diagnosis. Implied criticism of the doctor or of past diagnosis was one class of patient comment that tended to be expunged by the interpreters (Davidson 2000:398).

Davidson (2000:4) concluded that:

> The linguistic data, both quantitative and qualitative, points strongly away from a conclusion that interpreters are acting as 'advocates' or 'ambassadors' for interpreted patients, but are acting, at least in part, as informational gate-keepers who keep the interview 'on track' and physician on schedule. While the interpreters do in fact convey much of what is said, they also interpret selectively, and appear to do so in a patterned (non-random) fashion.

Davidson noted that the interpreters at Riverview were professional in the sense that they were paid employees of the hospital; but that the training given to these interpreters was scant. There was no requirement of any formal degree in interpretation or translation. The only requirements for becoming an interpreter at Riverview were a good grasp of both English and Spanish, and the ability to translate 50 medical terms on a test with complete accuracy. There was no training in discourse processes, and the training for how medical interactions worked was on-the-job. Davidson reports that the physicians, for their part, received absolutely no training in how to use interpreters, beyond being told how to summon them.

Davidson's research is of interest in that it is based on actual data of the use of translation in medical encounters in a context that he suggests is broadly representative of widespread practice in the United States. Unfortunately, as he points out, it is far from best practice.

9.5 ADVERTISING: A TRUE CHALLENGE FOR INTERCULTURAL COMMUNICATION[1]

PET FOOD IN THE AMERICAS

Weller (1992) reports the difficulties inherent in the translation of an advertisement for cat food from English into Spanish and Portuguese. Her comments are based on a research project involving third-year undergraduate students from Mexico City and Rio de Janeiro.

TURN ON YOUR CAT

NEW Chef's Blend – made with real meat juices!

NEW MEAT TASTE

Chef's Blend

Now you can turn on your cat with the real taste of meat! because the

New Chef's Blend is made with real meat juices for real meat taste.

Each crunchy nugget gets its taste from real beef, chicken, liver and

turkey juices. Cats will love the real meat taste. 100% nutritionally

complete Chef's Blend Dry cat Dinners. To turn on your cat to the

new Chef's Blend with real meat taste from real meat juices!

Figure 9.1. Pet food advertisement
(Weller 1992)

The task was to translate the advertisement in Figure 9.1.

Weller reports that the first line of this translation wouldn't work in either language and so the following alternatives were provided for Brazilian Portuguese: *pegue o seu gato pelo estômago* ('the way to your cat's heart is through its stomach'), *conquiste de vez o seu gato* ('win your cat's heart for good'); and for Mexican Spanish *pon en onda a tu gato* ('help your cat get with it') and *agasaje a su gato* ('treat your cat to').

Translation of the English word 'juice' is not straightforward because the closest equivalent more typically refers to fruit juice in Mexico (even though you can say *jugo de carne* ('meat juice'), and even more so in Brazil, whereas *molto* ('sauce') or *caldo* ('broth') is more commonly used with dinner food. The term 'crunchy nuggets' also proved difficult.

Another problem was how to handle the brand name, 'New Chef's Blend'. Weller reports that many students kept the brand name in English (perhaps to take advantage of the novelty of something foreign), whereas others chose to translate it in part (*Nueva Chef's Blend*) or translated in full *Nueva Receta del Chef.*

Some student translators took advantage of the fact that imperatives, diminutives and augmentative suffixes can express endearment (-inho/ão in Portuguese and –ito/òn in Spanish) and used these to create extra appeal. Examples are words like *pedacinho* (little morsel) for nugget, *gatinho* (little kitten) or gatão (big cat or 'hunk' in colloquial American English) and *gostinho* (special flavour), among others.

Weller (1992:149) reports that further research, using the same advertisement, was conducted in Mexico by Murillo (1989). Murillo consulted with several advertising agencies and reported that these agencies thought that the translation students' versions were not creative enough and felt that in this case a whole rewrite was necessary, including the presentation of the product for a Mexican audience. In a culture where people feed their cats with table scraps, such advertising would need to introduce the concept of 'pet food'.

CHINESE TRAVEL

Bowe and Zhang (2001) examined some newspaper travel advertising in China and found that Chinese travel advertising draws heavily on images of the beauty of the vista and the changing seasons, and health and happiness deriving from the travel experience.

Chinese travel agencies have names which also draw on similar themes, for example, 'Spring and Autumn Travel Agency', 'Golden Bridge Travel Agency', 'Health and Splendour Travel Agency', and 'Golden Sea Travel Agency'.

The focal points in one advertisement include 'romantic journey', 'comfortable journey', 'unforgettable journey', 'sweet journey', and 'healthy journey'. At the centre of the advertisement there are two large overprints of the Chinese characters for happiness, with the meaning 'Double Happiness'.

Another advertisement contains famous lines from an ancient Chinese poet describing the natural beauty of the Mongolian region referring to the vast sky, boundless wilds, cattle and sheep, low grass and (gently) blowing winds.

One advertisement incorporated a western heart symbol with a more traditional invitation along the lines of 'Put my sincere heart into your palm and dissolve your confidence into my sincere heart'.

In none of the Chinese advertisements is price or value mentioned at all.

These advertisements contrast with travel advertising in newspapers in Western cultures where much travel advertising tends to involve price discounts and inclusive packages. In glossy magazines beauty is often appealed to through photographic images, rather than descriptive language, but health and happiness do not generally rate a mention. (Glossy magazines have not been widely affordable in China so no parallel can be drawn with them.)

This example of advertising from China illustrates again that cultural practice will determine, to a large extent, what is appropriate in an advertisement, although aspects of Western cultural practice are being incorporated as a result of globalisation.

9.6 THE DEVELOPMENT OF INTERPRETING/TRANSLATING SERVICES IN AUSTRALIA

Interpreting and translation services in Australia have developed in the context of an increasing awareness of the multicultural nature of Australian society. Such services were a response to community needs within Australia, much of which related to health, legal and social security areas. Nguyen (1993) suggests that by the 1970s, Australia had become a world leader in the provision of interpreting and translating services for migrant settlement purposes by introducing an innovative national interpreting network, the Telephone Interpreter Service (later called the Translation and Interpreting Service), and in establishing The National Accreditation Authority for Translators and Interpreters (see also Gentile 1991).

The ongoing effects of globalisation have resulted in Australia becoming more oriented towards international engagement and overseas markets and there is an increasing demand for business and conference interpreting.

Australia continues to have a special need for adequate interpreting services for Aboriginal and Torres Strait Islander people, notably in the legal and health areas. The provision of Auslan interpreters for the deaf has also become a matter of priority.

The National Accreditation Authority for Translators and Interpreters (NAATI 2003) points out that:

> ... whilst there is virtually no distinction between the international and Australian definitions of translator and interpreter, there are (some) differences between the role of Translators and Interpreters in Australia and the contexts in which they practice, as compared to the situations in which their overseas counterparts operate. Community interpreting and translating in Australia requires practitioners to have a wide range of skills, which enable them to interpret and translate in situations from general conversation through to those where a thorough knowledge of specialised subjects and terminology

is required. Community interpreters are normally required to interpret in *both* language directions. The particular needs of the migrant population have in fact helped create the special characteristics that distinguish the way Translating and Interpreting is practised here compared with overseas.

In addition to the community interpreting, Australia also requires the very highly skilled and experienced Translators and Interpreters for diplomatic missions, trade delegations, high level negotiations and international conferences.

INTERPRETING/TRANSLATING QUALIFICATIONS

Tertiary study programs in translating and interpreting are available in many countries, and there may also be some form of professional accreditation required as well. In Australia, NAATI is a government sponsored organisation set up to conduct the accreditation of translators and interpreters in Australia. According to Nguyen (1993) the major Australian employers of translators and interpreters have been government or government funded bodies, all of which support the NAATI accreditation system and seek to employ only NAATI accredited people.

NAATI has a two-tiered approach to accreditation/recognition depending on the level of applicant and employer/community demand. For languages of high use, accreditation can be obtained by passing a NAATI test. Alternatively, NAATI accreditation can be earned by successful completion of a NAATI approved course of study at an Australian or overseas institution.

NAATI tests examine the following:

- bilingual language skills
- interpreting and translating skills
- background and cross-cultural knowledge
- professional ethics
- confidentiality, impartiality.

NAATI ACCREDITATION LEVELS

The Australian National Accreditation Authority for Translators and Interpreters has established the following standards for translation and interpreting.

Accreditation may be obtained in one language direction (i.e. English into other language *or* other language into English) for Translator, Advanced

Translator and Advanced Translator (Senior), and for Conference Interpreter and Conference Interpreter (Senior).

In translation at the paraprofessional level and in interpreting at both the paraprofessional and first professional levels, accreditation is based on competence in both language directions.

NAATI provides translating and interpreting accreditation over four levels, plus a language aide accreditation for Government employees only:

- Language Aide (for Government employees only)
- Paraprofessional Interpreter/Translator
- Interpreter/Translator
- Advanced Translator/Conference Interpreter
- Advanced Translator (Senior)/Conference Interpreter (Senior)

The following detail is provided by NAATI to characterise each level.

LANGUAGE AIDE (FOR GOVERNMENT EMPLOYEES ONLY)

This is an elementary level of language use; it is *not* a translator/interpreter category. It is appropriate for persons who are required to use a minimal knowledge of a language for the purpose of simple communication. It is the required level for the first range of the Community Language Allowance (formerly LAPA).

Relevant tasks would include:

- counter work: answering general enquiries, usually on the language other than English
- assisting clients to complete a simple form in English
- assisting persons of non-English-speaking background by giving instructions or directions in the language other than English.

PARAPROFESSIONAL INTERPRETER/ TRANSLATOR

Paraprofessional Interpreter This represents a level of competence in interpreting for the purpose of general conversations, generally in the form of non-specialist dialogues.

Relevant tasks would include:

- interpreting in general conversations
- interpreting in situations where specialised terminology or more sophisticated information is not required

- interpreting in situations where a depth of linguistic ability is not required.

Paraprofessional Translator This represents a level of competence in translation for the purpose of producing a translated version of non-specialised information.

Relevant tasks would include:

- translation of texts which do not contain technical or specialised information or terminology
- very simple translation work, where some level of inaccuracy is acceptable.

INTERPRETER/TRANSLATOR

This represents the minimum level of competence for professional interpreting or translating. It may be regarded as the Australian professional standard.

Interpreter Interpreters convey the full meaning of the information from the source language and into the target language in the appropriate style and register. Interpreters at this level are capable of interpreting across a wide range of subjects involving dialogues at specialist consultations. They are also capable of interpreting presentations by consecutive mode.

Relevant tasks would include:

- interpreting in both language directions for a wide range of subject areas usually involving specialist consultations with other professionals, for example doctor/patient, solicitor/client, bank manager/client, court interpreting
- interpreting in situations where some depth of ability in *both* languages is necessary.

Translator Translators convey the full meaning of the information from the source language and into the target language in the appropriate style and register. Translators at this level work across a wide range of subjects involving documents with specialised content. Translators may choose to specialise. They are qualified to translate into one language only, or into both languages, depending upon their accreditation.

Relevant tasks would include:

- translation work that may include routine correspondence, reports, standard text material in the general field of scholarship

- translation of non-specialised scientific, technical, legal, tourist and commercial subjects
- translation work requiring a reasonable level of accuracy.

CONFERENCE INTERPRETER/ADVANCED TRANSLATOR

This represents the advanced level and a level of competence sufficient to handle complex technical and sophisticated translation and interpreting.

Conference Interpreter Conference interpreters practise both consecutive and simultaneous interpreting in diverse situations including at conferences, high-level negotiations, and court proceedings. Conference interpreters operate at levels compatible with recognised international standards, and may choose to specialise in certain areas.

Relevant tasks would include:

- tasks involving international conferences, diplomatic missions, trade negotiations, and other high-level negotiations
- tasks involving complex court proceedings
- interpreting in situations requiring accurate translation of complex, technical and sophisticated material.

Advanced Translator Advanced translators handle complex, technical and sophisticated material, compatible with recognised international standards. They may choose to specialise in certain areas, usually into one language only, that being their first language.

Relevant tasks would include:

- translation of specialist material for specialists, for example international conference papers, scientific papers in journals, legal documents, diplomatic agreements, etc.
- acting as revisers of work done by other translators.

ADVANCED TRANSLATOR (SENIOR)/ CONFERENCE INTERPRETER (SENIOR)

This is the highest level of NAATI accreditation and reflects both competence and experience. It represents an international standard together with demonstrated extensive experience and leadership.

Advanced Translator (Senior) Relevant tasks would include:
- translation tasks as for Advanced Translators
- tasks involving the management of translation of papers for international conferences
- providing advice for translation services within and outside Australia.

Conference Interpreter (Senior) Relevant tasks would include:
- interpreting tasks as for Conference Interpreters
- tasks involving the organisation of international conferences
- providing advice for interpreting services within and outside Australia.

NAATI TEST AVAILABILITY

NAATI has tests available in the following languages:

Albanian, Amharic, Arabic, Assyrian, Auslan, Bangla, Bosnian, Bulgarian, Burmese, Cantonese*, Chinese#, Croatian, Czech, Dari, Dutch, Eastern Arrernte, Filipino, Finnish, French, German, Greek, Hakka, Hindi, Hungarian, Indonesian, Italian, Japanese, Khmer, Korean, Kurdish (Kurmanji), Kurdish (Sorani), Lao, Macedonian, Malay, Maltese, Mandarin*, Persian, Pertame, Pitjantjatjara, Polish, Portuguese, Punjabi, Pushto, Romanian, Russian, Samoan, Serbian, Sinhalese, Slovak, Somali, Spanish, Tamil, Tetum, Thai, Tigrinya, Tongan, Turkish, Ukrainian, Urdu, Vietnamese.

(*Interpreter only, #Translator only)

Tests are scheduled for the above languages at least once per year at the Interpreter/Translator level. Testing at more advanced levels is conducted mainly on request.

In practice, accreditation at the Advanced and Senior levels seems to be relatively rare.

Languages for which NAATI (2006) does not plan to conduct tests in the immediate future, and for which 'recognition' has been awarded are as follows:

Afrikaans, Armenian, Azerbaijani, Bielorussian, Catalan, Cebuano, Chaldean, Cook Is. Maori, Danish, Dinka, Estonian, Fijian, Flemish, Fuzhou, Gajerrong, Garawa, Georgian, Gujerti, Hamun, Harari, Hazaragi, Hebrew, Hindustani, Hiri-Motu, Hokkien, Hmong, Ibo, Ilocano,

Javanese, Kazakh, Konkani, Latvian, Latin#, Lingala, Lithuanian, Malay-alam, Marathi, Melanesian, Miriuwung, Multani, Mongolian, Nepalese, Norwegian, Nuer, Oromo, Pidgin, Pukapukan, Pyribal, Shan, Slovene, Sun-danese, Swahili, Swatow, Swedish, Syric, Tetum T'oishan, Taiwanese, Tatar, Telegu, Teo Chiew, Tibetan, Tigre, Tigrinya, Timorese (Haaka), Uighuyre, Uzbek, Warlpiri, Wu (Shangainese), Yiddish.

(#Translation only)

DATABASES OF TRANSLATORS AND INTERPRETERS IN AUSTRALIA

NAATI maintains a database of accredited translators and interpreters.

The Australian Association for Interpreters and Translators (AUSIT), which is a professional association for translators and interpreters, also maintains a database of practising translators and interpreters.

9.7 SOME TIPS FOR TRANSLATING AND INTERPRETING IN THE BUSINESS CONTEXT

The following tips for addressing translation and interpreting issues in the business context are drawn from Victor (1992:38-45). We think these suggestions warrant inclusion here as they address some of the issues discussed above.

- Care must be taken with the selection of translators and interpreters and take account of reputability, experience, dialect familiarity, and expertise with business terminology. Victor (1992:41) reports that when General Motors entered the Belgian market it mistranslated its slogan 'Body by Fisher' into 'Corpse by Fisher' (Ricks 1983:83). Victor suggests that choosing a reputable translator reduces the likelihood of similar blunders.

- Adjust untranslated communication so that idiomatic speech, slang and colloquialisms are avoided. Victor reports a famous example of the failure of idioms to translate involved Pepsi's 'Come alive with Pepsi' campaign, in which the popular English language advertisement was mistranslated into German as 'Come out of the grave' and in Asia as 'Bring your ancestors back from the grave' (Ricks 1983:84).

- Personally review translated documents. Victor (1992:42) suggests that even if you don't understand the target language, you can review errors in the spelling of your own name, the names of other company members, company names, brands and trademarks, and check that the layout and print quality are appropriate.

- Pay attention to the pronunciation of names and key terms, and be aware of different customs concerning the sequencing of names and differing conventions concerning family names. Victor (1992:43) reports that for example, almost 10 per cent of the population, or well over 100 million people in the People's Republic of China are named Zhang, and in Korea, half of the population has one of four names: Kim, Lee, Park or Choi (Demente 1988, 1989). Victor suggests that in such countries it is imperative to remember the full names and usually the titles and company sections of business associates.

- Back-translation. Victor (1992:44) suggests that the most reliable means of discovering translation errors is the system called *back-translation* which is a two-step process involving the following:
  - first have the document translated into the new language
  - then have the document translated back into the original language
  - then compare the original manuscript with the back-translated document to determine errors or discrepancies. (You may find it interesting to try doing this with an internet translation tool!)

When speaking English to an audience for whom English is a second language, Victor (1992:40) suggests that it is a good idea to:

- rephrase frequently
- repeat key ideas in different words
- use written support because most people's written knowledge of a foreign language exceeds their spoken knowledge for that language.

Of course these principles would be of benefit in all intercultural communication to maximise interference from differences in pronunciation, rhythm and stress placement.

9.8   CONCLUSION

In this chapter we have examined key issues relating to the practice of translating and interpreting and related these to the broader issues of intercultural communication and illustrated these with research-based examples. Such research further enhances our understanding of translation and interpreting as a particular type of intercultural communication.

9.9   REVIEW

1. **Key Terms:** Interpreter, translator, simultaneous interpreting, chuchotage, sequential translation, pragmatic equivalence, impartiality, bilingual professional, language aide, adjustment of untranslated communication, back-translation, NAATI.

2. **Key Ideas**
   Having read this chapter you should:
   a. appreciate the difference between interpreting and translating
   b. be able to make appropriate decisions in the selection and employment of translators and interpreters, based on standard criteria
   c. appreciate the need for sensitivity to cross-cultural differences in the organisation and presentation of spoken and written material designed for international communication.

3. **Focus Questions**
   a. Semantic equivalence with pronouns
   In Chapter 7 we discussed the fact that in some cultures formal pronoun forms are widely used in public contexts and informal forms are reserved for close personal acquaintances; whereas in other cultures informal forms might be widely used in public discourse, the use of formal forms being reserved for extreme formality and for coding extreme social distance.
   (i) Given that the task of an interpreter is to render a client's speech into a second language, without changing the meaning, explain why it might be necessary when interpreting between certain languages for interpreters not to use the grammatically equivalent pronoun form, but to change from a formal form to an informal form.
   (ii) What reasons might an interpreter offer for not making such a switch?
   b. Business interpreting
   (i) In the business context, it might be advantageous for each of the negotiating parties to employ their own interpreter, rather than just use one. Explain why this might be so.
   (ii) What disadvantages might accrue from the two parties sharing the same interpreter?

    (iii) Explain why it might sometimes be in the business interests of a company for an interpreter not to be impartial. How can this ethical issue be resolved?

c. Employing staff with foreign language skills

    (i) If a hotel was seeking to employ customer service personnel with foreign language skills, what level of skills might be required to handle the following:

      – an enquiry about the location of a suitable restaurant

      – a complaint about the use of disrespectful language by a hotel employee

      – a major emergency at the hotel such as a large explosion.

    (ii) Are the NAATI accreditation levels helpful in describing the different levels of skill required?

    (iii) How might organisations such as international hotels best plan for the provision of interpreting and translation needs?

4. Research Analysis

    a. Explain exactly what went wrong with each of the following mistranslations:

    (i) The Belgian market mistranslated its slogan 'Body by Fisher' into 'Corpse by Fisher'.

    (ii) In Pepsi's 'Come alive with Pepsi' campaign, the popular English language advertisement was mistranslated into German as 'Come out of the grave' and in Asia as 'Bring your ancestors back from the grave'.

    b. What, exactly is difficult about translating the title of the cat food advertisement 'Turn on your cat'?

5. Research Exercise

    a. Locate a pair of magazines published in English and also in another language.

    b. Compare a text or advertisement in each language in terms of the features discussed in this chapter. (If you are comparing longer texts, you may need to also refer to the discussions in Chapter 8 on cultural differences in writing.)

    This exercise is suitable for bilingual students, or for students with complementary language skills working in pairs.

NOTE

1 This heading is taken from the title of Weller's (1992) article.

SUGGESTED FURTHER READING

Haffner, L. 1992 'Translation is not enough: Interpreting in a medical setting. In "Cross cultural medicine – a decade later"', Special issue. *Western Journal of Medicine*, vol. 157, pp. 255–9.

Larson, M. L. 1984 *Meaning-based Translation: A Guide to Cross-Language Equivalence*. Lanham, Maryland: University Press of America.

Munday, J. 2001 *Introducing Translation Studies: Theories and Applications*. London and New York: Routledge.

O'Hagen, M. & Ashworth, D. 2002 *Translation-Mediated Communication in a Digital World*. Clevedon, UK: Multilingual Matters.

Pym, A. 2004 *The Moving Text: Localization, Translation, and Distribution*. Amsterdam: John Benjamins.

Pym, A. 2004 'Propositions on cross-cultural communication and translation'. *Target: International Journal of Translation Studies*, vol. 16, no. 1, pp. 1–28.

10 | Intercultural communication issues in professional and workplace contexts

THIS CHAPTER WILL EXAMINE language issues relevant to a number of professional and workplace contexts. We will begin by discussing some further aspects of Béal's (1992) workplace intercultural communication difficulties between French and Australian co-workers, and then turn to reporting two studies involving intercultural business negotiation. The issue of the centrality of the question and answer sequences in medical and legal practice will also be explored and exemplified by one research study where different cultural expectations are evident in court proceedings. We will conclude with an account of some of the key findings of the intercultural workplace study conducted by Clyne (1994) at a number of workplaces in Melbourne, including a number of factories.

10.1 TWO DIFFERENT WORKPLACE CULTURES IN CONTACT

Béal (1990) reports some of the findings from her intercultural workplace study involving native speakers of French and native speakers of Australian English interacting within a single company in Melbourne. This part of her study related to differences in the ways in which French and Australian co-workers behaved when it came to **requests** and how the **two sets of sociolinguistic rules** could **clash**.

There has been considerable work on cross-cultural differences in requests (see Chapter 4). In Béal's study, reported here, we see examples of how such differences are actually played out within a single intercultural workplace. In particular, Béal identifies differences between speakers as to which politeness strategies they prefer to use when making a request, differences between speakers in the assessment of what constitutes a 'face-threatening' act and clashes between 'face wants' and other wants (Béal 1990:16).

Using Brown and Levinson's notions of **positive politeness** (aimed at satisfying the interlocutor's desire to be acknowledged and approved of) and **negative politeness** (minimising a potential threat to territory, privacy or freedom of action (Brown & Levinson 1987)), Béal found that French and Australian speakers tended to choose different **conventionalised forms** to minimise the threat to the face of the hearer when making a request. Unfortunately, in both directions, interlocutors misinterpreted the negative politeness strategies of their co-workers.

In French, negative politeness is accomplished most of the time by the use of an impersonal verb such as *Il faut* (literally, *It has to be* + past participle). In English one would typically use an indirect speech act such as *Could you possibly (do such and such)*.

Béal (1990:20) recounts the case of a young French employee who had only been in Australia for a few months having a rather serious falling out with one of the secretaries. In discussion with Béal after the incident, the employee exclaimed:

> honestly, I don't understand what I did wrong, I said 'this has to be done immediately' you know 'Il faut le faire toute de suite,' 'il faut': 'this has to be done' (toute de suite means 'immediately')

Béal observes that the explanation showed that the employee was carrying communication conventions from French to English and by insisting that she had correctly translated 'Il faut' she was emphasising the French rationale for choosing this particular strategy, which carries the idea 'this is not me asking, the order comes from above us – it is me and you versus the system'. To a native speaker of English, this form comes across as very abrupt because it lacks any personal touch.

In contrast, Béal reports that the English habit of asking 'Would you mind doing this for me', which can be regarded as acknowledging a personal debt (another instance of negative politeness), annoyed some of the French people, because in the workplace making requests personal seemed inappropriate and they interpreted the 'for me' as a case of 'me and the system versus you'.

More generally, Béal found that the French employees were more likely to use positive politeness strategies – by the use of in-group terminology, directness and turn overlap to emphasise their shared group affiliation. They therefore tended to interpret the conventionally indirect request forms used by Australian employees as deliberate attempts to keep social distance.

Béal (1990:31) suggests that her data identifies the need to reassess, to some extent, the accepted current models for the description of politeness phenomena. She suggests that tying up the notion of politeness almost exclusively to the notion of face, represents an essentially anglocentric approach which regards positive face strategies as 'less polite'. By ranking negative politeness as more polite than positive politeness, Béal suggests that the fundamental difference between positive and negative politeness is obliterated or becomes blurred, and the theory cannot account easily for examples like those in which French speakers feel insulted by tactful Australian negative politeness strategies.

Béal (1990:31) observes three basic differences between the nature of positive politeness and negative politeness. She suggests that positive politeness is global, rather than related to speech acts; is long term, rather than immediate; and escalating, rather than stable. Béal's point further exemplifies our observations in Chapter 3, that positive politeness, which relates to the acknowledgment of another person's worth, can be achieved not only by refraining from criticism of the person, and by building up solidarity through the use of shared colloquial expressions and other informal linguist in-group behaviour, but also by overt acknowledgment of the accomplishments of the individual, which may be expressed formally in many circumstances. As Béal points out, this forms part of an ongoing process of creating relationships. On the other hand, negative politeness, which relates to the management of face-threatening acts, refers to the particular situation of use, and to particular speech acts, that may involve face-threatening acts. Of course the impact of negative politeness will also be sensitive to what different people regard as face-threatening acts.

10.2 DIFFERENCES OF EXPECTATION IN INTERCULTURAL BUSINESS ENCOUNTERS

Marriott (1990) reports some very interesting conclusions from her case study of a business encounter between a Japanese businessman and an Australian businessman meeting for the first time. This study shows that miscommunication occurs significantly when the parties have different **expectations** of the particular phase of the negotiation. Marriott uses the term *norm discrepancy* to refer to the observation that the two parties each assume that the negotiation will proceed in certain (but quite different) ways according to the **norms** of each culture.

Marriott's methodology involved videotaping the actual business encounter between (J), the senior Japanese representative of a Japanese company located in Melbourne, who himself had been resident in Australia for two and a half months, and an Australian businessman (A), who was the managing director of his own, recently established, small cheese company. Marriott also conducted **follow-up interviews** with each participant during which the videotape was replayed segment by segment. These interviews and all comments by the participants were audio-taped. Marriott's use of follow-up interviews followed the approach advocated by Neustypný (e.g. Neustypný 1985) and proved to be of significant value.

Marriott (1990:40) reports that an examination of the discourse of the business negotiation and of the follow-up interviews revealed that the Australian and the Japanese interactants held disparate views on the function of their first dyadic interaction. The Australian's objective was clearly to introduce his product and to obtain from his Japanese addressee an indication of interest in proceeding to a further stage of the negotiation. The objective of the Japanese, on the other hand, was to obtain information about the Australian company and of its intention relating to future cooperation.

In the follow-up interview, Marriott (1990:47) reports that J declared that the purpose of his first meeting was to procure information about A's company and its plans. Simultaneously, he raised two socio-economic problems. One concerned the lack of the Australian company possessing a patent. The other related to the small size of the Japanese cheese market for such specialised cream cheese as that manufactured by A's company. However, J did not explicitly refer to the difficulties of entering into a cooperative arrangement with the Australian as the purpose of that meeting was just to gather information for reporting to head office.

Marriott suggests that although it could be argued that the Japanese businessman's behaviour was motivated by the desire to express politeness by avoiding an explicit display of disinterest, as is frequently contended in the popular literature, there is a much stronger case for arguing that his conduct was due to different **norms** concerning the function of the interaction. The cultural norm of the Japanese businessman certainly did not require him to make any commitment at this stage or even venture his own individual evaluation. Marriott concludes that the disparity of the norms in this regard was particularly strong, and since it was the Australian who, using his own native norm, noted and negatively evaluated a deviation in the conduct of the Japanese, it was he who was frustrated at the outcome of the negotiation.

This research of Marriott's illustrates the value of conducting **follow-up interviews** following the approach advocated by Neustypný (e.g. Neustypný 1985). Such interviews can provide the researcher with insight into the participants' intentions and concerns with respect to the encounter, and are the only way certain information relating to intercultural differences of expectations and misunderstandings concerning the encounter can be recovered.

Spencer-Oatey and Xing (2003) report on two Chinese–British business meetings held by the same British company to welcome groups of engineers from a Chinese company with which they had been doing business for some time. Spencer-Oatey and Xing (2003:38) report that despite many similarities between the meetings, both the British and the Chinese were very satisfied with the first meeting, while the Chinese were very annoyed with the second meeting. The seating arrangements were interpreted as conveying a negative 'status' message. The Chinese Delegation Leader expressed his concerns as follows:

> . . . it shouldn't have been that he was the chair and we were seated along the sides of the table. With equal status, they should sit along this side and we should sit along that side . . .

In other words, the Chinese felt that since the two teams were of equal status, they should have sat on opposite sides of the table, with the heads of each side sitting in the middle.

Spencer-Oatey and Xing also report two difficulties relating to the welcome speech offered by the British chairman. Firstly, the Chinese felt that the British chairman's comments on the Sino-British relationship were not weighty enough. Spencer-Oatey and Xing (2003:39) explain that the Chinese had heard on the grapevine that the British company was in serious financial difficulties, and they believed it was the Chinese contracts that had saved them from bankruptcy. This was expressed by a Chinese sales manager in the following terms:

> It is understandable for them to praise their own products, but by doing so they in fact made a big mistake. Why? Because, you see, because for a company when they haven't got new orders for their products for several years it is a serious problem for them, but they didn't talk about it . . . he should have said that you have made great efforts regarding [the sale of] our

products, right? And hope you continue. They should have said more in this respect. He didn't mention our orders. So in fact this is a very important matter. It is not a matter of just receiving us . . .

Spencer-Oatey and Xing conclude that the British were not strong enough in their compliments towards the Chinese, and in the degree of gratitude they expressed.

The research of Marriott (1990) and Spencer-Oatey and Xing (2003) are excellent examples of ideal research practice in the area of intercultural business negotiations. In both cases, actual business meetings were video-recorded and post-meeting comments were collected from participants and used in the analysis of the data.

Although opportunities to conduct such research are difficult to arrange because of commercial confidentiality, Spencer-Oatey and Xing (2003) point out that such authentic intercultural discourse data is vital if we are to advance our understanding of intercultural communication.

10.3 INFORMATION GATHERING IN MEDICAL AND LEGAL PRACTICE

Western approaches to medical and legal practice are very reliant on language because questions and answers form an important component of both.

Within the Western biomedical approach to medicine, health professionals, especially doctors, ask patients questions in order to establish their medical history. Davidson (2000:383) characterises medical interviews as a type of verbal and physical investigation:

> a matching of unorganized experiences against familiar patterns and processes of human vulnerability to disease. The overt elaborated goals of the medical interview are; (1) from the data provided, determine what, if anything, is wrong with the patient; (2) elaborate a plan of treatment for the ailment; and (3) convince the patient of the validity of the diagnosis so that treatment can be followed.

Davidson suggests that the 'creation' of medical 'facts' through medical practice is heavily influenced by a social evaluation of the meaning and importance of whatever facts are uncovered or created (Foucault 1963; Waitzkin 1991). Davidson thus sees diagnosis as an 'interpretive process in which the patient's physical and verbal data is passed, by physicians, through a grid of medical meanings (biological and social) and re-analysed, so that 'irrelevant' input from the patient may be excluded and the story of the disease constructed'.

The issue of differences in cultural expectations of communication, and of expectations regarding medical in general, as well as the inherent **asymmetrical knowledge/power** relationship between the doctors and patients, thus makes intercultural medical encounters particularly complex.

Since the diagnosis and subsequent decision making regarding treatment rely so heavily on input from the patient, any difficulties in information gathering may undermine the process significantly.

Much of the work of the legal profession, likewise, involves the **gathering of information** from clients and witnesses, and relies heavily on **questions and answers**. It is thus crucial that medical and legal practitioners are aware of the complexities involved in information gathering in general, and particular issues involved in intercultural contexts.

The following discussion illustrates some differences of expectation regarding the gathering of information involving Indigenous Australians in the courtroom.

10.4   AUSTRALIAN INDIGENOUS CLIENTS IN THE COURTROOM

Pauwels, D'Argaville and Eades (1992) observe that although Australian Aboriginal people use direct questions in routine situations, such as to find out who a person is related to, or where they come from, in situations where Aboriginal people want to find out significant information, they do not use direct questions.

In Aboriginal interactions, information is sought as part of a **two-way exchange**. Hinting, volunteering information for confirmation or denial, silence, and waiting until people are ready to give information, are all central to Aboriginal ways of seeking any substantial information. It is important not to rush people or put them on the spot, and not to invade their personal privacy with direct questions about substantial issues.

Pauwels, D'Argaville and Eades (1992:103–4) provide the following fictionalised example, drawn from a number of actual cases, which contrasts the way an Aboriginal English speaker gives information about the time of an event, firstly in courtroom questioning, and secondly, in answer to investigation by an Aboriginal Field Officer. They point out that it would be a mistake to conclude that the speaker is vague or uncertain about the timing of the event in question. He is able to give much precise information relevant to this, in his own terms, **relating the incident to other events** that happened on the same morning. On the other hand, his courtroom evidence, which is tied down to clock times, may give the false impression that the speaker is unsure about the event, or inconsistent, or an unreliable witness.

EXAMPLE 1: ABORIGINAL WITNESS IN COURT

Examination-in-chief (Defence Counsel (DC), Aboriginal witness (A)):

DC: What time did this happen?
A: I don't know . . . I know we's working . . .
DC: Well, what time was it?
A: About 10 o'clock.

Cross-examination Public Prosecutor (PP), Aboriginal witness (A):

PP: When did this happen?
A: It was in the morning sometime . . .
PP: Was it late in the morning?
A: Yeah, pretty late.
PP: Say, 11.30?
A: Yeah, 11.30.

EXAMPLE 2: ABORIGINAL WITNESS INTERACTING WITH AN ABORIGINAL FIELD OFFICER

FO: When that thing you talking about happened?
A: I don't know . . . I know we's working . . . morning, or afternoon . . . I don't really know.
FO: You fellas already had 'smoko'?
A: Well, we have smoko already, then old Aunt Bessie come down – she was lookin' for that cousin belong to what's-'is-name, used to live up there along the riverbank before. She stopped for a while, then she went up to the hospital – that cousin might be there, eh? – then we's working again a bit more. Then that's when the boolimun [policeman] came, like I'm telling you.
FO: Them school kids, they already came back for lunch?
A: No, boolimun come before that.

In a more recent article, Eades (2000) examines the reaction of Aboriginal witnesses in a New South Wales country town to various types of questions, and shows that even although several of these witnesses are able, to their advantage, to use Yes/No questions as an invitation to tell an explanatory narrative, such leeway seems to be restricted to the provision of evidence that the Defence Counsel or the Judge feels is relevant. In cases in which these narratives relate family relationships and other aspects of contemporary Aboriginal social organisation that seem less relevant to the same officers of the court, they tend to restrict the Aboriginal witness's answers, effectively 'silencing' that part of the witness's testimony.

10.5 WORKPLACE COMMUNICATION: FROM FACTORY TO OFFICE

The major research project reported in Clyne (1994) involved a series of Melbourne workplaces with diverse ethnolinguistic composition which results from and comprised two car factories, one of American origin and one of Japanese origin, a textile factory of Australian origin, an electronics factory of German origin, the catering section of a migrant hostel, two government offices and meetings of a multicultural parents' group. In all, a total of 182 hours of audio recordings were analysed. Clyne's monograph contains an excellent account of theoretical perspectives underpinning the methodology, and analysis of a wide range of features of intercultural communication.

Of a total of 26 instances of **communication breakdown** in the corpus, Clyne reports that 18 of them were resolved through **negotiation of meaning**. Six of the instances involved problems in understanding the content and/or context or the communication, seven involved vocabulary or grammatical decoding difficulties and another six were discourse problems related to cultural background. The example discussed in Chapter 4 of an apology offered by a Polish female operator taking considerable time to be accepted by her workplace supervisor of Malaysian–Chinese background, is an instance of the last type.

Several of the instances of miscommunication were those in which the addressee did not understand 'small-talk', which was intended by the speaker as friendly phatic communication but, perhaps, mainly due to it referring to activities and people outside the context of the workplace, was not understood at all. One instance was the result of intolerance of a longer pause than met the expectations of the communication partner.

Clyne's observation (1994:147) that the resolution of almost all the instances of communication breakdown in the corpus, and the attempted resolution of all of them, speak for the intercultural expertise that has been acquired in Australian society and the Australian workplace. Clyne's methodology served as a springboard for the research of Bowe and Neil reported in the following chapter.

10.6 CONCLUSION

In this chapter we have seen a variety of features of intercultural communication drawing on research conducted in actual intercultural professional and workplace contexts. Such research further enhances our understanding of the nature of intercultural communication which ultimately constitutes a basis for intercultural competence.

10.7 REVIEW

1. **Key Terms:** Communication conventions, cultural expectations/ assumptions, norms, norm-discrepancy, follow-up interviews, information gathering, question and answer sequences, asymmetric power, communication breakdown, miscommunication, negotiation of meaning (from Chapter 3, positive and negative politeness).

2. **Key Ideas**
   Having read this chapter you should:
   a. understand the importance of expectations and norms in relation to communication in general, and intercultural communication in particular
   b. appreciate the potential for communication failure in such contexts, and be able to identify some of the causes of communication breakdown
   c. be able to use an understanding of these issues for the purpose of smooth intercultural interaction.

3. **Focus Questions**
   a. Positive and negative politeness strategies of French and Australian co-workers
   Consider the examples of positive and negative politeness provided by Béal in the research reported in section 10.1 and identify which strategies you might use in a similar context. Are you more inclined to use positive or negative politeness strategies?

b. **The importance of norms in understanding intercultural communication**

Much of the material in this chapter provides examples of miscommunication that has occurred in intercultural communication, often due to differences in what we call cultural norms or cultural expectations. One of the problems with differences in cultural norms/expectations is that the speaker is usually unaware that there is a particular expectation or norm involved. Speakers usually regard their own communication style as 'sensible' and 'appropriate'. In view of this, do you think that either of the terms 'cultural expectation' or 'cultural norm' is more suitable than the other? (You need to consider what is meant by 'expectation' in this context.)

c. **Questions and answers in contexts of asymmetrical power**

In Table 2.1 Speech Acts (Chapter 2) Searle (1969) outlines a number of conditions for the speech act question. Consider in what way the conditions identified by Searle may be helpful in understanding why people in positions of relatively little power, such as patients in the medical context, and witnesses in the legal context, often have difficulty answering the questions that are put to them.

4. **Research Analysis**
Aboriginal witnesses in the courtroom

Which of the utterances provided by the Australian Indigenous witnesses in the scenarios in section 10.4 would contribute to a conclusion that Aboriginal people are uncooperative in the courtroom? Discuss.

5. **Research Exercise**

The research reported in Chapter 10 is all based on authentic intercultural communication data.

a. What do you think are the reasons that there is more cross-cultural research (where two cultures are compared), than intercultural research (where speakers from different cultures are engaged in some activity)?

b. Check a recent research journal on intercultural communication, or intercultural pragmatics, and determine whether or not this is the case for the research reported in the journal you choose.

SUGGESTED FURTHER READING

Clyne, M. 1994 *Inter-cultural Communication at Work: Cultural Values in Discourse*. Cambridge: Cambridge University Press.

Eades, D. 2000 'I don't think it's an answer to the question: Silencing Aboriginal witnesses in court'. *Language in Society,* vol. 29, pp. 161–95.

Endomoto, S. 1998 'The management of politeness in Japanese tour guiding discourse'. *Japanese Studies,* vol. 18, no. 3, pp. 295–310.

Lakoff, R. 1989 'The limits of politeness: Therapeutic and courtroom discourse'. *Multilingua,* vol. 8, pp. 101–29.

Marriott, H. 1990 'Intercultural business negotiations: The problem of norm discrepancy'. *Australian Review of Applied Linguistics,* Series S, vol. 7, pp. 33–65.

Sarangi, S. & Roberts, C. (eds) 1999 *Talk, Work and Institutional Order: Discourse in Medical, Mediation and Management Settings.* Berlin: Mouton de Gruyter.

Spencer-Oatey, H. & Xing, J. 2003 'Managing rapport in intercultural business interactions: A comparison of two Chinese–British welcome meetings'. *Journal of Intercultural Studies,* vol. 24, no. 1, pp. 33–46.

11 Towards successful intercultural communication

RESEARCH INVOLVING PARTICIPANTS from different cultures, who are engaged in natural communication in a language that is not a first language to any of the speakers, shows that individuals can develop ways to construct **common ground** and avoid many of the problems inherent in intercultural communication.

In this chapter we report the findings of two research studies (Bowe 1995; Neil 1996) conducted in multicultural workplaces in Australia that show that individuals engaged in intercultural communication can draw on **creative discourse strategies** to circumvent some aspects of potential miscommunication.

We also briefly discuss the Giles (1977:322) notion of **accommodation**, and Sharifian's notion of **conceptual renegotiation** (Sharifian forthcoming); two further perspectives which seek to explain how individuals adapt to the challenges of intercultural communication.

11.1 THE ELABORATION OF REPETITION AS A CREATIVE STRATEGY TO HELP AVOID MISCOMMUNICATION

Using similar methodology to that developed by Clyne (1994), Heather Bowe examined discourse between migrant workers in the automotive industry. This study, conducted mainly on the factory floor, used tape-recorded samples of communication between supervisors and operators who were almost all immigrants to Australia. Spoken communication between supervisors and operators typically involves messages concerning health and safety in the factory, productivity, quality control, training and staff organisation, as well as general communication of a more personal nature which functions to maintain rapport. In many cases, supervisors are carrying out tasks originating from production meetings and quality control reports.

This research found that there was a considerable difference in the style of discourse adopted by supervisors who had an Anglo–Australian background and those who were migrants from a non-English-speaking background.[1] A prominent feature of the English discourse of non-English-speaking migrants was the use of repetition (with relevant intonation) in place of the more minimal responses such as *m-hm* and *uh-huh* (see section 5.4). Such use of repetition ensures not only that the listener is attending to what is being said, but that the propositions on which the feedback is based are able to be checked.

In cases where the proposition was correctly restated, the repetition functions as the appropriate response, that is, agreement, assent, query and so on. In cases where the proposition was misunderstood, the response in the form of repetition can expose the source of the misunderstanding and the proposition can be corrected.

The data that was collected from the shop floor contained numerous examples of repetition of several kinds, some of which are presented here. (In these examples overlapping words are indicated with [. . .]. For other symbols, please refer to the transcription conventions listed on page xii.)

a. **Repetition as a means of acknowledging receipt of information**
In this example, Sombat, a Laotian group leader, informs his Tongan team member that his long service leave application has been approved. The team member repeats *approved* followed by *yes okay* in acknowledgment of having received the information.

> *Sombat*   Tupou ++ your application for + long service leave + has
> been approved
> *Tupou*   ↑ah
> *Sombat*   it's [approved]
> *Tupou*   **[approved] yes [okay]**
> *Sombat*   [yes] ++ eight weeks you're going for +
> *Tupou*   thank you

b. **Repetition as a means of confirming information**
In this example, Frank, the Italian group leader, reminds his Serbian team leader, Stefan, that there will be a safety check on Thursday. Stefan reiterates *Thursday* to show he is aware of the arrangement.

> *Frank*   we have to do something about it + the other part over there
> ++ and no forget we + on **Thursday** we have safety check

Stefan **Thursday [yeah]**
Frank [yeah] otherwise we have nothing xxxx

c. Repetition as an expression of solidarity

In this example, there is a problem in the paint shop which seems to be occurring infrequently. Sometimes the cars come through with defects, while on other occasions there are no faults at all. The Greek team member, Panteli, explains this to his Vietnamese team leader, Alfred, by saying that (the cars are) '*sometime alright sometime no good*'. Alfred repeats the utterance *sometime alright sometime no good* to indicate that he is listening and taking notice.

Alfred how job the paint shop ++ what you think the job the paint shop
Panteli where
Alfred in the paint shop + job come ↑okay +3+ ↑why
Panteli <I don't know xxxxx xxxxx xxxxx + <**sometime alright sometime no good**
Alfred **sometime alright sometime no good** + what the ↑problem + ↑roof + or frame or
Panteli xxxxx xxxxx xxxxx frame
Alfred xxxxx ↑frame + xxxxx frame
Panteli xxxxx like that like this
Alfred like frame frame buff cut or ↑something

In a similar conversation between two native speakers of English, a more minimal response such as 'aha' or 'mm' would have been more likely. However, the use of repetition accomplishes the same function while providing opportunities for picking up misunderstandings.

d. Repetition as a means of confirming speaker's hypothesis

In the following example, Spiro, the Greek team leader, and Alfonso, the Italian team leader, discuss forthcoming soccer finals. There is some confusion as to which teams will be playing and when the matches will be held. Alfonso is talking about which teams will play 'tomorrow night'. Spiro asks about 'Wollongong' and Alfonso replies that this team has to play too. Spiro then clarifies 'tomorrow too'. Alfonso's repetition 'tomorrow too' confirms Spiro's hypothesis.

Spiro Juventus play tonight
Alfonso [no tomorrow]
Spiro [xxxxx]
Alfonso tomorrow night

Spiro	er Wollongong who with er xxxxx no play ↑anymore
Alfonso	yeah they have to play too
Spiro	**tomorrow too**
Alfonso	**tomorrow too** and ah Sunday
Spiro	Hellas Marconi
Alfonso	Marconi

e. Repetition as a means of answering a negative question

In the following example, we see Marco an Italian team leader speaking to his Lebanese team member, Hassan. Hassan wants to check that Jim, another team member, is not coming in to work. Marco's reply, *yeah Jimmy no in today* is in fact a repetition of the relevant details of Hassan's utterance with the addition of the word *no* to negate the proposition. However, Marco has prefaced the reply with the affirmative 'yeah' to indicate agreement with Hassan. Had Marco simply replied *no* without any additional information, this may have resulted in misunderstanding because of the fact that in some languages *no* in this context would indicate disagreement with the foregoing proposition meaning that Jimmy was in fact going to come in to work.

| *Hassan* | what ↑**Jim. not coming today** |
| *Marco* | **yeah Jimmy no in today** ++ now + I wanna you . . . |

f. Repetition as a query

In the following conversation, Colin, an Anglo–Australian team leader, uses repetition (with rising intonation) as a means of requesting confirmation of what he thought he heard. Ian, a Sri Lankan (Burgher) team leader asks Colin to get him some plastic tape. Colin queries *plastic tape* and Ian repeats the key words of his initial utterance *yeah sure, plastic plastic* as a way of letting Colin know that he has correctly understood the directive.

Ian	my best buddy friend + er ++ would you be able to **get me some plastic + tape** please
Colin	**plastic ↑tape**
Ian	yeah sure + plastic plastic

The use of repetition as a query is a strategy often used by Anglo–Australians.

g. Repetition as a means of acknowledging the correction of a wrong hypothesis

This example is from a conversation between Ian, the Sri Lankan (Burgher) team leader, and Toby, an Afghan team member. Ian asks

Toby whether his niece was born in Afghanistan. Toby replies *Pakistan* and Ian repeats this as a way of acknowledging the correction.

Ian   but she was born in Australia [↑wasn't she]
Toby   [no no]
Ian   [in Afghanistan]
Toby   [xxxxx **Pakistan**]
Ian   **Pakistan ++**

h. Repetition as a means of framing a question

In the following example, Van, a Vietnamese team leader, informs his Italian group leader, Frank, that he may be leaving early on Friday. He says *maybe maybe Friday I go home early*. In response to this, Frank wants to know the reason Van will be leaving earlier than usual. Instead of simply asking *why* he also repeats the important details of Van's utterance *you go home early on Friday* then adds the interrogative *why*.

Van   hey Frank +2+
Frank what +2+
Van   maybe maybe **Friday ++ I go home early ++**
Frank **you go home early on ↑Friday ↑why +**
Van   because . . .

By employing this repetitive discourse strategy, communication breakdown can be avoided. In the example above, Frank makes it clear to Van what his interrogative question *why* actually refers to by repeating the important details of Van's utterance, that is, the details Frank wishes to know more about.

i. Routine repetition exposing miscommunication

In the following example, Sammy, a Laotian panel beater, tells Tim, the Cambodian team leader, how many years he has been working at Rising Sun Motors. Tim repeats the number of years (with upward intonation) indicating surprise as well. It turns out that he had misheard the number, and because he had repeated what he thought he had heard, the miscommunication was able to be corrected.

Sammy after after xxxxx after um + this year is **sixteen ++**
Tim   ↑**sixty**
Sammy <**sixteen**
Tim   **one six**
Sammy [**oh one six**]
Tim   [alright] +

This research has shown that a prominent feature of the English discourse of factory workers from a non-English-speaking background is the use of repetition for a range of discourse functions including agreement, assent, affirmation, and acknowledgment. These are precisely the types of functions for which researchers such as Duncan (1973, 1974), Sacks, Schegloff and Jefferson (1978), Schegloff (1982) and Levinson (1983) have identified the use of minimal responses such as *m-hm* and *uh-huh*.

The use of repetition (with relevant intonation), rather than the more minimal responses such as *m-hm* and *uh-huh*, is a creative strategy to ensure that intercultural communication occurs in an unambiguous way, despite different cultural expectations and the difficulties of having to use a second language with limited grammatical competence.

11.2 TURN-SHARING AS COLLABORATION BETWEEN NON-ENGLISH-SPEAKING WORKERS: ANCILLARY STAFF AT A MELBOURNE HOSPITAL

Neil's (1996:97) research reports that **collaborative strategies** are a significant feature of the intercultural communication of hospital ancillary staff from a non-English-speaking background, using English as a lingua franca in a Melbourne hospital.

> In intercultural communication, the need for both speakers' participation is heightened if the interaction is going to proceed smoothly and be optimally effective. Speakers must take an active, joint responsibility for constructing and sustaining talk which is mutually comprehensible. In this way, joint text production in intercultural discourse has the social function of engaging speakers equally in successfully producing meaning.

Neil illustrates that **turn-sharing** is a significant feature of the joint discourse production of her subjects.

Building on the work of Sacks (1967–8), Lerner (1991), Ferrara (1992) and others, Neil (1996:98) distinguishes between turn completions which are *pre-emptions*, usually the initiative of the interlocutor, and those which result after *petering out* on the part of the speaker, which can act as a tacit invitation to the interlocutor to complete the turn. In the first case, one speaker offers an anticipatory completion of a turn, which was begun by the other speaker. By contrast, in the latter case, the interlocutor's completion is more likely to be invited by the speaker when words fail and his/her turn begins to peter out.

Neil (1996:104) provides the following example of *pre-emptive* turn-sharing between Hien, a Vietnamese woman who speaks Cantonese at home, and her supervisor Juana, whose first language is Tagalog.

> *Hien*   you go to the dentist for, for ∼∼ (0)
> *Juana*   (0) private? yeah
> *Hien*   yeah, how much? one [twenty!]

Neil suggests that Juana's contextual knowledge of the conversation and her familiarity with her interlocutor make the nature of Hien's question predictable for Juana. She therefore latches onto Hien's 'for – ', marked by a level tone, which prompts Juana to realise that Hien is searching for the next word and to pre-empt this word. Juana's use of question intonation may indicate that this is a suggestion being offered, not a definitive statement.

The following is an example provided by Neil (1996:107) of an utterance begun by Theona being completed by her conversation partner Juana, because Theona's first utterance *peters out*.

> *Theona*   I don't know! too many <XplaceX what's it called? I forgot where they test the –
> *Juana*   oh yeah, they test th+e ∼∼
> *Theona*   yeah
> *Juana*   the <XglucoseX>
> *Theona*   (0) yeah, them or another place. (0)

Neil explains that Theona has used the routine formula 'What's it called?' to signal that she is struggling for a word. Inherent in this formulation is the invitation for Juana to intercept with the right word. But rather than pausing to await Juana's response, Theona continues with the turn. The additional information supplied by 'I forgot where they test the –' makes it easier for her interlocutor to identify the word she means. The petering out also sets the scene for Juana's turn completion; Theona's utterance peters out at the point in her turn where the word must be supplied.

Neil argues (1996:120) that contrary to the view articulated by Zuengler (1989) that finishing another's statement is a dominating move; collaborative productions, or utterance completions, are an indication of the solidarity and close social organisation that enables workers from language backgrounds other than English to communicate successfully using English as a lingua franca.

Neil's 1996 monograph provides a well-documented inventory of collaborative strategies found in her data, including several different turn-sharing strategies, the collaborative use of repetition, the collaborative use of paraphrase, clarification strategies and the use of information questions for topic development.

11.3 THE RESPONSE OF THE INDIVIDUAL TO THE CHALLENGES OF INTERCULTURAL COMMUNICATION

The research of Clyne (1994) and Marriott (1990) discussed in Chapter 9 reports instances of miscommunication in intercultural communication, due mostly to different cultural conventions relating to language. However, the research findings of Bowe's study of automotive manufacturing workers and of Neil's (1996) study of hospital ancillary staff, described in this chapter, overwhelmingly reveal the ability of speakers from different language and cultural backgrounds to creatively use the discourse of a language with which they have only a limited familiarity, to communicate effectively in intercultural contexts.

These two quite different sets of findings illustrate both the potential for miscommunication in intercultural contexts, and also the potential of individuals to overcome this.

Giles (1977:322), from the perspective of Language and Social Psychology, observes that successful communicators are often motivated to adjust their speech (verbal and non-verbal) to **accommodate** to the conventions of others, as a means of expressing positive values, attitudes and intentions towards them. Giles' **Communication Accommodation Theory** examines the social motivation for speakers to accommodate to the language conventions of the addressee, including factors such as individual identity, group identity, and whether the speaker is a member of a dominant group or a subordinate group (see also Gallois et al. 1988 and articles in Giles & Robinson 1990). Coupland et al. (1988) incorporate the notion of **conversational needs** into the Communication Accommodation Theory model. This focus on the others' *interpretive competence* (ability to understand) leads to a set of *interpretability* strategies that include decreasing diversity of vocabulary or simplifying syntax, the modification of pitch, loudness and tempo, and to **discourse management** strategies including topic choice (maintaining topic coherence and thematic development), sharing topic selection and sharing management of turn-taking.

The intercultural discourse strategies identified by Bowe and Neil seem to be motivated by a **shared responsibility for making meaning** in a mutually challenging context. These participants do not seem to be primarily motivated to accommodate to each other's conventions, but rather they are using discourse strategies in a creative way that seems to be mutually useful in the language context in which they find themselves. These strategies relate more closely to the extensions to Accommodation Theory proposed by Coupland et al. (1988).

11.4 THE EMERGENT AND DISTRIBUTED NATURE OF CULTURAL COGNITION: THE LOCUS OF NEW CONCEPTUAL INTERPRETATIONS

By way of conclusion to this book, we will turn to some recent research which provides insight into the nature of the interaction between culture and cognition, and the way in which **cultural conceptualisations** are **integrative** and thus amenable to **reinterpretation**. This research comes from the tradition of cognitive linguistics and draws upon the connectionist models (e.g. Rumelhart et al. 1986).

Sharifian (2003, 2004, 2005, forthcoming) provides a model of the complex processes that relate **cultural cognition**, **conceptualisation** and **language**. (See Chapter 3 for Sharifian's analysis of the cultural schema known as *sharmandegi* (sometimes translated as 'being ashamed') in the Persian language (Farsi)).

The multifaceted nature of the relationship between cultural cognition, conceptualisation and language provides an explanation of how individuals can respond to the challenges of intercultural communication.

Sharifian (forthcoming) explains that research on cultural cognition draws on the fields of cognitive psychology, cognitive linguistics, cultural linguistics and cognitive anthropology. He draws on Sperber and Hirschfeld's (1999:cxv) characterisation of the relationship between culture and cognitive activity:

> The study of culture is of relevance to cognitive sciences for two major reasons. The first is that the very existence of culture, for an essential part, is both an effect and a manifestation of human cognitive abilities. The second reason is that the human societies of today culturally frame every aspect of human life, and, in particular, of cognitive activity.

It is the observation that **culture** is both an 'effect and a manifestation of human cognitive abilities' that seems most relevant to our discussion here.

Sharifian (2004:120 ff.) draws a distinction between cognition at the level of the individual, or what may be termed **psychological cognition**, and cognition at the level of the cultural group, or what may be termed **cultural cognition**. He suggests that cultural knowledge is the collective knowledge of the members of a cultural group, not just the knowledge shared by members of a cultural group, but rather '**a pool of knowledge that is represented in a distributed fashion across the minds in a cultural group**' (Sharifian 2004:121). In other words, although aspects of the knowledge can be seen to be distributed across the entire group, not all members of the group necessarily command each aspect. Sharifian (forthcoming) further presents an integrative view of cognition as a '**system that emerges from the interactions between members of a cultural group**'. He suggests that '(m)embers of a cultural group negotiate and renegotiate their **emergent cultural cognition** across time and space'.

It would seem that it is the **emergent** and **distributed** nature of cultural cognition, as defined by Sharifian (forthcoming), that provides the means by which individuals can adapt the conceptualisations of their immediate culture to negotiate new interpretations and to expand their own conceptual inventory through the study of, and engagement in, intercultural communication.

11.5   CONCLUSION

The principle of **accommodation** identified by Giles (1977), the **collaborative discourse strategies** identified by Bowe (1995) and Neil (1996), the process of **conceptual renegotiation** identified by Sharifian, are thus three facets of the process of intercultural communication, and represent three levels of relevant activity. Accommodation is related to attitudes to communication with those from different cultural backgrounds; collaborative discourse strategies are born out of the process of conversation itself; and conceptual renegotiation is possible because of the potential of human cognition.

Depending on an individual's exposure and experience as a communicator in intercultural contexts, they may be at a different stage in the development of an awareness of the ways in which sociocultural conventions shape language use. In the early stages, individuals may approach intercultural communication through the ethnocentric prism of their own immediate culture and misread the intentions of their intercultural communication partners. We have seen the potential for this in the research on cross-cultural comparisons of a number of perspectives, particularly the research on cross-cultural realisations of speech acts (Blum-Kulka, House & Kasper 1989). Much of the research on intercultural communication in the workplace shows that conventions of a speaker's language and cultural background do influence many speakers engaged in intercultural interaction, regardless of whether the encounters are of relatively short duration or whether the interaction is part of a full-time job.

The richness of language use that allows speakers to conventionally code meaning in non-literal ways, means that the job of negotiating language meaning is an ongoing one, even for speakers who share the same language and culture.

We hope that the presentation in this book of the many processes involved in intercultural communication will not only enable readers to communicate more effectively in the intercultural world, but will also enable researchers from different disciplines to incorporate some of the perspectives presented here into their own research.

11.6   REVIEW

1. Key Terms: Common ground collaborative discourse strategies, repetition, accommodation, turn-sharing, pre-emption, cultural schema, cultural cognition, conceptualisation, conceptual renegotiation.

2. Key Ideas
   Having read this chapter you should:
   a. be aware of some of the ways in which speakers can engage in collaborative discourse strategies to minimise potential misunderstanding in intercultural contexts
   b. be aware of the process of accommodation and its potential role in intercultural communication
   c. be able to consider cognitive aspects of intercultural communication such as conceptual renegotiation.

3. Focus Questions
   a. Collaborative discourse strategies
      (i) In what kinds of communicative contexts might you have used collaborative discourse strategies such as turn-sharing, turn completion, repetition and paraphrase?
      (ii) What was your motivation?
   b. Accommodation
      (i) In what kinds of communicative contexts have you used language accommodation?
      (ii) What was your motivation?

4. Research Analysis
   Consider the data in section 11.1 and decide whether, in a parallel conversation, it would seem more natural for you, as a fluent speaker of English, to use minimal responses such as *m-hm* and *uh-huh* instead of the repetition used by the speakers with minimal English skills in each of the examples.

5. Research Exercise
Cultural schema and cultural conceptualisations
Until relatively recently, many English speakers used to offer a Christian prayer to mark the beginning of a meal. It was known as *Grace*, and was usually offered by the head of the household, typically a male, and was an important part of the social context of family life. This would be an example of what cognitive linguists such as Sharifian refer to as a cultural schema. More recently this practice has fallen out of use, leaving a bit of a vacuum. Australian English speakers tend to adopt expressions from other languages, such as the French *Bon appetit* to fulfil this function. Conduct a survey among your classmates, or friends and acquaintances and find out whether they have a conventional way of beginning a meal, who performs it and what cultural ideas and values attach to it.

NOTE

1 The term 'migrant' is used in Australia to refer to the many people who have taken up permanent residence in Australia and have the right to take up citizenship. Their situation is thus quite different from the large numbers of immigrant workers who are temporary residents in many countries of the world.

SUGGESTED FURTHER READING

Gallois, C., Franklyn-Stokes, A., Giles, H. & Coupland, N. 1988 'Communication accommodation in intercultural encounters'. In Kim Y. Y. & Gudykunst W. B. *Theories in Intercultural Communication.* Newbury Park: Sage Publications, pp. 157–85.

Giles, H. 1977 *Language, Ethnicity and Intergroup Relations.* Academic Press, London.

Neil, D. 1996 *Collaboration in Intercultural Discourse: Examples from a Multicultural Australian Workplace.* Frankfurt am Main: Peter Lang.

Sharifian, F. 2003 'On cultural conceptualizations'. *Journal of Cognition and Culture*, vol. 3, no. 3, pp. 188–207.

Sharifian, F. 2004 'Cultural schemas and intercultural communication: A study of Persian'. In Leigh J. & Loo E. *Outer Limits: A Reader in Communication Across Cultures.* Melbourne: Language Australia, pp. 119–30.

Sharifian, F. (forthcoming) 'Distributed, emergent cultural cognition, conceptualisation and language'. In Frank R. M., Dirvan R., Ziemke T. & Bernárdez E. (eds) *Body, Language and Mind (Vol. 2): Sociocultural Situatedness.* Berlin/New York: Mouton de Gruyter.

References

Adegbija, E. 1989 'A comparative study of politeness phenomena in Nigerian English, Yoruba and Ogori'. *Multilingua,* vol. 8, no. 1, pp. 57–80.

Agha, A. 1998 'Stereotypes and registers of honorific language'. *Language in Society,* vol. 27, pp. 151–93.

Albert, S. & Kessler, S. 1976 'Processes for ending social encounters: The conceptual archaeology'. *Journal for the Theory of Social Behaviour,* vol. 6, pp. 147–70.

Albert, S. & Kessler, S. 1978 'Ending social encounters'. *Journal of Experimental Social Psychology,* vol. 14, pp. 541–53.

Allan, K. 1986 *Linguistic Meaning,* 2 vols. London: Routledge & Kegan Paul.

Allan, K. 1991 'Cooperative principle'. In Bright W. (ed.) *Oxford International Encyclopedia of Linguistics.* New York: Oxford University Press.

Allan, K. 1994 'Speech act theory: An overview'. In Asher R. E. et al. (eds) *Encyclopedia of Languages and Linguistics.* Edinburgh: Pergamon and University of Aberdeen Press.

Anderson, B. 1990 'Language, fantasy, revolution: Java, 1900–1945'. *Prisma,* vol. 50, pp. 25–39.

Appel, R. & Muysken, P. 1987 *Language Contact and Bilingualism.* London: Hodder Headline Press.

Austin, J. L. 1962 *How to Do Things with Words.* Oxford: Oxford University Press.

Austin, J. L. 1970 *Philosophical Papers.* Oxford: Clarendon Press.

Bader, J. 2002 *Schriftlichkeit und Mündlichkeit in der Chat-Kommunikation,* Networx Nr. 29, <www.mediensprache.net/networx/networx-29.pdf (accessed 7 January 2007).

Banks, S. P. 1989 'Power pronouns and the language of intercultural understanding'. In Ting-Toomey S. & Korzenny F. (eds) *Language Communication and Culture.* Newbury Park: Sage Publications, pp. 180–98.

Bargiela, F., Boz, B. C., Gokzadze, L., Hamza, A., Mills, S. & Rukhadze, N. 2002 'Ethnocentrism, politeness and naming strategies'. *Working Papers on the Web,* vol. 3, pp. 1–17, <www.shu.ac.uk/wpw/politeness/bargiela.htm> (accessed 26 October 2006).

Bargiela-Chiappini, F. & Harris, S. J. 1996 'Requests and status in business correspondence'. *Journal of Pragmatics,* vol. 28, pp. 635–62.

Bateson, G. 1980 *Naven,* London: Wildwood House.

Bays, H. 1998 'Framing and face in internet exchanges: A socio-cognitive approach'. *Linguistik Online,* vol. 1, pp. 1–20, <www.linguistik-online.de/bays.htm> (accessed 7 January 2007).

Béal, C. 1990 'It's all in the asking: A perspective on problems of cross-cultural communication between native speakers of French and native speakers of Australian English in the workplace'. *Australian Review of Applied Linguistics*, Series S, vol. 7, pp. 16–32.

Béal, C. 1992 'Did you have a good weekend? Or why is there no such thing as a simple question in cross-cultural encounters?' *Australian Review of Applied Linguistics*, vol. 15, no. 1, pp. 23–52.

Beale, P. 1990 'And so Nobby called to Smudger . . . nicknames associated with individual surnames'. *Lore and Language*, vol. 9, no. 1, pp. 3–18.

Bialystok, E. 1993 'Symbolic representation and attentional control in pragmatic competence'. In Kasper G. & Blum-Kulka S. (eds) *Interlanguage Pragmatics*. Oxford: Oxford University Press, pp. 43–63.

Blum-Kulka, S. 1987 'Indirectness and politeness in requests: Same or different?' *Journal of Pragmatics*, vol. 11, pp. 131–46.

Blum-Kulka, S. 1989 'Playing it safe: The role of conventionality in indirectness'. In Blum-Kulka S., House J. & Kasper G. (eds) *Cross-cultural Pragmatics: Requests and Apologies*. Norwood, New Jersey: Ablex, pp. 27–70.

Blum-Kulka, S. 1990 'You don't touch lettuce with your fingers: Parental politeness in family discourse'. *Journal of Pragmatics*, vol. 14, pp. 259–88.

Blum-Kulka, S. 1992 'The metapragmatics of politeness in Israeli society'. In Watts R. J., Ide S. & Ehlich K. (eds) *Politeness in Language: Studies in Its History, Theory and Practice*. Berlin: Mouton de Gruyter, pp. 255–80.

Blum-Kulka, S. & House, J. 1989 'Cross-cultural and situational variation in requesting behavior'. In Blum-Kulka S., House J. & Kasper G. (eds) *Cross-cultural Pragmatics: Requests and Apologies*. Norwood, New Jersey: Ablex, pp. 123–54.

Blum-Kulka, S., House, J. & Kasper, G. (eds) 1989 *Cross-cultural Pragmatics: Requests and Apologies*. Norwood, New Jersey: Ablex.

Blum-Kulka, S. & Katriel, T. 1991 'Nicknaming practices in families: A cross-cultural perspective'. In Ting-Toomey S. & Korzenny F. (eds) *Cross-Cultural Interpersonal Communication*. Newbury Park: Sage Publications, pp. 58–78.

Blum-Kulka, S. & Olshtain, E. 1984 'Requests and apologies: A cross-cultural study of speech act realisation patterns'. *Applied Linguistics*, vol. 5, no. 3.

Bowe, H. 1994 'Developing successful communication with recently arrived migrants in industry'. Research Report submitted to DEET National Priority Reserve Fund.

Bowe, H. 1995 'The elaboration of repetition as a creative discourse strategy in the multilingual workforce'. Paper read at the Australian Linguistics Conference, Canberra.

Bowe, H. & Zhang, M. 2001 'Travel agency advertisements in Chinese newspapers'. Lecture notes provided as part of LIN3160 *International Cultural Interaction*, Monash University, Berwick.

Braun, F. 1988 *Terms of address: Problems of Patterns and Usage in Various Languages and Cultures*. Mouton de Gruyter, Berlin.

Brown, P. 1998 'How and why are women more polite: Some evidence from a Mayan community'. In Coates J. (ed.) *Language and Gender: A Reader*. London: Blackwell Publishers.

Brown, R. & Ford, M. 1961 'Address in American English'. *Journal of Abnormal and Social Psychology*, vol. 67, pp. 375–85.

Brown, R. & Gilman, A. 1960 'The pronouns of power and solidarity'. In Sebeok T. A. (ed.) *Style in Language*. New York: Technology Press of MIT.

Brown, P. & Levinson, S. 1978 'Universals in language usage: Politeness phenomena'. In Goody E. (ed.) *Questions and Politeness.* Cambridge: Cambridge University Press, pp. 56–289.

Brown, P. & Levinson, S. 1987 *Politeness: Some Universals in Language Usage.* Cambridge: Cambridge University Press.

Bungarten, T. (ed.) 1981 *Wissenschaftssprache.* Munich: Fink.

Cameron, J. 1996 *Titanic: A Screenplay.* Twentieth Century Fox.

Clark, H. 1996 *Using Language.* Cambridge: Cambridge University Press.

Clark, H. & French, J. 1981 'Telephone goodbyes'. *Language in Society,* vol. 10, no. 1, April.

Clyne, M. 1980 'Writing, testing and culture'. *Secondary Teacher,* vol. 11, pp. 13–16.

Clyne, M. 1983 'Communicative competences in contact'. In Smith L. (ed.) *Readings in English as an International Language.* Oxford: Pergamon, pp. 147–63.

Clyne, M. 1987 'Cultural differences in the organisation of academic discourse'. *Journal of Pragmatics,* vol. 11, pp. 211–47.

Clyne, M. 1991a 'Trying to do things with letters: Letters of request and complaint in the university domain'. In *Linguistics in the Service of Society: Essays in Honour of Susan Kaldor.* Institute of Applied Language Studies, Perth: Edith Cowan University.

Clyne, M. 1991b 'The sociocultural dimension: The dilemma of the German-speaking scholar'. In Hartmut Schröder (ed.) *Subject-oriented Texts,* Berlin: Mouton de Gruyter, pp. 49–67.

Clyne, M. (ed.) 1992 *Pluricentric Languages.* Berlin: Mouton de Gruyter.

Clyne, M. 1994 *Inter-cultural Communication at Work: Cultural Values in Discourse.* Cambridge: Cambridge University Press.

Clyne, M., Fernandez, S. & Muhr, R. 2003 'Communicative styles in a contact situation: Two German national varieties in a third country'. *Journal of Germanic Linguistics,* vol. 15, no. 2, pp. 95–154.

Clyne, M. & Kreutz, H. 1987 'The nature and function of digression and other discourse structure phenomena in German academic writings'. Working Papers. In *Migrant and Intercultural Studies 8.*

Clyne, M. & Platt, J. 1990 'The role of language in cross-cultural communication'. In *Proceedings of the Conference on Cross-Cultural Communication in the Health Profession.* National Centre for Community Languages in the Professions, Melbourne: Monash University, pp. 38–55.

Coates, J. (ed.) 1998 *Language and Gender. A Reader.* London: Blackwell Publishers.

Cohen, A. & Olshtain, E. 1981 'Developing a measure of sociocultural competence: The case of apology'. *Language Learning,* vol. 31, no. 1, pp. 113–34.

Connor, U. 2003 'Changing currents in contrastive rhetoric: Implications for teaching and research' In Knoll B. (ed.) *Exploring Dynamics of Language Writing.* New York: Cambridge University Press, pp. 218–41.

Connor, U. & Kaplan, R. B. (eds) 1987 *Writing Across Cultures.* Reading, Massachusetts: Addison-Wesley.

Cordella, M. 1990 'Spanish speakers apologizing in English: A cross-cultural pragmatic study'. *Australian Review of Applied Linguistics,* vol. 14, pp. 115–38.

Cordella, M. 1991 'Apologizing in Chilean Spanish and Australian English: A cross-cultural perspective'. *Australian Review of Applied Linguistics,* Series S, vol. 7, pp. 66–92.

Coulmas, F. (ed.) 1981 *Conversational Routines.* The Hague: Mouton.

Coupland, N., Coupland, J., Giles, H. & Henwood, K. 1988 'Accommodating the elderly: Invoking and extending a theory'. *Language in Society,* vol. 17.

Davidson, A. I. 1986 'Archaeology, genealogy and ethics'. In Hoy D. C. (ed.) *Foucault: A Critical Reader*. Oxford: Basil Blackwell, pp. 221–33.

Davidson, B. 2000 'The interpreter as institutional gatekeeper: The social-linguistic role of interpreters in Spanish–English medical discourse'. *Journal of Sociolinguistics*, vol. 4, no. 3, pp. 379–405.

Demente, B. 1988 *Korean Etiquette and Ethics in Business*. Lincolnwood, Illinois: NTC Business Books.

Demente, B. 1989 *Chinese Etiquette and Ethics in Business*. Lincolnwood, Illinois: NTC Business Books.

Descartes, R. 'La Recherche de la vérité'. In *Oeuvres Complètes*.

Doi, T. 1973 *The Anatomy of Dependence*. John Bester (trans.), Tokyo: Kodansha.

Duncan, S. 1973 'Towards a grammar for dyadic conversation'. *Semiotica*, vol. 9, pp. 29–46.

Duncan, S. 1974 'On the structure of speaker interaction during speaking turns'. *Language in Society*, vol. 2, pp. 161–80.

Eades, D. 2000 'I don't think it's an answer to the question: Silencing Aboriginal witnesses in court'. *Language in Society*, vol. 29, pp. 161–95.

Edwards, J. 1985 *Language, Society and Identity*. Oxford: Blackwell Publishers.

Eggington, W. 1987 'Written academic discourse in Korean'. In Connor U. & Kaplan R. B. *Writing Across Cultures*. Reading, Massachusetts: Addison-Wesley, pp. 153–68.

Ehlich, K. 1992 'On the historicity of politeness'. In Watts R. J., Ide S. & Ehlich K. (eds) *Politeness in Language*. Berlin: Mouton de Gruyter, pp. 71–107.

El-Dash, L.G. & Busnardo, J. 2001 'Perceived in-group and out-group stereotypes among Brazilian foreign language students'. *International Journal of Applied Linguistics*, vol. 11, no. 2, pp. 224–37.

Endomoto, S. 1998 'The management of politeness in Japanese tour guiding discourse'. *Japanese Studies*, vol. 18, no. 3, pp. 295–310.

Errington, J. 1985 *Language and Social Change in Java: Linguistic Reflexes of Modernisation in a Traditional Royal Polity*. Ohio: Ohio University Press.

Ervin-Tripp, S. M. 1972 'Sociolinguistic rules of address'. In Pride J. B. & Holmes J. (eds) *Sociolinguistics*. Harmondsworth: Penguin.

Fairclough, N. 1989 *Language and Power*. Harlow: Longman Group.

Fairclough, N. 2000 *New Labour, New Language*. London: Routledge.

Fairclough, N. & Wodak, R. 1997 'Critical discourse analysis'. In van Dijk T. A. (ed.) *Discourse as Social Interaction*. London: Sage Publications, pp. 258–84.

Ferguson, C. A. 1976 'The structure and use of politeness formulas'. *Language in Society*, vol. 5, pp. 137–51.

Ferrara, K. 1992 'The interactive achievement of a sentence: Joint productions in therapeutic discourse'. *Discourse Processes*, vol. 15, pp. 207–28.

Foucault, M. 1963 (1973) *The Birth of the Clinic: An Archaeology of Medical Perception*. New York: Vintage Books.

Foucault, M. 1978 *The History of Sexuality: Volume 1: An Introduction*. Hurley R. (trans.), Harmondsworth: Penguin Books.

Foucault, M. 1980 *Power/Knowledge: Selected Interviews and Other Writings, 1972–1977*. New York: Pantheon.

Fraser, B. 1975 The concept of politeness. Paper presented at the NWAVE Meeting. Georgetown University.

Fraser, B. 1990 'Perspectives on politeness'. *Journal of Pragmatics*, vol. 14, pp. 219–36.

Fraser, B. & Nolen, W. 1981 'The association of deference with linguistic form'. *International Journal of the Sociology of Language*, vol. 27, pp. 93–109.

Gallois, C., Franklyn-Stokes, A., Giles, H. & Coupland, N. 1988 'Communication accommodation in intercultural encounters'. In Kim Y. Y. & Gudykunst W. B. *Theories in Intercultural Communication*. Newbury Park: Sage Publications, pp. 157–85.

Gavioli, L. 1995 'Turn-initial versus turn-final laughter: Two techniques for initial remedy in English/Italian bookshop service encounters'. *Discourse Processes*, vol. 19, pp. 369–84.

Geertz, C. 1976 'Linguistic etiquette'. In Pride J. B. & Holmes J. (eds) *Sociolinguistics*. New Hampshire: Penguin Books, pp. 167–79.

Gentile, A. 1991 'Working with professional interpreters'. In Pauwels A. (ed.) *Cross-cultural Communication in Medical Encounters*. Community Languages in the Professions Unit, Language and Society Centre NLIA, Melbourne: Monash University, pp. 26–48.

Giddens, A. 1982 *Profiles and Critiques in Social Theory*. London: Macmillan.

Giddens, A. 1993 *New Rules of Sociological Method*, 2nd edn. Cambridge: Polity Press.

Giles, H. 1977 *Language, Ethnicity and Intergroup Relations*. London: Academic Press.

Giles, H. & Robinson, W. P. 1990 (eds) *Handbook of Language and Social Psychology*. Chichester: John Wiley & Sons.

Givón, T. (ed.) 1983 *Topic and Continuity in Discourse: A Quantitative Cross-language Study*. Amsterdam: Benjamins.

Goddard, C. 1989 'Issues in natural semantic metalanguage'. *Quaderni di Semantica*, vol. 10, no. 1, pp. 51–64 (Round table on Semantic Primitives, 1).

Goddard, C. 2005 'The lexical semantics of culture'. *Language Sciences*, no. 27, pp. 51–73.

Goddard, D. 1977 'Same setting, different norms: Phone call beginnings in France and in the United States'. *Language in Society*, vol. 6, pp. 209–19.

Goffman, E. 1955 'On facework: An analysis of ritual elements in social interaction'. *Psychiatry*, vol. 18, pp. 213–31.

Goffman, E. 1967 *Interaction Ritual: Essays on Face to Face Behavior*. New York: Doubleday.

Goffman, E. 1968 *Stigma: Notes on the Management of Spoiled Identity*. London: Penguin.

Goffman, E. 1971 *Relations in Public*. New York: Basic Books.

Gottlieb, N. 1998 'Discriminatory language in Japan: Burakumin, the disabled and women'. *Asian Studies Review*, vol. 22, no. 2, pp. 157–73.

Gottlieb, N. 2006 Book review: Fushimi, N., Matsuzawa, K., Kurokawa, N., Yamanaka, T., Oikawa, K., Noguchi, K. 2002, 'Okama' wa sabetsu ka: 'Shūkan Kinyōbi no *Sabetsu Hyōgen* Jiken [Does 'okama' have discriminatory connotations? The discriminating expression case in the weekly magazine *Shūkan Kinyōbi*] *Intersections: Gender, History and Culture in the Asian Context*, issue 12, January <http://wwwsshe.murdoch.edu.au/intersections/issue12/gotlieb_review.html>

Grice, H. P. 1975 'Logic and conversation'. In Cole P. & Morgan J. (eds) *Syntax and Semantics 3: Speech Acts*. New York: Academic Press.

Gu, Y. 1990 'Politeness phenomena in modern Chinese'. *Journal of Pragmatics*, vol. 14, pp. 237–57.

Gumperz, J. 1992 'Interviewing in intercultural situations'. In Drew P. & Heritage J. (eds) *Talk at Work*. Cambridge: Cambridge University Press, pp. 302–27.

Haffner, L. 1992 'Translation is not enough: Interpreting in a medical setting in "Cross cultural medicine – a decade later"'. Special issue, *Western Journal of Medicine*, vol. 157, pp. 255–9.

Harkins, J. 1990 'Shame and shyness in the Aboriginal classroom: A case for practical semantics'. *Australian Journal of Linguistics*, vol. 10, pp. 293–306.

Herbert, R. K. 1990 'Sex based differences in compliment behaviour'. *Language in Society*, vol. 19, pp. 201–24.

Herbert, R. K. 1995 'The sociolinguistics of personal names: Two South African case studies'. *South African Journal of African Languages*, vol. 15, no. 1, pp. 1–8.

Hess-Lüttich, E. W. B. & Wilde, E. 2003 'Der Chat als Textsorte und/oder als Dialogsorte?' *Linguistik online*, vol. 13, no. 1, pp. 161–80 <www.linguistik-online.de/13_01/hessLuettichWilde.pdf> (accessed 26 October 2006).

Heydon, G. 2005 *The Language of Police Interviewing : A Critical Analysis.* New York: Palgrave Macmillan.

Hill, B., Ide, S., Ikuta, A., Kawasaki, T. & Ogino, T. 1986 'Universals of linguistic politeness'. *Journal of Pragmatics*, vol. 10, pp. 347–71.

Hinds, J. 1980 'Japanese expository prose'. *Papers in Linguistics: International Journal of Human Cognition*, vol. 131, no. 1, pp. 117–58.

Hinds, J. 1983a 'Contrastive rhetoric: Japanese and English'. *Text*, vol. 3, pp. 183–95.

Hinds, J. 1983b 'Contrastive studies of English and Japanese'. *Annual Review of Applied Linguistics*, vol. 3, pp. 78–84.

Hobbs, P. 2003 'The medium is the message: Politeness strategies in men's and women's voice mail messages'. *Journal of Pragmatics*, vol. 35, pp. 243–62.

Hofstede, G. 1980 *Culture's consequences: International differences in work-related values.* Beverly Hills, California: Sage Publications.

Hofstede, G. 1983 'Dimensions of national cultures in fifty countries and three regions'. In Deregowski J. B. & Dziurawiec S. et al. (eds) *Explications in Cross-cultural Psychology.* Netherlands: Swets & Zeitlinger, pp. 335–55.

Hofstede, G. 1991 *Cultures and Organizations: Software of the Mind.* New York: McGraw-Hill.

Hofstede, G. 1998 'Think locally, act globally: Cultural constraints in personnel management'. *Management International Review*, Special issue, vol. 38, no. 2, pp. 7–26.

Hofstede, G. & Bond, M. H. 1984 'Hofstede's cultural dimensions'. *Journal of Cross-Cultural Psychology*, vol. 15, pp. 417–33.

Hogg, M. A. & Abrams, D. 1988 *Social Identifications: A Social Psychology of Intergroup Relations and Group Processes.* London: Routledge.

Holmes, J. 1988 'Paying compliments: A sex-preferential politeness strategy'. *Journal of Pragmatics*, vol. 12, pp. 445–65.

Holmes, J. 1998 'Women's talk: The question of sociolinguistic universals'. In Coates J. (ed.) *Language and Gender. A Reader.* London: Blackwell Publishers.

House, J. & Kasper, G. 1981 'Politeness markers in English and German'. In Coulmas F. (ed.) *Conversational Routines.* The Hague: Mouton, pp. 157–85.

Hvoslef, E. 2001 'The social use of personal names among the Kyrgyz'. *Contemporary South Asia*, vol. 20, no. 1, pp. 85–95.

Ide, S. 1989 'Formal forms and discernment: Two neglected aspects of universals of linguistic politeness'. *Multilingua*, vol. 8, nos 2/3, pp. 223–38.

Ide, S. 1990 'How and why do women speak more politely in Japanese?' In Ide S. & McGloin N. H. (eds) *Aspects of Japanese Women's Language.* Tokyo: Kuroshio Publishers, pp. 63–79.

Ide, S., Hill, B., Carnes, Y. M., Ogino, T. & Kawasaki, A. 1992 'The concept of politeness: An empirical study of American English and Japanese'. In Watts R. J., Ide S. & Ehlich K. (eds) *Politeness in Language.* Berlin: Mouton de Gruyter, pp. 281–93.

Janney, R. W. & Arndt, H. 1992 'Intracultural tact versus intercultural tact'. In Watts R. J., Ide S. & Ehlich K. (eds) *Politeness in Language.* Berlin: Mouton de Gruyter, pp. 21–41.

Jary, M. 1998 'Relevance theory and the communication of politeness'. *Journal of Pragmatics*, vol. 30, no. 1, pp. 1–19.

Johnson, D. M. & Roen, D. J. 1992 'Complimenting and involvement in peer review: Gender variation'. *Language in Society*, vol. 21, pp. 27–57.

Kachru, Y. 1988 'Writers in Hindi and English'. In Purves A. C. (ed.) *Writing Across Languages and Cultures*. Newbury Park: Sage Publications, 109–37.

de Kadt, E. 1998 'The concept of face and its applicability to the Zulu language'. *Journal of Pragmatics*, vol. 29, pp. 173–91.

Kageyama, T. & Tomori, I. 1976 'Japanese whimperatives'. *Papers in Japanese Linguistics*, vol. 4, pp. 13–53.

Kaplan, R. B. 1972 'Cultural thought patterns in inter-cultural education'. In Croft K. (ed.) *Readings in English as a Second Language*. Cambridge, Massachusetts: Winthrop, 246–62.

Kaplan, R. B. 1988 'Contrastive rhetoric and second language learning: Notes toward a theory of contrastive rhetoric'. In Purves A. C. (ed.) *Writing Across Languages and Cultures*. Newbury Park: Sage Publications, pp. 275–304.

Kasher, A. 1986 'Politeness and rationality'. In Johansen J. D. & Sonne H. (eds) *Pragmatics and Linguistics: Festschrift for Jacob Mey*. Odense: Odense University Press, pp. 103–14.

Kasper, G. 1990 'Linguistic politeness'. *Journal of Pragmatics*, vol. 14, pp. 193–218.

Kasper, G. & Blum-Kulka, S. (eds) 1993 *Interlanguage Pragmatics*. Oxford: Oxford University Press.

Katriel, T. 1986 'Talking straight: *Dugri* speech in Israeli Sabra culture'. Cambridge: Cambridge University Press.

Kirkpatrick, A. 1991 'Information sequencing in Mandarin letters of request'. *Anthropological Linguistics*, vol. 33, no. 2, pp. 183–203.

Kjaerbeck, S. 1998 'The organization of discourse units in Mexican and Danish business negotiations'. *Journal of Pragmatics*, vol. 30, pp. 347–62.

de Klerk, V. & Bosch, B. 1997 'The sound patterns of English surnames'. *Language Sciences*, vol. 19, no. 4, pp. 289–301.

Knapp, M. L., Hart, R. P., Friedrich, G. W. & Shulman, G. M. 1973 'The rhetoric of goodbye: Verbal and nonverbal correlates of human leave-taking'. *Speech Monographs*, vol. 40, pp. 182–98.

Koentjaraningrat, R. M. 1989 *Javanese Culture*. Singapore: Oxford University Press.

Koyama, T. 1992 *Japan: A Handbook in Intercultural Communication*. Sydney: Macquarie University Press.

Kretzenbacher, H. L. 2005 'Hier im großen internetz, wo sich alle dududuzen', Internet discourse politeness and German address. Paper given at the Third International Conference on Language Variation in Europe (IClaVE), Amsterdam, pp. 1–15.

Lakoff, R. 1973 'The logic of politeness: Or, p's and q's'. In Corum C. et al. (eds) Papers from the *Ninth Regional Meeting of the Chicago Linguistic Society*. Chicago Linguistic Society, pp. 292–305.

Lakoff, R. 1979 'Stylistic strategies within a grammar of style'. In Orasanu J. et al. (eds) *Language Sex and Gender*. Annals of the New York Academy of Sciences, pp. 53–80.

Lakoff, R. 1989 'The limits of politeness: Therapeutic and courtroom discourse'. *Multilingua*, vol. 8, pp. 101–29.

Lambert, B. 2001 Bilingual women and terms of address, Unpublished honours dissertation, Linguistics Department. Melbourne: Monash University.

Larson, M. L. 1984 *Meaning-based Translation: A Guide to Cross-Language Equivalence*. Lanham, Maryland: University Press of America.

Lebra, T. S. 1976 *Japanese Culture and Behaviour: Selected Readings*, rev. edn. Honolulu: University Press of Hawaii.

Leech, G. 1983 *Principles of Pragmatics*. New York: Longman.

Lee-Wong, S. M. 1994a 'Imperatives in requests: Direct or impolite, observations from Chinese'. *Journal of Pragmatics*, vol. 4, pp. 491–515.

Lee-Wong, S. M. 1994b 'Qing/Please: A polite or requestive marker? Observations from Chinese'. *Multilingua*, vol. 13, no. 4, pp. 343–60.

Leibnitz, G. W. 1903 'De organo sive arte magna gogitanti'. In *Opuscules et Fragments Inédits* (ed.) L. Couturat, Paris.

Lerner, G. 1991 'On the syntax of sentences-in-progress'. *Language in Society*, vol. 20, pp. 441–58.

Levinson, S. C. 1983 *Pragmatics*. Cambridge: Cambridge University Press.

Levinson, S. C. 1985 'What's special about conversational inference?' Paper presented to the British Psychological Society Annual Meeting, Swansea, April 1985.

Locke, J. 1775 'An essay concerning human understanding'. *London 1775*, vol. 2.

Mao, Lu Ming, R. 1994 'Beyond politeness theory: "Face" revisited and renewed'. *Journal of Pragmatics*, vol. 21, pp. 451–86.

Marriott, H. 1990 'Intercultural business negotiations: The problem of norm discrepancy'. *Australian Review of Applied Linguistics*, Series S, vol. 7, pp. 33–65.

Matsumoto, Y. 1988 'Reexamination of the universality of face: Politeness phenomena in Japanese'. *Journal of Pragmatics*, vol. 12, pp. 403–26.

Matsumoto, Y. 1989 'Politeness and Conversational Universals: Observations from Japanese'. *Multilingua*, vol. 8, pp. 207–21.

Mauss, M. 1974 *Oeuvres 2*. Paris: Editions de Minuit.

Meier, A. J. 1995a 'Defining politeness: Universality in appropriateness'. *Language Sciences*, vol. 17, no. 4, pp. 345–56.

Meier, A. J. 1995b 'Passages of politeness'. *Journal of Pragmatics*, vol. 24, pp. 381–92.

Mitzutani, O. & Mitzutani, N. 1987 *How to Be Polite in Japanese*. Tokyo: Japan Times.

Montgomery, M. 1996 *An Introduction to Language and Society*. London: Routledge.

Moreno, M. 2002 'The address system in the Spanish of the Golden Age'. *Journal of Pragmatics*, vol. 34, no. 1, pp. 15–47.

Morgan, J., O'Neil, C. & Harre, R. 1979 *Nicknames: Their Origins and Social Consequences*. London: Routledge & Kegan Paul.

Mühlhäusler, P. 1996 *Linguistic Ecology: Language Change and Linguistic Imperialism in the Pacific Region*. London: Routledge.

Munday, J. 2001 *Introducing Translation Studies: Theories and Applications*. London and New York: Routledge.

Murillo, A. 1989 'Do translated ads sell?' *Coming of Age, 30th Annual Conference ATA, Washington DC* (eds) Hammond D. & Medford N. J. New Jersey: Learned Information.

NAATI (National Accreditation Authority for Translators and Interpreters) 2003 *NAATI Information Booklet*.

NAATI <www.naati.com.au> (accessed 26 October 2006)

Neil, D. 1996 *Collaboration in Intercultural Discourse: Examples from a Multicultural Workplace*. Frankfurt am Main: Peter Lang.

Neustypný, J. V. 1985 'Language norms in Australian–Japanese contact situations'. In Clyne M. (ed.) *Australia, Meeting Place of Languages*. Canberra: Pacific Linguistics, pp. 161–70.

Nguyên, C. 1991 'Barriers to communication between Vietnamese and non-Vietnamese'. *Journal of Vietnamese Studies*, vol. 1, no. 4, pp. 40–5.

Nguyen, D. 1993 'Interpreting and translating in Australia'. *Digest of Australian Language and Literacy*, Issue no. 1, August, Canberra: National Languages and Literacy Institute of Australia.

Nida, E. & Taber, C. 1974 *The Theory and Practice of Translation*. Leiden: E. J. Brill

Noor, R. 2001 'Contrastive rhetoric in expository prose: Approaches and achievements'. *Journal of Pragmatics*, vol. 33, no. 2, pp. 255–69.

Ochs, E. 1992 'Indexing gender'. In Duranti A. & Goodwin C. (eds) *Rethinking Context: Language as an Interactive Phenomenon*. Cambridge: Cambridge University Press.

O'Hagen, M. & Ashworth, D. 2002 *Translation-Mediated Communication in a Digital World*. Clevedon, UK: Multilingual Matters.

De Oliveira, S. M. 2003 'Breaking conversational norms on a Portuguese users network: Men as adjudicators of politeness?' *Journal of Computer-Mediated Communication*, vol. 9, no. 1, p. 22 <http:((jcmc.indiana.edu/vol9/issue1/oliveira.html> (accessed 26 October 2006).

Olshtain, E. & Cohen, A. 1983 'Apology: A speech-act set'. In Wolfson N. & Judd E. (eds) *Sociolinguistics and Language Acquisition*. Rowley, Massachusetts: Newbury House, pp. 18–36.

Ostler, S. 1987 'English in parallels: A comparison of English and Arabic prose'. In Connor U. & Kaplan R. B. (eds) *Writing Across Cultures*. Reading, Massachusetts: Addison-Wesley, pp. 169–85.

Pandharipande, R. 1983 'Contrastive studies of English and Marathi'. *Annual Review of Applied Linguistics*, vol. 3, pp. 118–36.

Pauwels, A., D'Argaville, M. & Eades, D. 1992 'Problems and issues of cross-cultural communication in legal settings'. In Pauwels A. (ed.) *Cross-cultural Communication in Legal Settings*. Language and Society Centre, National Languages and Literacy Institute of Australia, Melbourne: Monash University, pp. 77–105.

Pavlidou, T. 1991 'Universality and relativity in cross-cultural politeness research'. Paper delivered at the International Conference on Contrastive Linguistics, Innsbruck, Austria, May 1991.

Pennycook, A. 2001 *Critical Applied Linguistics: A Critical Introduction*. London: Lawrence Erlbaum Associates.

Pilkington, J. 1998 'Don't try and make out that I'm nice! The different strategies women and men use when gossiping'. In Coates J. (ed.) *Language and Gender: A Reader*. London: Blackwell Publishers.

Poynton, C. 1989 'Terms of address in Australian English'. In Collins P. & Blair D. (eds) *Autralian English*. Australia: University of Queensland Press, pp. 53–69.

Precht, K. 1998 'A cross-cultural comparison of letters of recommendation'. *English for Specific Purposes*, vol. 17, no. 3, pp. 241–65.

Pym, A. 2004 *The Moving Text: Localization, Translation, and Distribution*. Amsterdam: John Benjamins.

Pym, A. 2004 'Propositions on cross-cultural communication and translation'. *Target: International Journal of Translation Studies*, vol. 16, no. 1, pp. 1–28.

Richards, J. C. & Sukwiwat, M. 1983 'Language transfer and conversational competence'. *Applied Linguistics*, vol. 4, pp. 113–25.

Ricks, D. A. 1983 *Big Business Blunders: Mistakes in Multinational Marketing*. Homewood, Illinois: Dow-Jones Irwin.

Rumelhart, D. E., Smolensky, P., McClelland, J. L. & Hinton, G. E. 1986 'Schemata and sequential thought processes in PDP models'. In McClelland J. L., Rumelhart D. E.

& the PDP Research Group (eds) *Parallel Distributed Processing: Explorations in the Microstructure of Cognition, Vol. 2, Psychological and Biological Models.* Cambridge, Massachusetts: MIT Press, pp. 7–57.

Ryden, K. C. 1993 *Mapping the Invisible Landscape: Folklore, Writing, and the Sense of Place.* Iowa City: University of Iowa Press.

Sacks, H. 1967–8 *Lectures on Conversation,* 2 vols (ed. G. Jefferson 1992). Cambridge, Massachusetts: Blackwell Publishers.

Sacks, H. 1992 *Lectures on Conversation, I–II* (ed. G. Jefferson). Oxford: Blackwell Publishers.

Sacks, H., Schegloff, E. A. & Jefferson, G. 1974 'A simplest systematic for the organization of turn-taking in conversations'. *Language,* vol. 59, pp. 941–2.

Sarangi, S. 1996 'Conflation of institutional and cultural stereotyping in Asian migrants' discourse'. *Discourse & Society,* vol. 7, pp. 359–87.

Sarangi, S. & Roberts, C. (eds) 1999 *Talk, Work and Institutional Order: Discourse in Medical, Mediation and Management Settings.* Berlin: Mouton de Gruyter.

Schegloff, E. A. 1968 'Sequencing in conversational openings'. In Gumperz J. & Hymes D. (eds) *Directions in Sociolinguistics: The Ethnography of Communication.* New York: Holt, Rinehart & Winston, pp. 346–80.

Schegloff, E. A. 1982 'Discourse as an interactional achievement: Some uses of "Uh huh" and other things that come between sentences'. In Tannen D. (ed.) *Analyzing Discourse: Text and Talk.* Georgetown University Round Table in Languages and Linguistics 1981, Washington DC: Georgetown University Press.

Schegloff, E. A. & Sacks, H. 1973 'Opening up closings'. *Semiotica,* vol. 8, pp. 289–327.

Schiano, D. 1997 'Convergent methodologies in cyber-psychology: A case study, Behavior Research Methods'. *Instruments and Computers,* vol. 29, no. 2, pp. 270–3.

Schulze, M. 1999 'Substitution of paraverbal and nonverbal cues in the written medium of IRC'. In Naumann B. (ed.) *Dialogue Analysis and the Mass Media. Proceedings of the International Conference in Erlangen,* April 2–3, 1998, Niemeyer (Beiträge zur Dialogforschung 20), Tübingen, pp. 65–82.

Scollon, R. & Scollon, S. Wong 2001 *Intercultural Communication: A Discourse Approach.* 2nd edn. Oxford: Blackwell.

Searle, J. R. 1969 *Speech Acts.* Cambridge: Cambridge University Press.

Searle, J. R. 1975 'Indirect speech acts'. In Cole P. & Morgan J. (eds) *Syntax and Semantics 3 (Speech Acts).* New York: Academic Press.

Searle J. R. 1979 *Expression and Meaning: Studies in the Theory of Speech Acts.* Cambridge: Cambridge University Press.

Searle, J. R. 1995 *The Construction of Social Reality.* New York: Free Press.

Sharifian, F. 2003 'On cultural conceptualizations'. *Journal of Cognition and Culture,* vol. 3, no. 3, pp. 188–207.

Sharifian, F. 2004 'Cultural schemas and intercultural communication: A study of Persian'. In Leigh J. & Loo E. *Outer Limits: A Reader in Communication Across Cultures.* Melbourne: Language Australia, pp. 119–30.

Sharifian, F. 2005 'The Persian cultural schema of shekasteh-nafsi: A study of complement responses in Persian and Anglo–Australian speakers'. *Pragmatics and Cognition,* vol. 13, no. 2, pp. 337–61.

Sharifian, F. (forthcoming) 'Distributed, emergent cultural cognition, conceptualisation and language'. In Frank R. M., Dirvan R., Ziemke T. & Bernárdez E. (eds) *Body, Language and Mind (Vol. 2): Sociocultural Situatedness.* Berlin/New York: Mouton de Gruyter.

Sifianou, M. 1989 'On the telephone again! Differences in telephone behaviour: England versus Greece'. *Language in Society*, vol. 18, pp. 527–44.

Smith, J. S. 1992 'Women in change: Politeness and directives in the speech of Japanese women'. *Language in Society*, vol. 21, pp. 59–82.

Smith, R. 1983 *Japanese Society: Tradition, Self, and the Social Order.* Cambridge: Cambridge University Press.

Sneddon, J. 1996 *Indonesian Reference Grammar.* Australia: Allen & Unwin.

Spencer-Oatey, H. & Xing, J. 2003 'Managing rapport in intercultural business interactions: A comparison of two Chinese–British welcome meetings'. *Journal of Intercultural Studies*, vol. 24, no. 1, pp. 33–46.

Sperber, D. & Hirschfeld, L. 1999 'Culture, cognition and evolution'. In Wilson R. & Kiel F. (eds) *MIT Encyclopedia of the Cognitive Sciences.* Cambridge, Massachusetts: MIT Press, pp. cxi–cxxxii.

Sperber, D. & Wilson, D. 1986 *Relevance.* London: Routledge & Kegan Paul.

Stafford, L. & Kline, S. L. 1996 'Women's surnames and titles: Men's and women's views'. *Communication Research Papers*, vol. 13, no. 2, pp. 214–24.

Sugimoto, N. 1998 'Norms of apology depicted in U.S. American and Japanese literature on manners and etiquette'. *International Journal of Intercultural Relations*, vol. 22, no. 3, pp. 251–76.

Suszczyńska, M. 1999 'Apologizing in English, Polish and Hungarian: Different languages, different strategies'. *Journal of Pragmatics*, vol. 31, pp. 1053–65.

Suzuki, T. 1976 'Language and behavior in Japan: The conceptualization of personal relations'. *Japan Quarterly*, vol. 23, no. 3, pp. 255–66.

Svartvik, J. & Quirk, R. (eds) 1980 *A Corpus of English Conversation.* Lund: Gleerup.

Tajfel, H. 1982 'Social identity and intergroup relations'. Cambridge: Cambridge University Press.

Takahashi, T. & Beebe, L. M. 1993 'Cross-linguistic influence in the speech act of correction'. In Kasper G. & Blum-Kulka S. (eds) *Interlanguage Pragmatics.* Oxford: Oxford University Press, pp. 138–57.

Tannen, D. 1981 'Indirectness in discourse: Ethnicity as conversational style'. *Discourse Processes*, vol. 4, pp. 221–38.

Tannen, D. 1986 *That's Not What I Meant.* New York: William Morrow.

Tannen, D. 1994 *Talking From 9 to 5: How Women's and Men's Conversational Styles Affect Who Gets Heard, Who Gets Credit, and What Gets Done at Work.* New York: Avon Books.

Teo, P. 2000 'Racism in the news: A critical discourse analysis of news reporting in two Australian newspapers'. *Discourse & Society*, vol. 11, no. 1, pp. 7–49.

Thomas, J. 1995 *Meaning in Interaction: An Introduction to Pragmatics.* London: Longman.

Trosborg, A. (ed.) 1994 *Interlanguage Pragmatics: Requests, Complaints and Apologies* (Studies in Anthropological Linguistics 7). Berlin/New York: Mouton de Gruyter.

Tylor, E. B. 1871 *Primitive Culture: Researches into the Development of Mythology, Philosophy, Religion, Art, and Custom, Volume I.* London: John Murray, Albemarle Street.

Usami, M. 2002 *Discourse Politeness in Japanese Conversation: Some Implications for a Universal Theory of Politeness.* Tokyo: Hitsuji Shobo.

Van Dijk, T. 1987 *Communicating Racism: Ethnic Prejudice in Thought and Talk.* Newbury Park, California: Sage Publications.

Van Dijk, T. 1996 'Discourse, power and access'. In Caldas-Coulthard C. R. & Coulthard M. (eds) *Texts and Practices: Readings in Critical Discourse Analysis.* London: Routledge, pp. 84–104.

Victor, D. 1992 'Issues in language in international business communication'. In *International Business Communication*. New York: Harper Collins.

Victor, D. 1992 *International Business Communication*. New York: Harper Collins.

Waitzkin, H. 1991 *The Politics of Medical Encounters: How Patients and Doctors Deal With Social Problems*. New Haven/London: Yale University Press.

Watts, R. J. 1989 'Relevance and relational work: Linguistic politeness as politic behavior'. *Multilingua*, vol. 8, pp. 131–66.

Watts, R. J. 2003 *Politeness*. Cambridge: Cambridge University Press.

Watts, R. J., Ide, S. & Ehlich, K. 1992 *Politeness in Language: Studies in its History, Theory and Practice*. Berlin/New York: Mouton de Gruyter.

Weller, G. 1992 'Advertising: A true challenge for cross-cultural translation'. In Moore C. N. & Lower L. (eds) *Translation East and West: A Cross-Cultural Approach: Selected Conference Papers*. Honolulu: University of Hawaii.

Widdowson, H. G. 1978 *Teaching Language and Communication*. London: Oxford University Press.

Wierzbicka, A. 1972 *Semantic Primitives* (Linguistische Forschungen 22). Frankfurt: Athenäum.

Wierzbicka, A. 1980 *Lingua Mentalis: The Semantics of Natural Language*. Sydney/New York: Academic Press.

Wierzbicka, A. 1985 'Different cultures, different languages, different speech acts'. *Journal of Pragmatics*, vol. 9, pp. 145–78.

Wierzbicka, A. 1991 *Cross-Cultural Pragmatics: The Semantics of Human Interaction*. Berlin: Mouton de Gruyter.

Wierzbicka, A. 1994a 'Cognitive domains and the structure of the lexicon: The case of emotions'. In Hirschfeld L. A. & Gelman S. A. *Mapping the Mind: Domain Specificity in Cognition and Culture*. Cambridge: Cambridge University Press, pp. 771–97.

Wierzbicka, A. 1994b 'Cultural scripts: A semantic approach to cultural analysis and cross-cultural communication'. In *Pragmatics and Language Learning*. Bouton L. & Kachru Y. (eds) Urbana-Champaign: University of Illinois, pp. 1–24.

Wierzbicka, A. 2003 *Cross-cultural Pragmatics: The Semantics of Human Interaction*, 2nd edn. Berlin: Mouton de Gruyter.

Wierzbicka, A. & Goddard, C. 2004 'Cultural scripts: What are they and what are they good for?', *Intercultural Pragmatics*, vol. 1, no. 2, pp. 153–66.

Wilson, S. 1998 *The Means of Naming: A Social and Cultural History of Personal Naming in Western Europe*. London: OCL Press.

Wittermans, E. P. 1990 'Indonesian terms of address in a situation of rapid social change'. *Social Forces*, pp. 48–51.

Wodak, R. 1996 *Disorders of Discourse*. London: Addison Wesley Longman.

Young, L. W. 1983 'Inscrutability revisited'. In Gumperz, J. J. (ed), *Discourse Strategies*. Melbourne: Cambridge University Press, pp. 72–84.

Zadjman, A. 1995 'Humorous face-threatening acts: Humour as strategy'. *Journal of Pragmatics*, vol. 23, pp. 325–39.

Zimin, S. 1981 'Sex and politeness: Factors in first- and second-language use'. *International Journal of the Sociology of Language*, vol. 27, pp. 35–58.

Zuengler, J. 1989 'Performance variation in native speaker–non native speaker interactions: Ethnolinguistic differences or discourse domain?'. In Gass S., Madden C., Preston D. & Selinker L. (eds) *Variation in Second Language Acquisition, Volume 1: Discourse and Pragmatics*. Cleveland: Multilingual Matters.

Index